My
Digital
Travel
for Seniors

Jason R. Rich

AARP®
Real Possibilities

que®
800 East 96th Street,
Indianapolis, Indiana 46240 USA

My Digital Travel for Seniors

ISBN-13: 978-0-7897-5795-1

ISBN-10: 0-7897-5795-8

Library of Congress Control Number: 2016952406

Printed in the United States of America

1   16

Trademarks

Warning and Disclaimer

Special Sales

For information about buying this title in bulk quantities, or for special sales opportunities (which may include electronic versions; custom cover designs; and content particular to your business, training goals, marketing focus, or branding interests), please contact our corporate sales department at corpsales@pearsoned.com or (800) 382-3419.

For government sales inquiries, please contact governmentsales@pearsoned.com.

For questions about sales outside the U.S., please contact intlcs@pearson.com.

Editor-in-Chief
Greg Wiegand

Senior Acquisitions Editor
Laura Norman

Marketing Manager
Stephane Nakib

Director, AARP Books
Jodi Lipson

Development Editor
Charlotte Kughen,
The Wordsmithery LLC

Managing Editor
Sandra Schroeder

Senior Project Editor
Tonya Simpson

Indexer
Publishing Works, Inc.

Proofreader
Paula Lowell

Technical Editor
Jeri Usbay

Editorial Assistant
Cindy Teeters

Cover Designer
Chuti Prasertsith

Compositor
Studio Galou

Contents at a Glance

Find the online chapters and other helpful information on this book's website at quepublishing.com/title/9780789757951.

Table of Contents

Find the online chapters and other helpful information on this book's website at quepublishing.com/title/9780789757951.

About the Author

Jason R. Rich (www.jasonrich.com) is an accomplished author, journalist, and photographer, as well as an avid world traveler. Some of his recently published books include *My Digital Photography for Seniors*, *My Digital Entertainment for Seniors*, and *iPad and iPhone Tips and Tricks*, Fifth and Sixth Editions (all from Que Publishing).

Jason's photographic work (www.jasonrich.photography) appears with his articles published in major daily newspapers, national magazines, and online, as well as in his various books. He also works with professional actors, models, and recording artists to develop their portfolios and take their headshots. Jason also pursues opportunities in travel and animal photography.

Through his work as an enrichment lecturer, he often offers workshops and classes about digital photography, the Internet, and consumer technology aboard cruise ships operated by Celebrity Cruise Lines, Norwegian Cruise Lines, Princess Cruises Lines, and Royal Caribbean, as well as through adult education programs in the New England area. Please follow Jason R. Rich on Twitter (@JasonRich7) and Instagram (@JasonRich7).

About AARP and AARP TEK

AARP is a nonprofit, nonpartisan organization, with a membership of nearly 38 million, that helps people turn their goals and dreams into *real possibilities*™, strengthens communities, and fights for the issues that matter most to families such as healthcare, employment and income security, retirement planning, affordable utilities, and protection from financial abuse. Learn more at aarp.org.

The AARP TEK (Technology Education & Knowledge) program aims to accelerate AARP's mission of turning dreams into *real possibilities*™ by providing step-by-step lessons in a variety of formats to accommodate different learning styles, levels of experience, and interests. Expertly guided hands-on workshops delivered in communities nationwide help instill confidence and enrich lives of the 50+ by equipping them with skills for staying connected to the people and passions in their lives. Lessons are taught on touchscreen tablets and smartphones— common tools for connection, education, entertainment, and productivity. For self-paced lessons, videos, articles, and other resources, visit aarptek.org.

Dedication

This book is dedicated to my family and friends, including my niece Natalie, my nephew Parker, and my Yorkshire Terrier Rusty, who is always by my side as I'm writing.

Acknowledgments

Thanks once again to Laura Norman and Greg Wiegand at Que for inviting me to work on this project, and for their ongoing support. I'd also like to thank everyone who worked on the editing, design, layout, marketing, printing, and distribution of this book for their ongoing assistance, and offer my gratitude to everyone at AARP who helped to make this book possible.

We Want to Hear from You!

As the reader of this book, *you* are our most important critic and commentator. We value your opinion and want to know what we're doing right, what we could do better, what areas you'd like to see us publish in, and any other words of wisdom you're willing to pass our way.

We welcome your comments. You can email or write to let us know what you did or didn't like about this book—as well as what we can do to make our books better.

Please note that we cannot help you with technical problems related to the topic of this book.

When you write, please be sure to include this book's title and author as well as your name and email address. We will carefully review your comments and share them with the author and editors who worked on the book.

Email: feedback@quepublishing.com

Mail: Que Publishing
         ATTN: Reader Feedback
         800 East 96th Street
         Indianapolis, IN 46240 USA

Reader Services

Register your copy of *My Digital Travel for Seniors* at quepublishing.com for convenient access to downloads, updates, and corrections as they become available. To start the registration process, go to quepublishing.com/register and log in or create an account*. Enter the product ISBN, 9780789757951, and click Submit. When the process is complete, you will find any available bonus content under Registered Products.

*Be sure to check the box that you would like to hear from us to receive exclusive discounts on future editions of this product.

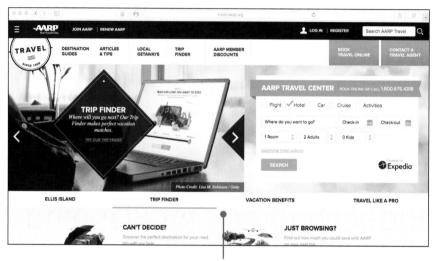

AARP Travel (travel.aarp.org) is an integrated travel website for generating ideas for planning, and booking your travel.

This chapter shows you ways to use your Internet-enabled computer, smartphone, and/or tablet to easily handle a range of travel-related tasks. You'll discover

→ How technology can help you make travel plans
→ What equipment you'll need to research, plan, book, and manage your trips
→ What types of travel-related services are available via the Internet
→ Ways you can save time and money planning trips using technology

Using Technology for Planning Travel

Travel enriches our lives. It opens the door to discovery, personal growth, wellness, and living our best lives. It connects us to family and friends. It's no wonder people love to travel! Every year consumers spend billions of dollars on both domestic and international leisure travel: everything from weekend getaways and road trips to visits to relatives and friends to vacation dreams of a lifetime. People also travel for business, caregiving, medical procedures, sports, and life events such as weddings, graduations, and funerals.

Consumers Spend a Fortune on Leisure Travel

According to the U.S. Travel Association, in 2015, consumers around the world spent $650.8 billion on domestic and international travel, and 79 percent of all trips taken were for leisure travel. Americans took 1.7 billion leisure trips in 2015. The most popular reasons for leisure travel were to visit relatives, go shopping, visit friends, experience fine dining, and bask in the sun on a gorgeous beach.

As with most other aspects of our lives, technology has made travel easier, more convenient, and, in many cases, more affordable. Technology affects how consumers learn about travel opportunities and destinations; research travel plans; and book and pay for flights and trains, accommodations, rental cars, tours, and related services. While we're on the go, technology can provide maps and navigation services, information about nearby attractions and restaurants, real-time language translation—even restroom locators. And during and after our trips, technology lets us share our experiences.

The technology that's built in to your Internet-enabled smartphone, tablet, smart watch, or computer can serve as a powerful time- and money-saving tool when it comes to travel, and it also enables you to easily manage virtually all aspects of your trips and puts a tremendous amount of pertinent information at your fingertips.

>>>*Go Further*
WHAT "INTERNET-ENABLED" MEANS

When a device is "Internet-enabled," it means that it has access to the Internet and can send and receive data, content, and information that's relevant to what you're doing.

A computer can connect to an established Internet connection in a home, office, or public location wirelessly, via a wireless connection (Wi-Fi), or by connecting a cable from the computer to a modem (and/or a router) that physically connects that location (and your equipment) to the Internet.

A mobile device, such as a smartphone or tablet, can connect to the Internet using a Wi-Fi connection when it's within the signal radius of a Wi-Fi hotspot or home wireless network, for example. Wireless hotspots can also readily be found in hotels, offices, coffee shops, Internet cafes, airports, hotels, libraries, restaurants, and many other public locations around the world.

Smartphones and some tablets can also connect to the Internet using a cellular data connection. This means that the device accesses the Internet via a wireless 3G, 4G, or LTE cellular signal that's provided by a cellular service provider. One part of a mobile device's wireless service plan is wireless data access. Some plans offer unlimited wireless data, but most include a monthly wireless data allocation, such as 1GB or 5GB.

Many of the travel-related tasks you'll be using your device to handle require Internet access. So, once you leave on your trip, you'll probably want to have a plan in place to access the Internet while on the go. As you'll discover from Chapter 14, "Connecting Your Computer, Smartphone, or Tablet While Traveling," you have several options available for connecting to the Internet while you're traveling, but some are far more cost-effective than others.

Don't Be Afraid of Technology

Thanks to technology, the travel industry has changed, and traditional travel agents play a smaller role. Today, instead of using the services of a travel agent, people are able to use their smartphones, tablets, and computers to manage travel-related tasks, including the following:

- Researching travel-related opportunities and destinations
- Obtaining trip-related recommendations/advice
- Planning a travel itinerary
- Shopping for the best prices and deals
- Making reservations for airfare, hotels, rental cars, tours, travel packages, and cruises
- Staying in touch with friends, family, and coworkers while traveling
- Sharing travel-related experiences and photos online via social media

There are some incredible benefits and conveniences that result from making your own travel arrangements. For example,

- Your travel itinerary can automatically be imported into the scheduling/calendar program you use on your computer.
- You can manage your whole trip using a trip-management service or mobile app, such as TripIt.com.
- You can be notified in real time on your smartphone, smartwatch, or tablet of flight delays, gate changes, bad weather conditions, or other changes to your itinerary as they happen.

If you're new to using the Internet to make your travel plans, you might feel intimidated by the available choices or fear you'll make a mistake. When it comes to overcoming mistakes and technology-related fears, *My Digital Travel for Seniors* can help you. Even if you don't consider yourself to be tech-savvy, this book walks you through using your device to handle many common travel-related tasks —while saving time and money! You'll also learn how to acquire the knowledge and confidence you need to effectively, securely, and safely use today's technology to handle many aspects of travel and take advantage of free information, tools, and tips from AARP Travel (travel.aarp.org), whether or not you're an AARP member.

What You Need to Get Started

To take advantage of technology to handle travel-related tasks, you need a device—computer, smartphone, or tablet—with Internet access. You can use any Windows-based PC or any Mac-based computer, whether it's a desktop or notebook computer, for example, and any Android or Apple mobile device.

From your computer, you can then use any web browser, such as Chrome, Firefox, Microsoft Edge (Windows PCs), or Safari to access any of the travel-related online services and websites described in this book.

Visit your favorite travel-related websites using your computer's web browser.

Remember, if you decide to manage various aspects of your travel from a smartphone or a tablet, the mobile device must have Internet access via a Wi-Fi or cellular data connection. Although you can use a mobile device's built-in web browser to access online-based travel services and websites, you'll typically find it much easier to use travel-related mobile apps, which you can download and install onto your mobile device. How to find, download, and install these mobile apps is explained later in this chapter, in the "Find, Download, and Install a Mobile App" section.

What's a Mobile App?

Your smartphone or tablet operates using a proprietary operating system—such as Android, iOS, or Windows Mobile—and comes with a handful of preinstalled apps. In addition, you can download and install other optional apps, which are independent programs that add specialized features or functionality to your mobile device.

Hundreds of optional travel-related mobile apps are available for your smartphone or tablet. Some optional mobile apps are free; others require you to pay a one-time fee to acquire them; and some are initially free but require you to make in-app purchases to make use of more robust features or functions.

You get apps for your mobile device from the online app store that's associated with your device. For example, if you're an iPhone or iPad user, to find, acquire, download, and install apps onto your device, launch the preinstalled App Store app. Internet connectivity is required.

Although all your travel information can be stored in your computer or mobile device, it's often convenient to print out information, such as your travel itinerary, reservation confirmation letters, or airline boarding passes, so you have a hard copy readily accessible while on the go. To make this possible, you need a printer that connects to your computer, smartphone, or tablet.

When you have this common equipment at your disposal, you'll need to access and use the various travel-related websites, online services, and mobile apps that are discussed throughout this book. The next section walks you through finding and downloading apps.

Find, Download, and Install a Mobile App

The app stores for the various devices include millions of apps that you can acquire, download, and install. Regardless of whether you use an Android, iOS, or Windows Mobile smartphone or tablet, finding, downloading, and installing optional apps works in pretty much the same way, although the look of the screens, menus, and app icons varies. The following steps outline how to find, download, and install an app onto an iPhone that's running iOS 9 . (If your iPhone/iPad is running the iOS 10 operating system, the steps to follow are virtually identical.)

(1) From the Home screen, launch the App Store app on your smartphone or tablet.

Use the App Store's Search Field for iPhones and iPads

If you know the name of the app you're looking for, launch the App Store app, tap the Search icon, and type the title of the app in the Search field. From the listing of search results, tap the desired app listing to view its app Description screen, and then skip to step 6.

(2) Tap the Featured icon, and then tap Categories.

(1) App Store App icon

Categories Option   (2)

Featured icon

3 Scroll through the Categories list, and tap Travel.

4 Browse through the app listings in the Travel category. Swipe horizontally under a heading to scroll through app listings displayed under each specific heading, and swipe up to view additional headings.

Discover the Best Selling and Most Popular Travel Apps

To view listings for the most popular and best-selling travel-related apps, launch the App Store app and tap on the Top Charts icon. Tap on the Categories option, and then tap on the Travel category option. Tap on the Paid, Free, or Top grossing tab, and then scroll through the listing of apps, which are displayed starting with the most popular first. From the listing of search results, tap on the desired app listing to view its app Description screen, and then skip to step 6.

5 Tap an app listing that's of interest to view its Description screen.

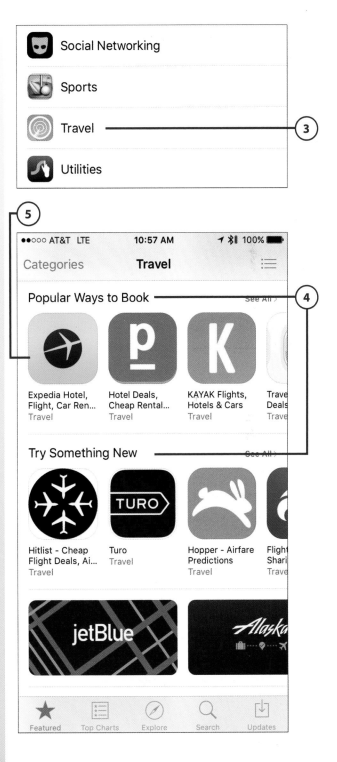

6 Tap the Details tab to view sample screenshots from the app, and then swipe up to view a description of the app.

7 Tap the Get button (on free apps—the button says Price for paid apps) to begin the download and installation process.

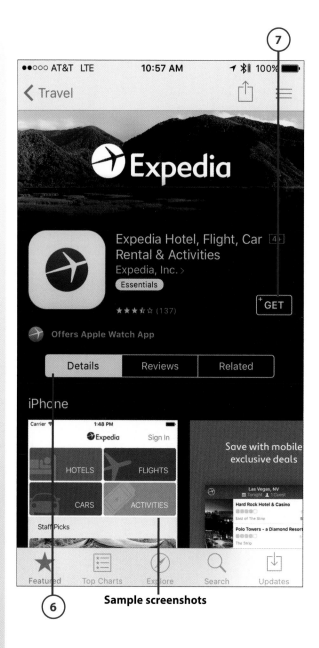

Sample screenshots

8. Tap the Install button to confirm your decision. For paid apps, tap the Buy button to confirm your decision.

9. Enter your Apple ID password, or place your finger on the iPhone or iPad's Touch ID sensor to approve the acquisition. The app begins to download immediately after you've provided approval.

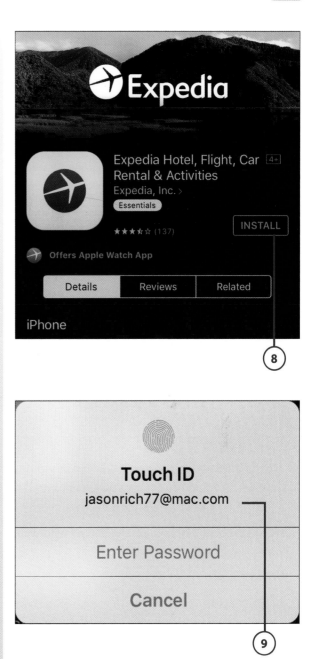

10 Tap the Open button to launch the app. Alternatively, return to the Home screen, and tap the app's icon.

>>>Go Further

MOBILE APP RATINGS AND REVIEWS

Every mobile app includes a text-based description that's created by the app's developer. However, in addition to relying on this information to determine what the app does, whether it functions as described, and to learn what other users think about the app, be sure to review the app's star-based ratings and text-based reviews before downloading and installing it.

The app's average star-based rating is displayed near the top of an app's Description screen. One star is the worst possible rating, and five stars is the best rating.

To the immediate right of the rating is a number displayed in parentheses, which indicates how many people have rated the app and how many ratings the average star-based rating is based upon.

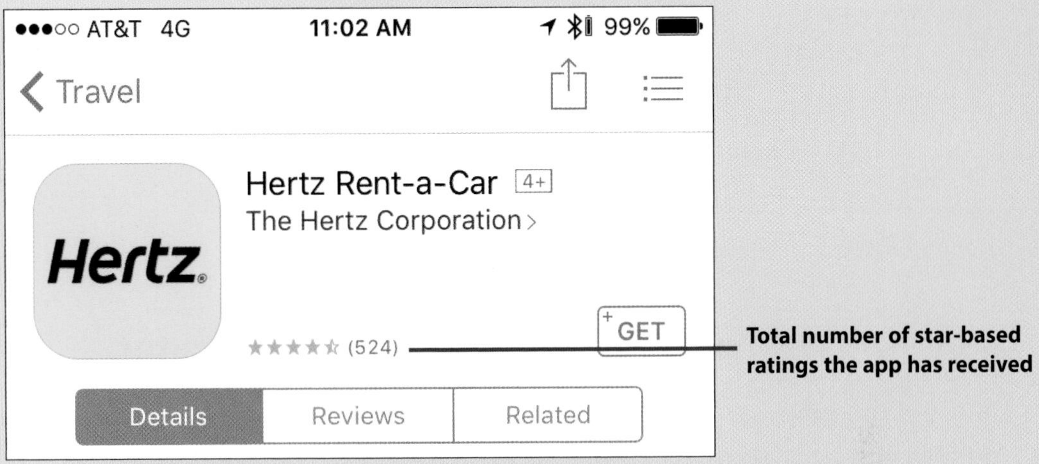

●●●○○ AT&T   4G   11:02 AM   ✈ ✳ 99% ▇

‹ Travel   ⬆   ☰

Hertz Rent-a-Car 4+
The Hertz Corporation ›

Hertz.

★ ★ ★ ★ ☆ (524) ——————— ⁺ GET ——— **Total number of star-based ratings the app has received**

| Details | Reviews | Related |

To view a more detailed chart that shows the breakdown of ratings, tap the Reviews tab and then look under the Ratings and Reviews heading.

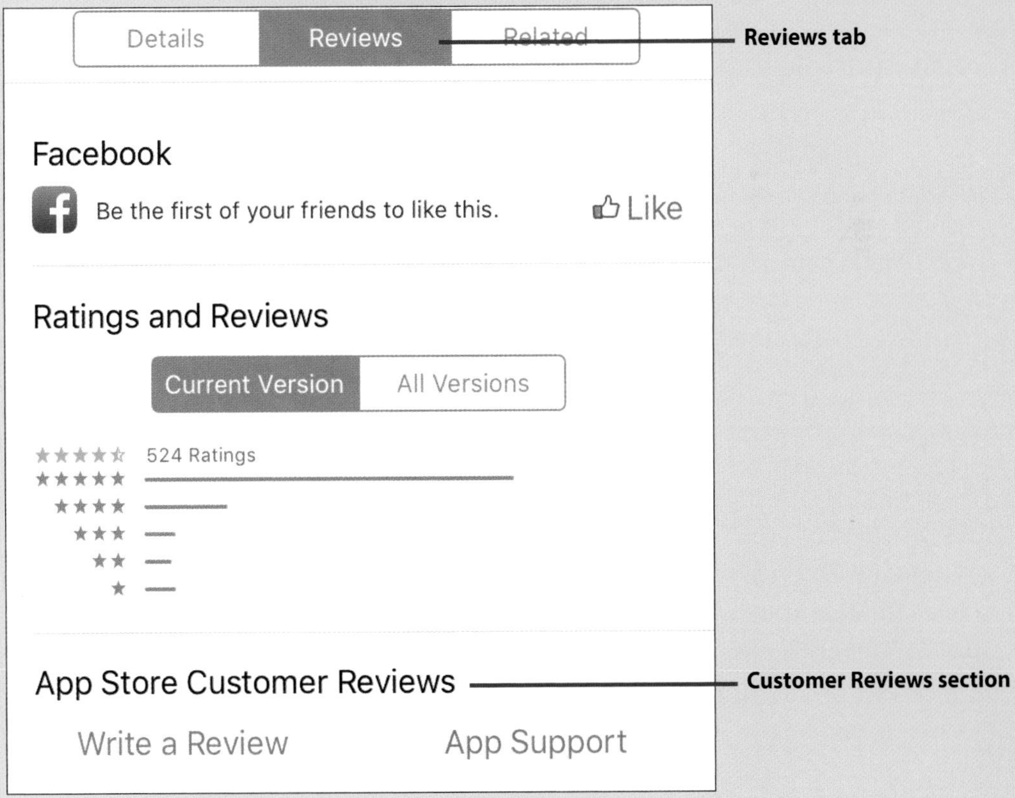

| Details | Reviews | Related ———— **Reviews tab** |

Facebook
🅵 Be the first of your friends to like this.   👍 Like

Ratings and Reviews

| Current Version | All Versions |

★ ★ ★ ★ ☆ 524 Ratings
★ ★ ★ ★ ★ ————————————————
★ ★ ★ ★ ————
★ ★ ★ —
★ ★ —
★ —

App Store Customer Reviews ———— **Customer Reviews section**

Write a Review   App Support

You also can read reviews written by other mobile device users. After tapping the Reviews tab, swipe up to see the App Store Customer Reviews heading, and then keep swiping up to read each review.

Any app that's received dozens, hundreds, or thousands of four- or five-star ratings is well designed, works as described, and will most likely serve you well. As a general rule, avoid apps that have received an abundance of one-, two-, or even three-star ratings.

Working with a Desktop or Notebook Computer

Most of the travel-related tasks for which you'll be using your computer will be online, and you'll use your computer's web browser. For example, to visit the online-based AARP Travel, launch your web browser, and in the address bar, type **travel.aarp.org**.

Visit Multiple Websites When Planning a Trip

According to research conducted by PhoCusWright, the average consumer visits 3.6 travel-related websites while shopping for an airline ticket. Using web browser bookmarks, you can store the website addresses (URLs) for your favorite travel-related websites, like travel.aarp.org, Booking.com, Hotwire.com, Travelocity.com, and Trivago.com, for quick and easy access later.

It's a good idea to create bookmarks for the various online services and websites you use so you can return to them quickly in the future. To better organize your webpage bookmarks, consider creating a bookmark folder, called Travel, for example.

The process for creating a bookmarks folder and storing bookmarks varies based on which web browser you're using. If you're using the Safari web browser on a Mac, for example, select the Bookmarks menu and click the Add Bookmark option. Select the folder in which you want to store the bookmark and, if desired, edit the webpage title. Click the Add button to save that bookmark.

Bookmarks menu

If you're using the Microsoft Edge web browser on a Windows PC (running Windows 10), click the star-shaped Favorites icon. You're then able to edit the Name field (which displays the name of the webpage), and adjust the Save In field (to determine in which folder the bookmark will be saved). Click the Add button to save the bookmark.

Favorites icon

Later, when you want to revisit a bookmarked website, access your list of bookmarks, and click the desired website in the list.

Putting Travel Technology to Work

Between travel-related websites and online services you can access from your computer (via a web browser) or from your mobile device using a specialized app, many different travel-related tasks can easily be handled using technology.

Travel-Related Websites, Online Services, and Mobile Apps

Many online travel-related services (websites and mobile apps) were originally designed to handle specific tasks. But as these sites and services have evolved, the line between what the specific tasks are has blurred. In other words, more and more online travel services and mobile apps are striving to become a one-stop-shop for most or all of your needs.

Let's take a quick look at some of the common tasks you can use your computer or mobile device to handle.

No Endorsements Are Implied

Throughout *My Digital Travel for Seniors* you'll read about many services, websites, and mobile apps. What's included in this book, however, is only a small sampling of what's actually available to you.

The services, websites, and mobile apps featured in this book are included for demonstration purposes only. In many cases, the most popular services, websites, and mobile apps are described or featured. Inclusion should not be considered an endorsement by the book's author, publisher, or AARP.

Researching Travel Destinations

Thanks to online and app-based travel guides, and countless digital travel magazines, online-based blogs, and destination-specific websites, as well as websites operated by the department of tourism for almost every city, country, and popular tourist destination in the world, as you're doing your trip planning you can find tools and resources to help you determine where to go, when to go, how to fit your travel budget, what to see, and all manner of information about specific destinations, historical sites, and attractions.

The Frommer's website

It's Not All Good

Always Pay Attention to the Source of Information

When doing travel-related research, pay close attention to the source of the information you're gathering to make sure it's timely, accurate, and unbiased.

An independently published travel guide, written by professional travel writers or journalists from a well-respected source, such as AAA Travel (www.aaa.com/travel), AARP Travel (travel.aarp.org), Fodor's (www.fodors.com), Frommer's (www.frommers.com), Lonely Planet (www.lonelyplanet.com), or Rough Guides (www.roughguides.com), will typically be timely and unbiased. But a website operated by a specific tour operator, resort, travel provider, or vacation destination could be somewhat biased and have a more sales-oriented approach.

You can also look to online travel resources, such as CruiseCritic.com or TripAdvisor.com, that publish ratings and reviews directly from travelers. When using this type of resource, don't put too much weight into any single review. Instead, choose a particular destination, travel provider, hotel, or tour operator, for example, and read a handful of reviews. Determine whether the majority of published reviews are highly positive, neutral, or very poor, keeping in mind that the reviews are written by consumers and travelers like you, not professional travel writers or journalists. This is also the case with many independently published travel-related blogs.

Finding and Booking Airline Tickets

When it comes to shopping for and booking airfares online, you can use an online travel agency website or service, such as travel.aarp.org, Hotwire.com, Orbitz.com, or Travelocity.com, that works with many different airlines and lets you compare prices among multiple airlines at once. You can also use a website or mobile app operated by a specific airline to shop for and book airline tickets from that airline.

The Southwest Airlines website

Every Major Airline Has Its Own Website

Chapter 5, "Finding and Booking the Best Airfares," introduces you to a handful of websites, online travel services, and mobile apps to use for shopping for and booking airline tickets.

Finding and Booking Hotels or Other Accommodations

In addition to popular online-based travel services like AAA Travel, AARP Travel, Hotwire, Orbitz, Priceline, or Travelocity, there are many online services (and mobile apps) dedicated to finding and booking hotel rooms, such as Booking.com, Hotels.com, and Trivago.com. If you prefer to stay at a hotel or a resort operated by a specific chain, such as Best Western, Choice Hotels, Hilton, Sheraton, or Starwood Hotels, you can visit the website or use the mobile app operated specifically by that hotel chain.

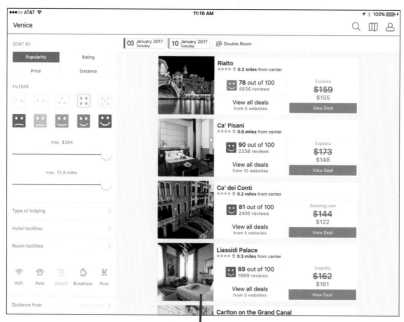

The Trivago app on the iPad

Use a Price Comparison Website to Save on Hotel Rooms

Many price-comparison websites allow you to choose a destination city, travel dates, number of beds needed, and a desired hotel/motel's star rating, and then quickly browse through a selection of chain and independent hotels and motels, compare prices, and often save between 30 and 70 percent off published nightly room rates.

Keeping in mind that rooms rates fluctuate daily based on a variety of criteria including season and demand, to find the lowest hotel rates, always check with at least three different travel services and websites before making a reservation.

Some of these services require pre-payment in full, and do not allow changes or cancellations after the reservation is made. Others offer the capability to cancel or change the reservation, either for free or for a fee, so read the fine print carefully before booking your reservation. In some instances, you'll find the lowest rate for a hotel directly from that hotel's website rather than on a price comparison website.

To learn more about how to save money when booking a hotel using your computer, smartphone, or tablet, read Chapter 7, "Finding and Booking Accommodations."

Finding and Booking Rental Cars

With services such as AAA Travel, AARP Travel, Hotwire, Orbitz, Priceline, or Travelocity, you can compare rental car prices among a handful of rental car companies in a specific city, or you can use a price-comparison service that deals only with car rentals, like AAA (www.rezserver.com/AAA-Travel), Carrentals.com, or Rentalcars.com. If you prefer to work with a specific car rental company, like Alamo, Avis, Budget, Dollar, Enterprise, Silvercar, or Thrifty, be sure to visit the website or use the mobile app for that specific company.

Discover Money-Saving Tips for Renting Cars

Be sure to read Chapter 6, "Finding Ground Transportation," to learn how to use specific websites and mobile apps to find the best deals when renting a car. For example, you can often save an additional 10 to 20 percent on a rental car if you reserve the car online at the same time you make your airline or hotel reservation using a popular online travel service.

The Hertz app running on an iPhone

Finding and Booking All-Inclusive Resorts, Cruises, or Travel Packages

Along with the general travel-related websites and services that allow you to compare prices for airfares, hotels, and rental cars, there are niche services that focus more on all-inclusive resorts, cruises, and specialized travel (like safaris in Africa or travel packages for solo travelers).

Chapter 8, "Finding and Booking a Cruise," covers how to find, book, and save money on cruise vacations, and Chapter 9, "Finding All-Inclusive Vacations and Vacation Package Deals," addresses how to discover money-saving deals when booking all-inclusive resorts and other types of vacations.

Finding and Booking Tours and Attraction Tickets

Some of the popular travel websites allow you to research and book tours and attraction tickets at the same time you book your airfare, hotel, and/or rental car. There are also specialized services and mobile apps that focus specifically on finding and booking city-specific tours and localized attraction tickets. For example, with Viator.com, you can find and book a vast selection of tours and attraction tickets all over the world.

The Viator mobile app on the iPad

The Ship Mate app (https://shipmateapp.com) is ideal for finding and booking independently operated shore excursions associated with a cruise vacation. Sight-Seeing (www.city-sightseeing.com) offers hop-on/hop-off city tours in dozens of cities throughout the world.

Comparing Prices and Finding Travel Deals

In addition to individual price-comparison websites and online-based travel agencies, meta search sites, like Kayak.com, allow you to perform airfare, hotel, or rental car searches across dozens, or even hundreds, of individual travel websites at once. From there, you're transferred to the website that's offering the deal you're looking for. In other words, these meta search sites help you find the best deals, and then direct you to the website(s) offering them.

Travelzoo.com Can Help You Find Travel Deals

Travelzoo.com (and the free Travelzoo mobile app) continuously scours the Internet in search of the very best travel deals and publishes its findings online. Every week Travelzoo contacts more than 1,000 travel providers and publishes a list of the top 20 best deals it finds. The Travelzoo Top 20 (www.travelzoo.com/top20) often lists money-saving offers for all-inclusive vacations and travel packages that include airfares, hotel, rental car, meals, tours, and admission to various attractions.

Reading Ratings and Reviews

Many services used for booking hotels and other travel services publish online reviews and ratings created by fellow travelers. In addition, online services like CruiseCritic, Family Vacation Critic, and TripAdvisor offer vast databases containing millions of consumer reviews of airlines, hotels, rental car companies, tourist attractions, tour operators, restaurants, and other travel-related services. Other mobile apps and websites, like Apple Maps, Google Maps, and Yelp!, also publish consumer-written reviews of local businesses, restaurants, local services, and attractions.

Purchasing Travel Insurance

Especially when traveling abroad, seriously consider acquiring travel insurance. Depending on the travel insurance you acquire from a company like Travelex or TravelGuard, you're financially protected if you experience a medical emergency, missed flight, lost/delayed luggage, or your trip is delayed or cancelled due to weather. Travel insurance typically costs about five percent of your total trip price, and it offers a variety of benefits if something bad happens during a trip. Chapter 12, "Finding and Purchasing Travel Insurance," offers information about how to purchase travel insurance from your computer or mobile device before you leave on a trip, as well as how to file a claim if the need arises.

Managing Your Travel Itineraries

Online-based services such as Tripit.com, as well as many different mobile apps such as FlightTrack Pro, let you manage your travel itineraries in real time. In addition to displaying your airfare, hotel, rental car, and tour details all in one place, these services alert you immediately if a flight is cancelled or delayed or if there's a last-minute gate change at the airport. Many of these services and apps sync information directly with the calendar/scheduling program you already use on your computer or mobile device. You can find more information about these services and mobile apps in Chapter 13, "Services for Managing Travel Itineraries."

Using Interactive Tour Guides and Navigation

Regardless of where you travel, chances are there's a mobile app you can install onto your smartphone or tablet that serves as an interactive tour guide and assists you in navigating any city or tourist destination. To use these services and mobile apps, however, you have to have Internet connectivity for the GPS capabilities of your smartphone or tablet to work. So, if you're traveling abroad, you'll need to turn on international data roaming (which can be costly) or purchase a pre-paid SIM chip for a local cellular service provider in the country you're visiting. More information about how to do this is covered in Chapter 14.

Using Language and Currency Translators

If you'll be traveling to a foreign country where they speak a language in which you're not fluent, consider one of the many optional mobile apps that serve as language translators. When using some of these apps, you simply type a word or sentence and the app translates it from one language to another. With other apps, you speak into the smartphone or tablet in your native language and the app translates in real time what you say into a selected foreign language. The mobile device then plays what you say in the selected language and displays the relevant text on the screen.

From the various app stores, you can also download currency-conversion apps that will come in handy when you're abroad.

If you have some time before traveling overseas, you can check out online services and mobile apps that employ technology to help you more easily learn to speak a foreign language. Rosetta Stone is an example.

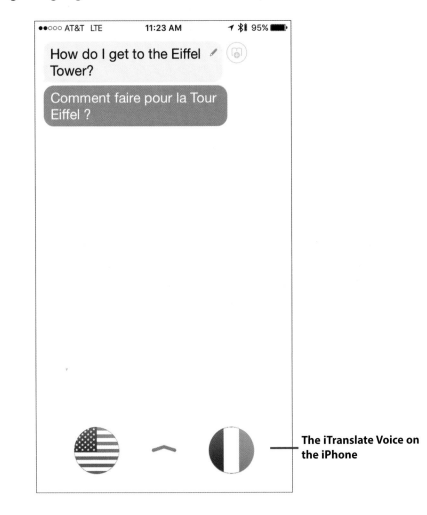

The iTranslate Voice on the iPhone

Connectivity for Language Translation and Currency Conversion

Most language-translator and currency-conversion apps require Internet access to function properly. Ideally, you need a cellular data connection so you can take advantage of these apps virtually anywhere. Keep in mind that these apps work just as well, and in some cases, faster if you're within the signal radius of a Wi-Fi hotspot.

You'll learn more about these websites and mobile apps in Chapter 10, "Mobile Apps to Use at Your Destination."

Reviewing Travel Experiences

As you experience travel, you might want to share your own reviews and opinions with other travelers. If this is the case, you can set up a free account on services like CruiseCritic, TripAdvisor, Yelp!, or one of the travel websites that publishes reviews, and then write and publish your own thoughts, reviews, and opinions and post photos. Check out Chapter 15, "Chronicle and Share Your Experiences," for step-by-step directions on how to publish and share your travel-related reviews and opinions.

Sharing Your Travel Photos Online

Using the cameras that are built in to your smartphone or tablet, it's possible to take pictures during your travels and then instantly edit and publish them online via social media. Services like Facebook, Instagram, SnapChat, and Twitter, along with online photo-sharing services such as Flickr, Google Photos, PhotoBucket, and SmugMug, offer free and public forums for sharing your travel photos. In some cases you can also create photo albums or galleries and share them only with specific friends or family members that you specifically invite to view your images.

>>>*Go Further*

REAP THE BENEFITS OF USING AARP TRAVEL AND THE AARP NOW APP

Whereas some online travel services and mobile apps are designed to handle only specific travel-related tasks, others, like AARP Travel (travel.aarp.org), offer a plethora of features, functions, and services that let you handle many aspects of travel from a single website, plus can save you money in the process.

Whether or not you're an AARP member, you can learn travel tips, research destinations, and get trip recommendations based on your individual interests. In addition, AARP members automatically qualify for a variety of discounts on airfares, hotels, rental cars, cruises, tours, attraction admission tickets, travel insurance, and other related services.

Chapter 11, "Online Travel Discounts by Association," explains how to navigate your way around the AARP Travel website, use the AARP Now app, and take full advantage of the travel-related perks your AARP membership automatically includes, such as dining.

Using Technology to Become Your Own Travel Agent

Now that you've gathered the technology you need and understand some of the ways you can use your computer, smartphone, and tablet as a powerful travel-related tool, it's time to become more technologically savvy and learn how to handle these tasks.

By following the directions and strategies in this book, in no time you'll be able to confidently serve as your own travel agent, book and manage your own travel, save yourself money and time, and maintain peace of mind knowing that you've done your research and planning to find the best value.

Technology Will Help You Plan Your Trips

Research conducted by AARP showed people 50-plus spend between 30 and 36 hours a year online planning personal trips. Additionally, they spend about 18 hours a year online booking these trips. *My Digital Travel for Seniors* will help you maximize and possibly greatly reduce your time spent handling these tasks, while helping you become acquainted with how to best use the technology that's available to you right now.

So, if you're ready to get started planning your next road trip, weekend getaway, or trip of a lifetime, Chapter 2, "Researching Travel Opportunities," explains how to use some of the online and mobile app tools available for helping you learn about potential travel destinations.

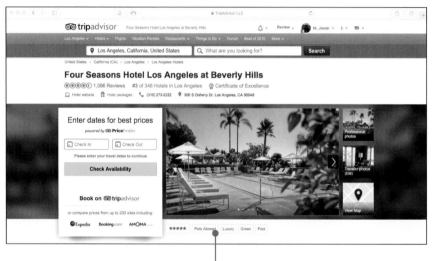

Use a consumer review website, such as TripAdvisor, to discover the opinions and experiences of other travelers before booking a hotel, restaurant reservation, or tour.

In this chapter, you discover what it takes to start planning a trip and find out how to use technologies to help you make important decisions. You'll learn

→ How to perform research about travel destinations using your Internet-enabled computer, smartphone, or tablet
→ Which online resources to rely on for the most timely, accurate, and relevant information
→ How to use AARP Travel
→ How to use Travelzoo
→ How consumer review sites, such as TripAdvisor and Yelp!, can be extremely helpful when planning your travel itinerary

Researching Travel Opportunities

Even if you're the most frugal traveler who invests a lot of time seeking out the very best travel deals, taking a trip can be costly. There are a lot of expenses and fees to consider. For example, it's important to determine

- How much you have to spend, and how you'll pay for the trip

- Where you want to travel, when you want to go, and how you'll get there

- How much transportation will cost

- Where you'll be staying, and the cost of accommodations

- What you want to experience during the trip, and what those activities will cost

- How much you need to budget for additional trip-related expenses, such as travel insurance, care for your pet while you're away, meals, and the cost associated with using your smartphone or tablet abroad (if applicable)

By making important decisions early during the trip-planning process, you can better cater to the wants, needs, and expectations of everyone you'll be traveling with (including yourself), and then use the technology that's at your disposal to research various aspects of your trip, which lets you make intelligent choices that will ultimately save you money without compromising your travel experience.

It's Not All Good

Travel Often Involves Many "Hidden" Fees

When it comes to booking airfares, choosing accommodations, renting a car, picking a cruise ship, or selecting an all-inclusive resort, in addition to the rate that's quoted, you can expect to pay a handful of additional fees that you should calculate into your travel budget.

For example, in addition to the advertised cost of an airline ticket, you might incur additional charges for taxes, airport fees, and potentially ticketing fees.

Plus, most airlines charge for some or all checked luggage and have a penalty fee for overweight or oversized bags. These fees can add $100.00 or more (each way, per passenger) to the cost of air travel. Southwest Airlines is one of the few remaining major airlines that not only offers reduced airfares for seniors but also allows all passengers to check two pieces of luggage for free, plus carry on one piece of carry-on-sized luggage and one personal item (such as a purse, briefcase, or backpack).

Many airlines now charge for snacks, premium drinks (alcohol), and meals. Some airlines also charge extra for reserving any seats or an upgraded seat with additional legroom.

Furthermore, unless you have special pre-boarding needs that you have requested in advance, many airlines charge passengers to pre-board an aircraft and charge extra for in-flight entertainment and Wi-Fi Internet access.

Chapter 5, "Finding and Booking the Best Airfares," focuses on how to calculate and, in some cases, avoid or reduce the extra charges imposed by airlines. Other chapters explain how to minimize or eliminate added fees imposed by rental car companies, hotels, cruise ships, and resorts.

Knowing what fees and extra charges to expect, and taking steps to minimize or avoid some of them, helps you set a more accurate travel budget and avoid unwanted surprises. The pre-trip research you perform helps you identify and potentially avoid these fees, or at least develop a realistic expectation.

Making the Important Decisions

Planning any travel requires making some decisions. Throughout this decision-making process, you can use your computer, smartphone, or tablet to help you research answers and make more educated, and potentially money-saving, choices.

For example, the first few decisions you need to make while planning any trip include

- Where do you want to travel?

- What do you and your fellow travelers want to get out of the trip?

- When do you want to travel?

- How will you get there?

- How long will your trip last?

- Where will you stay?

- How will you get around?

If you don't already have an answer to where you want to travel, using any of the online travel services that offer travel guides and travel-related articles can be very helpful.

After you determine where you're headed, you might then use the same travel guides and articles to help you develop realistic expectations about what that destination offers, so you can begin planning an itinerary based around the types of activities you and your fellow travelers will enjoy. For example, you can seek out adventurous activities, informative tours, details about spas, restaurant reviews, information about local attractions and historical sites you'd like to visit, facts about the local culture, and the weather forecast at your chosen destination.

Deciding when you want to travel is also an important decision, and one that affects cost. In general, you'll find lower airfares if you depart and return on a Tuesday, Wednesday, or Thursday and if you travel during the destination's off-peak or shoulder season.

>>>Go Further

UNDERSTANDING THE TRAVEL SEASONS

Every popular travel destination has a *peak, shoulder*, and *off-peak* season. Peak season is when the most people travel to that destination, so typically airfares and lodging will cost more. Peak season is also when you'll experience the largest crowds at tourist attractions, and you might discover it's harder to find dining reservations or tickets for theater or other events.

The peak travel season varies by destination. For example, in Cape Cod, peak season is the entire summer, whereas in parts of Colorado or Utah where skiing is popular, winter is the peak season.

The shoulder season is the gap between the peak and off-peak seasons. Prices are lower and crowds are less, but the tourist destination is still geared up for the peak season.

Off-peak season is when fewer tourists visit that destination. For example, the off-peak season in the Caribbean is during hurricane season (which lasts from June until November). During off-peak season, the weather might not be ideal or the activities that destination is known for might not be available. The benefits of traveling during a destination's off season are much smaller crowds and considerably lower prices.

If the information you need isn't prominently described in a travel guide or article about a particular destination, do a quick Internet search to determine the best times of the year to travel to particular destinations. In your web browser, open a search tool (such as Bing or Google) and type **peak travel season for [*destination*]** or **best time to visit [*destination*]** or **cheapest time to fly**.

Next, determine how you'll get to your destination and how long you'd like to stay. For domestic travel, you can drive, fly, or take a train (Amtrak) or a bus. Based on the distance and cost, which you can easily determine through online research, it's possible to find the fastest or most economical way to travel. For most international travel (unless you're going to Canada or Mexico from the United States or traveling around Europe), you'll probably need to fly or take a cruise ship, both of which offer their own benefits and perks, based on how you like to travel and what you want to experience during your trip.

The length of your trip is often based on your budget and the cost of travel, accommodations, meals, activities, and other travel expenses. Once again, by using some of the travel tools you'll soon be reading about, you can seek out low airfares, discounted accommodations, and/or complete package deals that allow you to save money and potentially extend the length of your trip while still staying within your budget.

Flexible Travel Dates Are Ideal

If your travel dates are flexible, you'll have more options when shopping around for lower airfares and accommodations. Sometimes you can alter your departure or return date by just a few days and save hundreds of dollars on your airfares. Likewise, if there are multiple airports in or near your departure or destination city, you'll sometimes find lower airfares by choosing a different airport.

Chapter 5 explains how to use the various online travel agents and travel services to find and book the lowest airfares.

When deciding where you'll stay when you reach your destination, you also typically have a wide range of options so you can pick one that best suits your personal preferences and budget. Each option offers advantages based on the services and amenities you're looking for. As described in Chapter 7, "Finding and Booking Accommodations," the following are some of your accommodation options:

- Brand-name hotel
- Boutique hotel
- Bed & breakfast
- Motel
- Timeshare property
- Airbnb
- Home or apartment rental

Don't Be Scared by High Hotel Prices

Websites for hotels located in or near a particular destination might advertise high nightly room rates, but when you start using online travel services, such as AARP Travel (travel.aarp.org), Booking.com, Hotels.com, or Trivago.com, you'll likely find the same or comparable accommodations at 30 to 70 percent off of those listed rates.

As with airfares, you might be able to save money if you have a little flexibility in your travel dates or a willingness to stay a slight distance away from a popular destination. By using a rental car, a taxi, Lyft, Uber, or public transportation to get to a popular area, you can often find much lower rates at lodgings located a few miles away from popular tourist destinations.

Another factor to consider is how you'll get around after you reach your travel destination. Many people immediately think they need a rental car. In some cases, though, a rental car is a costly nuisance. In addition to the daily cost of a rental car and frustration at navigating unfamiliar territory, you have to pay for gas and often rental car insurance and parking. In major cities, overnight parking at a hotel can cost an additional $30.00 to $75.00 per night. Plus, each time you arrive at a tourist destination, nearby parking often costs an additional $10.00 to $25.00 (or more).

Many cities offer public transportation systems, which are much easier to navigate when you use your smartphone with the Google Maps app (Android and iOS devices) or Maps app (iOS devices) or a specialized mobile app, which is covered in Chapter 10, "Mobile Apps to Use at Your Destination."

You might also discover it's less expensive to rely on taxis, Lyft, or Uber for transportation. The focus of Chapter 6, "Finding Ground Transportation," is using technology to discover and manage your local transportation options after you reach your destination.

>>>Go Further

THE LYFT AND UBER GROUND TRANSPORTATION ALTERNATIVE

Lyft and Uber are independent services that offer a much less expensive ground transportation option compared to a traditional taxi or limo service. Both of these services require the use of a proprietary mobile app on your Internet-enabled smartphone to request and pay for the service. While taxi or limo drivers and vehicles need to have special licenses, Lyft and Uber are staffed by independent drivers who use their own cars to transport people.

These services are available in many cities throughout the world, and a ride typically costs about half of what a traditional taxi charges, although in some places and during peak times, fees increase.

When you use the Lyft or Uber mobile app, your smartphone asks where you want to go, and then it determines your exact location when you request a pickup. The app locates a driver who is nearby and informs you when your ride arrives to your pickup location. After your trip, the app automatically charges the credit or debit card that's linked to the Lyft or Uber app when you reach your destination. Tipping the driver is not required.

Lyft and Uber mobile apps are available from the various apps stores. For more information, visit www.lyft.com or www.uber.com.

Using Your Devices to Conduct Pre-Trip Research

Throughout the trip planning process, and then once you reach your destination, your computer, smartphone, or tablet can be an indispensable tool that connects you to many information-packed resources.

Some popular travel websites, online services, and mobile apps serve you better than others in certain situations, so you'll benefit the most if you're willing to use a handful of different tools and resources during the trip-planning process and throughout your journey.

The following section describes the types of tools and resources that are available for travel-related research; Chapter 3, "Getting to Know Some Popular Travel Tools," focuses on teaching you about 12 of the most popular travel-related tools and resources and offers tips on how to best use them.

Digital Editions of Travel Magazines

Available for computers, smartphones, and tablets are digital editions of popular print publications and magazines, as well as publications that are only available in a digital format.

To find these digital publications, launch the app store app that comes preinstalled on your mobile device, and in the Search field, enter the phrase **travel magazines**.

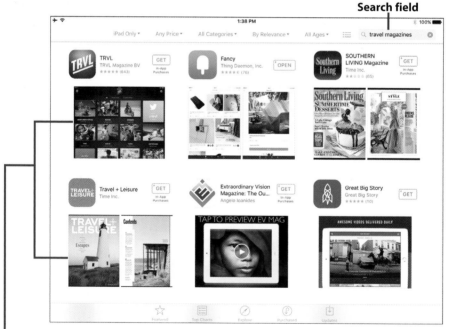

Search field

Digital magazine app listings

The search results will include apps for popular travel magazines and publications that offer a digital edition, such as *Budget Travel*, *Condé Nast Traveler*, *Cruise Travel*, *Golf & Travel*, *Lonely Planet Traveller*, *Luxury Escapes*, *National Geography Traveler*, *Romance Travel*, *Travel + Leisure*, and *World Travel*. In addition, you'll discover the digital edition of destination-specific magazines, such as *Escape! Asia*, *Hawaii Traveler*, and *Ontario Travel*, as well as city-specific editions of *Where* magazine and digital editions of airline magazines, all of which feature articles that can help you plan and experience an awesome trip.

Find Magazines in the App Store

To find the digital edition of any publication, simply enter the title in your app store's Search field. If a digital edition of that magazine is published, you'll be able to download the proprietary app for it and then acquire individual issues or a digital subscription.

Travel magazines are typically monthly publications written by professional travel journalists that you can read on your smartphone, tablet, computer, or eBook reader's screen. One great feature of the digital editions of these publications is that in the articles, you'll often find hyperlinks that you can tap or click to access additional relevant information. Plus, with a few extra taps or clicks, you can access past issues of the publication.

The Cost of Reading Digital Publications

The cost to acquire, download, and read a single digital issue of a popular magazine is typically about the same as buying a single issue of the printed magazine at your favorite newsstand. However, deep discounts are offered if you purchase an annual digital subscription to a particular publication. In some cases, if you're already a paid subscriber to a printed publication, the digital edition is available to you for free.

Another option is to install the free Texture mobile app on your smartphone or tablet, and then pay a flat monthly fee for unlimited access to hundreds of magazines, including dozens of popular travel and regional publications.

Public libraries offer their patrons digital magazines free of charge. The most common source is the digital newsstand Zinio, which offers libraries subscriptions. Overdrive is the other Library platform where you can find digital magazines.

Interactive Travel Guides

Interactive travel guides are just like traditionally printed guide books, but they're better because they're interactive and you don't have to lug around a heavy printed book! When your mobile device is connected to the Internet, it can access additional information and resources above and beyond what's printed in the actual travel guide.

Interactive travel guides are available online and via proprietary mobile apps. They're typically written by professional travel writers and published by highly reputable travel publishers. Examples are Fodor's, Frommer's, and Lonely Planet.

These guides are also city- or location-specific and include information about all aspects of that destination that's of interest to visitors, such as details about hotels, restaurants, tours, activities, tourist attractions, historical sites, and local transportation options.

Quickly Access Destination-Specific Travel Guides

To find an interactive travel guide while surfing the Internet, access any popular search engine and enter the search phrase, **[*City Name*] Travel Guide**. (You can use the same search phrase in your mobile device's app store.)

If the publisher of the travel guide website or mobile app isn't familiar to you, be sure to pay careful attention to the source of the information, as well as the mobile app's ratings and reviews (when applicable), to ensure the content is timely, accurate, and comes from a reputable source.

Popular Online Travel Services and Websites

Many of the travel services, websites, and mobile apps covered in the next chapter include comprehensive travel guides for popular destinations. This is true for services like AARP Travel (travel.aarp.org), Hotwire.com, Orbitz.com, and Travelocity.com.

Websites Operated by Individual Departments of Tourism

Every popular tourist destination, major city, and country throughout the world has a department of tourism or a convention and visitor's bureau (CVB). The sole purpose of these government agencies is to promote tourism and make it easier for prospective visitors to plan travel to that destination.

Finding a Department of Tourism or Convention and Visitor's Bureau

To quickly find the website for any department of tourism or CVB, launch your favorite web browser, and in the Search field, enter the phrase, **Department of Tourism, [*location*]** or **Convention & Visitor's Bureau, [*location*]**. Click or tap the search result that lists the official website for the tourism department or CVB you're looking for.

All these agencies have websites, and in many cases mobile apps, that offer information about flights, hotels, accommodations, restaurants, activities, historical sites, tourist attractions, and other information for that destination. The information is typically comprehensive, but it's important to bear in mind that the goal of a department of tourism or CVB is to attract tourists, so the content can be biased.

Visit Orlando tourism website

Despite possible bias, the website for a department of tourism or CVB can help you choose a travel destination, learn about what that destination offers, and then help with every aspect of your trip and itinerary planning process. Best of all, these resources are free of charge, and there's typically a toll-free phone number you can call to get your specific questions answered.

Map Apps on Your Smartphone or Tablet

Preinstalled in your iPhone or iPad is the Maps app. If you're using an Android-based mobile device, the Google Maps app comes preinstalled. (iPhone and iPad users can also download and install the free Google Maps app onto their mobile devices.) These two apps, as well as others like them, make use of the GPS capabilities and Internet connectivity that are also built in to your mobile device to provide powerful navigation tools that are useful pretty much anywhere in the world.

In addition to providing an interactive map and real-time navigation assistance, these apps contain vast databases that include informative listings about millions of points of interest, local businesses, restaurants, tourist attractions, historical sights, and other services.

These listings often include ratings and reviews about businesses, restaurants, and services, their hours of operation, and other pertinent details. So, if you're looking for a good pasta restaurant while exploring Venice, Italy, or want to find a highly rated steak restaurant in New York City, these apps can be extremely useful. Likewise, if you're looking for information about a specific museum to visit and need to know when it's open and how much the admission fee is, one of these apps can provide this information with a few onscreen taps.

In addition, as long as your mobile device has cellular Internet access, map apps can help you navigate, in real time, to your desired location by car, on foot, or using public transportation.

Digital Geography 101

For step-by-step information on how to use the Maps app on your iPhone or iPad or the Google Maps app on your Android-based mobile device, check out Chapter 10.

Using AARP Travel to Conduct Research

When you know where you want to go, AARP Travel is one of many online services that can help you figure out how to get there and pre-plan the best possible trip. If you don't yet know where you want to go, this service—for nonmembers and members—offers a quick, five-question quiz to help you choose travel destinations that match your interests. Anyone can use the site to conduct research, use travel tools, learn expert travel tips, and use the booking engine. You must be an AARP member to take advantage of member-only offers and discounts.

>>>Go Further

FEATURES OF AARP TRAVEL

You can find an ever-expanding selection of travel-related articles, travel tips, expert advice, and other content available in the AARP Travel website by visiting the site and clicking the Articles & Tips option that's displayed near the top of the screen.

For help selecting potential travel destinations, or to research destinations, click the Trip Finder option, and then follow the on-screen prompts to progress through the brief questionnaire.

Answer just five questions about your travel preferences, including how long of a trip you'd like to take, approximately when you want to travel, and with whom you'll be traveling. Within seconds after answering the questions, AARP Travel recommends a handful of destination suggestions, which you can then learn more about.

Use AARP Travel to Choose a Destination

1. Launch your computer's web browser (shown here is Safari running on a Mac).

2. Enter **travel.aarp.org** in the address field.

3. Click the Destination Guides option.

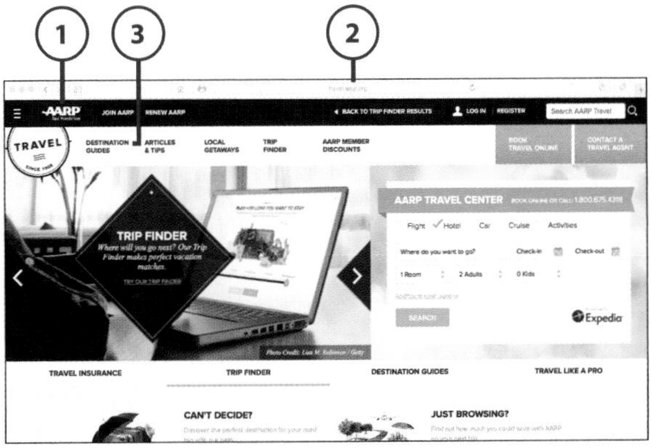

(4) Scroll through the options in the left sidebar and click on the one you want. The available guides are sorted by location, activity, environment, and alphabetically.

(5) Scroll through each section of a destination's guide or, when applicable, click the Restaurants, Shopping, Places to Explore, Hotels, Sights, Nightlife, Activities, or Travel Tips link to access more specific information about a location.

(6) Scroll to the Things You Can't Miss heading and click the Read More button that's associated with any of the listings.

Creating Hard Copies of Information

If you have a printer connected to your device, click the web browser's Print button to print the contents of the web page you're looking at. You can also click the Print icon near the top of each AARP Travel Destination Guide's webpage.

(7) Use the search window near the bottom of the Destination Guide page to shop for flights, a hotel, car, cruise, or activities related to that destination.

Using the Travelzoo Website and Mobile App

If you need help deciding where to go or want to research specific travel destinations and discover money-saving deals on vacation opportunities to those destinations, the Travelzoo online service and mobile app are useful tools.

Use the Travelzoo Website

(1) Launch your favorite web browser on your computer.

(2) Type **www.travelzoo.com** in the address field.

3 Click the Destinations option that's displayed along the left margin of the screen.

4 Select a specific destination.

5 In some cases, you will see one or more relevant articles, written by Travelzoo's experts.

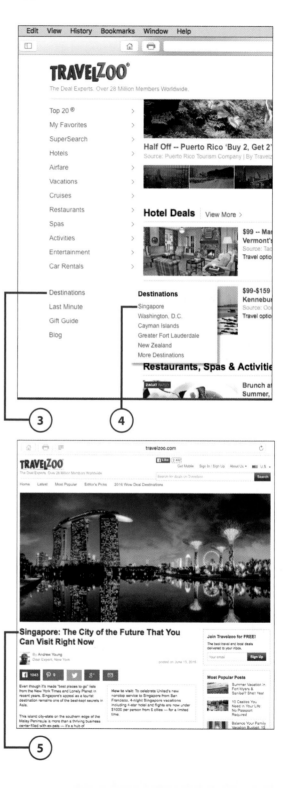

6 Click Top Deals for the selected destination to learn about money-saving offers from airlines, hotels, and tour operators and to get information about discounted travel packages, when available.

7 Alternatively, from the Travelzoo.com homepage, type your desired destination in the Search field (shown), or click the Last Minute option (when it appears) to find last-minute travel deals for specific destinations.

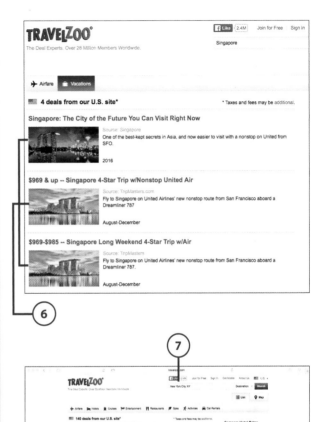

Join TravelZoo.com for Free

To unlock all the features and functions offered by TravelZoo, click the Join for Free option and set up a free Travelzoo account by providing your email address and ZIP code (or linking with your existing Facebook account).

Use the Travelzoo Mobile App

1 Launch your app store app, and type **Travelzoo** in the Search field. Download and install the free Travelzoo mobile app onto your smartphone or tablet. (Not shown.)

2 Launch the Travelzoo mobile app by tapping its app icon.

(3) The first time you use the app, tap the Allow button to allow the Travelzoo app to access your location. If you're using an iPhone or iPad, tap the OK button to allow the app to display notifications on your mobile device, when applicable. (Tap Don't Allow to prevent app-specific notifications from being generated and displayed.)

(4) Enter the desired travel destination to search for destination-specific deals. You can use a city, or a city and state, and/or a country.

(5) Tap the This Week's Top 20 option to display the week's 20 best deals from Travelzoo, or scroll down on the app's main screen to view nearby deals, based on where you're currently using the app.

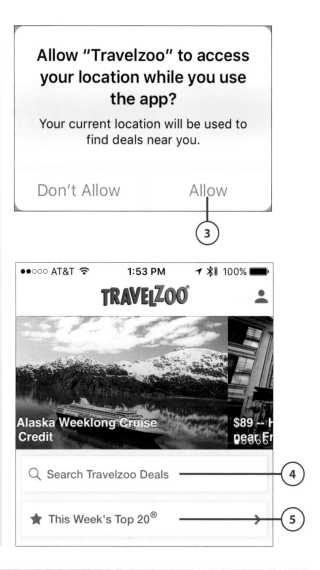

Many More Resources Are Available

Chapter 3 offers more useful information about online resources and mobile apps that allow you to easily and quickly conduct research about airlines, accommodations, tourist destinations, tour operators, and other services you might want to use during your trips.

Getting Advice from Fellow Travelers

Through its website or app, TripAdvisor offers the world's largest database (containing more than 350 million entries) of travel-related reviews and opinions that have been written by consumers like you. These reviews cover more than 6.5 million accommodations, attractions, and restaurants around the world.

More than 340 million unique users access TripAdvisor each month. The service can be a powerful tool for making intelligent decisions about where to stay, what to do, and where to eat when you're planning or experiencing a trip.

In general, the reviews published on TripAdvisor are unbiased and based on customers' actual experiences. However, never put too much emphasis on one single review. Instead, when looking up a particular hotel, attraction, or restaurant, read a handful of reviews to get a more realistic idea about what you should expect.

Get the Real Scoop About a Hotel

When a specific business on TripAdvisor has dozens or even hundreds of reviews associated with it, you can get a real sense of what you can expect when you stay at that location. For example, you'll hear from other travelers whether the rooms are clean, quiet, and well-equipped with amenities, or whether the staff was rude, the rooms were infested with bedbugs, or the expectations of visitors consistently go unmet.

You can access TripAdvisor from any Internet-enabled computer by pointing your web browser to www.TripAdvisor.com. If you want to access the same content from your smartphone or tablet, download and install the official TripAdvisor mobile app.

Set Up a Free TripAdvisor Account

To unlock all of TripAdvisor's free tools and resources, set up a free account the first time you visit the website or use the mobile app. To do this, click or tap the Join option. When prompted, share your Facebook, Google, or Email account information.

Use TripAdvisor on Your Computer

① Launch your favorite web browser on your computer.

② Type **www.tripadvisor.com** in the address field.

③ Type a city, state, and/or country in the Where Are You Going? field. Click the Search button to continue.

④ Alternatively click the What Are You Looking For? field. From the menu that appears, click what you're looking for, including options such as Overview of [*location*], Hotels in [*location*], and Vacation rentals in [*location*]. You can also type something specific, such as **Sheraton Hotel**.

⑤ You see a listing of what's available in the category you selected. From here, you can enter your desired check in and check out dates.

⑥ Sort the listing by various criteria by clicking on the appropriate tab.

⑦ Click a specific listing to read customer reviews of that location. In the listing title, you can also see its average rating. Click the Show Prices button to display rates for that hotel.

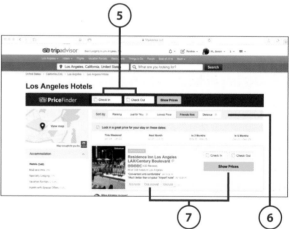

8 Find reviews about a specific hotel, attraction, or restaurant by entering the name and location, such as Sheraton Universal, Universal City, California in the What Are You Looking For? field. Click the Search button to continue.

9 You see the average TripAdvisor rating as well as details about the hotel.

10 Click the Overview tab to learn more about the specific hotel, or click the Reviews tab to see how many reviews have been posted about that hotel by travelers, and then read those reviews. Click the Photos option to view photos taken and published by TripAdvisor users.

Find Other Information

Instead of typing a hotel name in the search field or clicking the Hotels In [*location*] option, you can access similar reviews, ratings, and information about restaurants, attractions, and things to do in or near a desired location.

Use the TripAdvisor App

(1) Launch the App Store app, and in the Search field, type **TripAdvisor**. Download and install the free TripAdvisor mobile app onto your smartphone or tablet. (Not shown.)

(2) From the Home screen, launch the TripAdvisor mobile app and sign in or create an account. (Not shown.)

(3) Enter the name of a hotel, attraction, or restaurant followed by a comma and the city and state (or city, state, and country) in the Search field displayed. For example, type **Sheraton, New York Times Square**.

(4) You see an overview of that hotel, attraction, or restaurant, which includes its average TripAdvisor rating. Tap the Map icon to see a detailed map of the location where you requested is located. Tap the Call icon (if you're using a smartphone) to call the hotel, attraction, or restaurant. Tap the Been button to indicate you've been to that location, or tap the Save icon to save that listing.

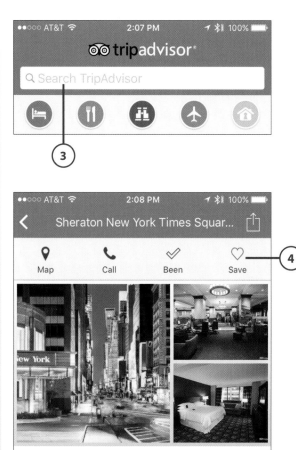

(5) Swipe up to see more details about a location's TripAdvisor ratings and, when applicable, sort the ratings and reviews by relevant criteria.

●●○○○ AT&T 📶 2:08 PM ⚹ ✱ 100% ▰▰

‹ Sheraton New York Times Squar... ⬆

PHOTOS   REVIEWS   NEARBY   **SHOW PRICES**

Reviews

#300 of 475 hotels in New York City

◉◉◉◉◯ 5,441 Reviews

Excellent		1688
Very good		2112
Average		1052
Poor		359
Terrible		230

Read reviews that mention:

All reviews   central park   the club lounge

times square   great location   new york

(6) Keep swiping up to read individual text-based reviews and see ratings created by TripAdvisor users. Tap any review to open and read it.

●●○○○ AT&T 🛜   2:08 PM   ✈ ✶🔋 100% ▬▬▬

<   Sheraton New York Times Squar...   ⬆️

PHOTOS   REVIEWS   NEARBY   **SHOW PRICES**

🔍 Search 5441 reviews   >

"Handy location and good for a city break "
◉◉◉○○ Jun 18, 2016

The Sheraton a Times Square could do with a bit of an update being little dated in parts but i...

"Exellent Location!!"
◉◉◉◉○ Jun 17, 2016

Stayed on this property with adult group tour travel for two nights. Excellent location, just a...

"Mixed Feelings"
◉◉◉◉○ Jun 17, 2016

Check in was swift and easy, as was finding our room....

"Our go-to hotel!"

(7) From the app's main screen, tap the Hotel, Dining, Attraction, or Flight Search icon to locate specific information relating to a destination you select, or tap the Near Me Now option to view a listing of reviews for hotels, attractions, and restaurants that are located near your current location (which is determined using your smartphone or tablet's built-in GPS).

(8) If you'll be traveling abroad and won't have Internet access from your smartphone or tablet, tap the Download Cities option. (Not shown.)

(9) Tap the Download a City button and select the city where you'll be traveling. Doing this before you leave will allow you to access location-specific content within TripAdvisor without requiring Internet access.

(10) Once you set up a free TripAdvisor account, you're encouraged to write and publish your own ratings, reviews, opinions, and travel photos. To do this from the mobile app, tap on the Write a Review option, and follow the on-screen prompts.

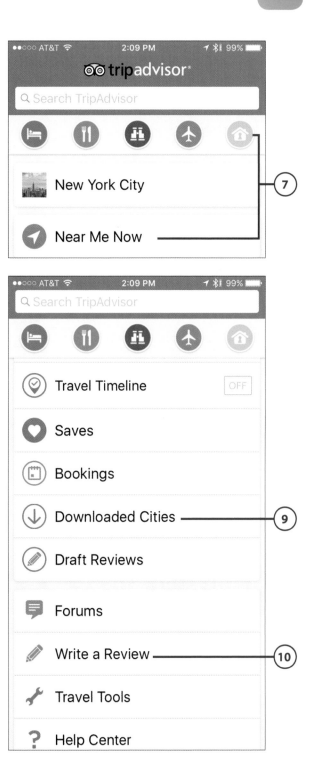

Other Sources for Consumer Reviews

TripAdvisor offers the largest collection of consumer-written reviews and opinions available online, but many popular travel services and websites, such as Booking.com and Hotels.com, also encourage their customers to rate and review their experiences. Reading these reviews before making plans and reservations will help you develop realistic expectations about what to expect and potentially avoid the pitfalls experienced by previous travelers.

Many online services and mobile apps, including Foursquare, OpenTable, Yelp!, Zagat, and Zomato (formerly UrbanSpoon) allow you to quickly find restaurants using a variety of search criteria (such as location, price, average rating, and/or food type) and then read customer reviews about each dining establishment before making a reservation.

Rely on Multiple Sources

To ensure you gather the most information possible and find the very lowest prices, always consider using at least three different online services, websites, or mobile apps when planning. The good news is that using any of these services to look up information takes just a few minutes.

Ultimately, by investing time to research the best travel deals online, you'll typically be able to have a better travel experience and save money.

Trivago.com is a well-designed service for finding and booking
hotels anywhere in the world.

This chapter introduces you to some popular online-based travel services, travel websites, and mobile apps that you can use for a wide range of tasks, including

→ Shopping for the lowest prices on airfares, rental cars, accommodations, cruises, travel packages, and other travel-related services
→ Booking your travel using a credit or debit card
→ Managing your travel itinerary

Getting to Know Some Popular Travel Tools

This chapter focuses on introducing you to some of the more popular travel-related services, websites, and mobile apps; outlines what you can use them for; and explains how to best use them.

Before You Book a Trip

Literally thousands of travel-related services and mobile apps allow you to shop for and book flights, accommodations, and rental cars, plus purchase other travel-related services. Many of them seem very similar, but in reality, there are often significant differences between these services. Thus, it's important that you understand what's being offered and what service-specific policies you'll have to abide by.

For example, each of the travel-related services that allow you to search multiple travel providers simultaneously to find the lowest prices has a different relationship, partnership, or deal with each travel provider (airline, hotel, rental car company, cruise line, and so on) that it represents. Thus, the prices each service can offer for airfares, hotels, rental cars, or other services vary, sometimes dramatically.

In addition, the travel providers that each service works with varies and constantly changes, so any single service will not allow you to shop for the lowest prices among all of the airlines, accommodations, or rental car companies that are available for the destination you're planning to travel to. This is why it's often beneficial to use three different services to shop for the lowest prices.

You'll also discover vastly different policies that go along with the deeply discounted prices you're being offered. For example, when you make a booking with many of these services, the reservations must be prepaid and can't be changed or cancelled.

Some services allow reservations to be changed but charge a hefty fee. Other services don't require prepayment for accommodations or rental cars (so you can easily cancel them), or offer different rates based on whether you prepay or opt to pay upon arrival.

In most cases, reservation holders must have a major credit card and photo identification (driver's license or passport) in their name to check in with the airport, hotel, rental car company, or cruise line. A debit card is often not accepted for check-in.

Meanwhile, some of the services that offer the deepest discounts don't tell you exactly which travel provider you'll be using until after you've prepaid for the noncancellable and nonchangeable reservation. For example, when booking a flight, you can choose the departure and destination city, as well as the departure and return dates, but not the actual airline or flight times. When booking a hotel, you can choose the star-based rating of a hotel, a room type, check-in and check-out dates, and an approximate location where you want to stay, but you can't select a specific hotel or hotel chain.

Some of these services advertise low prices then tack on extra fees and charges just prior to checkout, which dramatically increases the cost of what you're booking. In the case of hotels, for example, some now charge a mandatory "resort fee" (up to $25.00 per night), either per room or per person, that's typically not quoted as part of the nightly rate.

Some services advertise "price-match guarantees" but leave it up to you to find lower prices, call the service, and request the price match to be applied to your booking.

Also, when services offer star-based ratings for accommodations, many of them have their own star-based rating system that's different from industry standards. For example, a service might promote a specific hotel as being a four-star property (based on its own rating system), but every other established rating system gives that same hotel a three-star rating. So, the service advertises that you're getting a four-star hotel for the price of a three-star hotel, but by any other rating system this isn't the case.

All that being said, there are amazing travel deals to be found using the various online travel services, websites, and mobile apps. However, it's important that you understand exactly how each service works before paying for your bookings. Make sure to check for restrictions on making changes and cancellations before you click the button to purchase.

Whether you're traveling domestically or internationally, if you think you might need to change or cancel a trip, consider purchasing travel insurance from a third party, such as AIG Travel Guard, Allianz, or Travelex, with a "cancel for any reason" option, which often costs a bit extra. Chapter 12, "Finding and Purchasing Travel Insurance," offers more information on the benefits of travel insurance.

When you book a flight, hotel, rental car, tour, activity, cruise, or another travel-related service online, you generally receive a confirmation email, typically within minutes. At that point, it's a smart strategy to call the travel provider directly, confirm the reservation, and provide any additional information that's necessary, such as airline seat requests, hotel room requests, or meal preferences.

Special Needs?

If you need wheelchair assistance, other help in an airport, or special meals on your flight, call the airline in advance. Let airport employees and in-flight crew members know of your needs during the trip as well.

This chapter includes information, listed alphabetically, about 12 travel-related websites, online-based services, and mobile apps that will help you plan, book, and manage your travel. As you read about each service that's offered, you'll discover what sets each apart from its competition and learn about some of the pros and cons related to using it. Keep in mind that this is only a small sampling of the many popular travel-related websites, online-based services, and mobile apps that are available to you. Throughout this book, you'll be reading about additional options as well. A service's inclusion in this chapter should not be considered an endorsement by the author, the publisher, or AARP.

Airbnb

One of the best ways to immerse yourself in a local culture when traveling abroad, or to see how the locals live in a city you're visiting domestically, is to stay in a home or apartment rather than a traditional hotel or motel. Renting a home or apartment is also considerably less expensive than a traditional hotel or motel.

Airbnb (www.airbnb.com) is an online marketplace and community that lets travelers find and book unique accommodations through local hosts in more than 191 countries (encompassing more than 34,000 cities). An Airbnb host is someone who offers a room in their home or apartment, an entire home or apartment, or some other type of unique accommodation (such as a castle) for a nightly or weekly rate. These are not traditional hotels, motels, or bed and breakfasts, but peoples' private homes or properties.

Airbnb has more than 2 million listings worldwide, which makes finding the perfect place to stay and connecting with a host using the Airbnb website or mobile app extremely easy.

One advantage to Airbnb is that accommodations can be booked weeks or months in advance or the day before your planned arrival, and the nightly rate is not affected. Plus, most hosts are very accommodating when it comes to changing or cancelling reservations without incurring financial penalties.

Use the Airbnb Website or Mobile App

When you're planning your trip and need a clean and comfortable place to stay, all you need to do is launch the Airbnb website (www.airbnb. com) or mobile app, set up a free account and profile (which you do only once), and then follow these steps (shown here using the Airbnb mobile app running on an iPad):

(1) Tap on the Search icon (which looks like a magnifying glass), and type your desired destination in the search field. Tap the Search key to continue.

(2) Enter your desired travel dates using the calendar. Tap Next to continue.

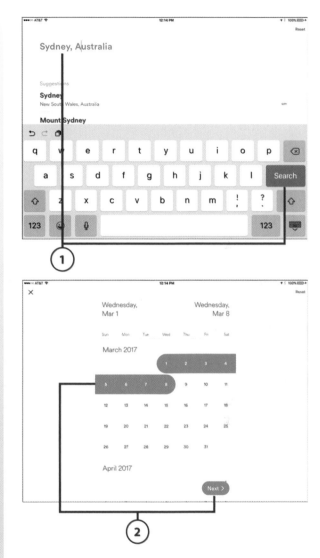

3 Select the type of accommodation you're looking for. Your options include Entire Place, Private Room, or Shared Room. Tap Next to continue.

4 Enter how many people you're traveling with and need accommodations for, and disclose whether you'll be traveling with pets. Swipe up to see all of the available options. Tap Save to continue.

Get Your Questions Answered

If you have a question about a particular listing, contact a host directly through the Airbnb website or mobile app by sending an email or text message. In some cases, you're invited to call the host directly. No matter which communication method you choose, you typically receive a reply very quickly.

5. Select how many beds, bedrooms, and/or bathrooms you require. Tap Save to continue.

6. Optionally, you can choose the amenities you'd like available, such as TV, Internet, wheelchair access, kitchen, and so on. Tap Save to continue.

7. Enter a price range per night using the slider. (This step is not required.) Tap Save to continue. (If you want to view all available options regardless of price, don't tap the Price Range option.)

Pay Attention to Each Host's Policies

Included within each Airbnb listing are the host's policies. For example, some hosts do not allow smoking or pets on their property. To avoid problems, be sure you understand and are willing to adhere to the host's rules.

Each Airbnb listing also includes a list of amenities offered and describes whether guests will have their own bathroom or a shared bathroom. Some hosts offer full use of their kitchen or include daily breakfast. You can also determine whether free Wi-Fi, the use of laundry facilities, and other essentials (including clean towels, shampoo, and soap) are included.

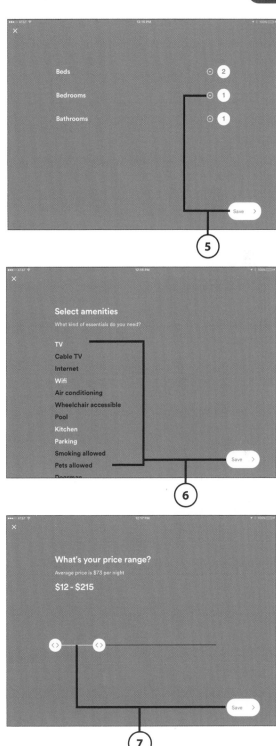

8 Tap the See [*insert number*] Homes banner to view individual listings that match the criteria you set. Each listing includes details about the property, information about the host, photos of the property, the average star-based rating the host has received (and the number of reviews from past guests), a list of amenities that are offered, and the nightly rate. To view an expanded version of each listing, tap its thumbnail image or adjust the display option by tapping the display icon.

9 Tap the Request to Book button for the listing where you want to stay. The host receives your request, views your profile, and either accepts or rejects the booking.

10 After the booking is accepted, payment in full is made using a credit or debit card. You receive a reservation confirmation and will be connected directly with the host via email or text message so you can discuss the details of your arrival. (Not shown.)

Display icon

Airbnb Alternatives

Airbnb is just one of several home sharing services. Competitors that offer similar services include HomeAway.com, HomeStay.com, PerfectPlaces.com, Tripping.com, and VRBO.com.

Airbnb Hosts

It's important to understand that when you use Airbnb to book accommodations, you're not working with a hotel, motel, or professionally operated bed and breakfast. Instead, you're working with individuals who are making some or all of their homes (or properties they own) available to you for a nightly fee that's typically much less than a hotel.

Many Airbnb hosts are willing to show you around their city and serve as an informal guide. Others include daily breakfast or are willing to provide a local's perspective and offer their suggestions as you're planning your itinerary or choosing restaurants. From a listing and the host's profile, you can determine how involved they're willing to be prior to and during your stay.

Booking.com

Booking.com and the Booking.com mobile app provide a fast and easy way to find and make accommodation reservations almost anywhere in the world. This service publishes a new selection of money-saving deals every day and offers listings for more than 945,000 properties worldwide (across more than 224 countries), including vacation rental homes. Each property listing is accompanied by verified reviews and star-based ratings from Booking.com customers.

Two other things that set Booking.com apart from other services are that most reservations can be changed or cancelled and, at the time of booking, guests can make special requests directly with the hotel. The hotel replies to that request, typically within a few hours. For example, you can request a room with a specific bed configuration, a nonsmoking room, or a room on a higher or lower floor within the hotel.

Booking.com never charges extra booking fees and offers a Best Price Guarantee, which means if you find a lower price for the same accommodations, for the same travel dates, Booking.com refunds the difference.

More About Booking Accommodations

Booking.com is an example of a service that's used exclusively for finding and booking accommodations. For more information on booking accommodations, and tips for saving money in the process using Booking.com or a competing service, read Chapter 7, "Finding and Booking Accommodations."

Use the Booking.com Service

Launch your computer's web browser and visit www.booking.com (shown in these steps) or install the Booking.com mobile app on your smartphone or tablet. You set up a free account, in which you store your name, address, credit card details, and other information so that you can make and confirm reservations much faster in the future.

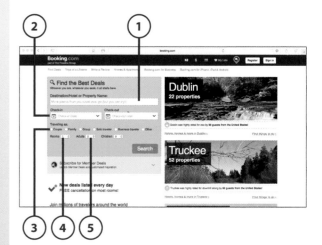

1. Type your destination city (or city, state, and country), or if you prefer to stay with a particular hotel chain, you can enter a specific name, such as **Hilton, Paris, France**.

2. Provide your check-in and check-out dates.

3. Select how you'll be traveling. Choices are Couple, Family, Group, Solo Traveler, Business Traveler, or Other.

4. Select the desired number of rooms.

5. Enter how many adults and children will be in your traveling party. If you indicate that you'll have children with you, you also need to enter their ages. Click the Search button.

6 You see a list of all accommodation options. Each property listing includes the name of the hotel, its average star-based rating, an icon indicting whether parking is available, and the cost per night. Click a specific listing to view more information or to choose a specific room type. (Keep in mind, requesting certain room types increases the room rate.)

7 Use the Filter By option to quickly narrow the list of available accommodations. For example, you can use the Set Your Budget Per Night filter to a specific price range. You can also display only accommodations with a specific star-based rating, or seek out listings for hotels that offer a free cancellation policy or the ability to book without using a credit card. It's also possible to narrow down the types of accommodations displayed or select your bed preferences (twin beds, double bed, queen size bed, or king size bed).

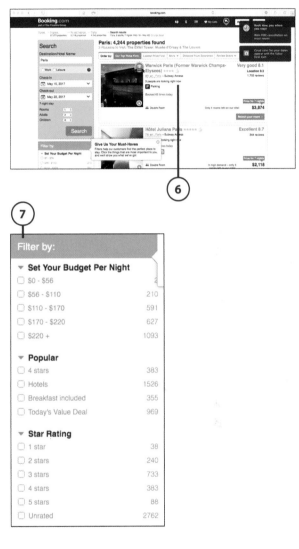

8 Scroll down in the Filter
By menu to select specific
amenities you want, such as
free Wi-Fi, a fitness center,
an airport shuttle, a spa, an
on-property restaurant, or a
swimming pool.

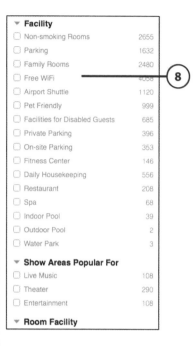

Pay Attention to Reviews and Ratings

Always check the hotel's average
star-based rating, and read some
of the reviews published on the
service prior to making your
reservation. Near the bottom of
each individual listing on Booking.
com is a heading that says,
"Reasons to Choose [*Hotel Name*]"
or "(#) Reasons Other Travelers
Love [*Hotel Name*]." Below either
heading, you see a handful of
bullet points outlining advantages
to that location.

Be sure to read the text displayed
below The Fine Print and House
Rules headings, so you fully understand the hotel-specific policies
prior to making your reservation.

9 Depending on the destination you've selected, it's often possible to narrow down your search by geographic region or district, or select specific hotel chains. After you've entered all your filter criteria, click a property listing to see details about that property.

10 You see photos of the property, along with a detailed text-based description. Scroll down to view and choose a specific room type. Click the Reserve button to begin booking your reservation.

District	
Paris City Center	2108
The Real Heart of Paris	3801
4th arr.	281
Les Halles	239
2nd arr.	274
3rd arr.	272
7th arr.	197
Le Marais	393
1st arr.	217
6th arr.	273
Pigalle	111
Latin Quarter	249
Saint Germain des Pres	288
5th arr.	244
Montmartre	183
Champs Elysées	314
8th arr.	304
16th arr.	217
18th arr.	276
11th arr.	223
9th arr.	290
15th arr.	256
10th arr.	218
17th arr.	225
14th arr.	150
12th arr.	108
Eiffel Tower Area	294
Belleville	17
Batignolles	51

Reserve button

Cruise Ship Mate

Cruise Ship Mate is a mobile app that handles several useful tasks for people looking to find a cruise. To begin, the app allows you to access information about every major cruise line, see details about the ships in each cruise line's fleet, and view upcoming cruise itineraries for each ship (sorted by date). This app does not let you book reservations for a cruise, but it does help you find a cruise so you can book it through another service, and it helps you manage details after you've booked your reservation. To use this app, you need to create a free account the first time you launch it.

Track the Location of Cruise Ships

After you book your cruise, you can track the location of your cruise ship in real time. This feature is useful for the friends and family you leave at home, so they can follow your high-seas adventure if they also install the Cruise Ship Mate app onto their mobile devices.

When you select a cruise, you can view the current price for it and set up a free Price Watch, which alerts you if the price drops. After you've booked the cruise, you're able to manage information about the sailing.

For example, the app displays your itinerary and offers an interactive packing list. You can also use the app's scheduling feature to keep track of dining, show, and spa reservations, as well as onboard activities you want to participate in.

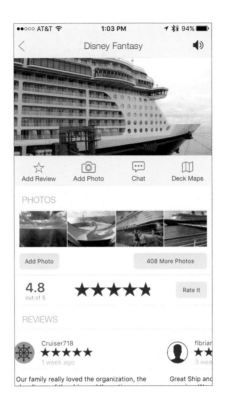

Tap the Excursions button to search for and independently book your own shore excursions at each port of call with Cruise Ship Mate's partners. Excursions booked through the Cruise Ship Mate app are typically less expensive than similar excursions booked through the cruise line.

It's Not All Good

Land Excursion Options

Although you have the option to book land excursions at each port of call through the Cruise Ship Mate app, or on your own once you go ashore, booking through the cruise line has some advantages even though you will pay more when you book shore excursions through the cruise line. However, if the excursion is delayed and you miss the all-aboard time, the cruise ship will wait for you as long as you have booked through the cruise line. Otherwise, you could find yourself missing the boat.

In addition, each tour operator the cruise line works with has been checked out by the cruise line and is insured, licensed, and uses well-maintained equipment, when applicable. This gives you added piece of mind when scuba diving, zip lining, jet skiing, taking a helicopter tour, or doing any activity that includes some level of danger.

In addition to the Cruise Ship Mate app, many cruise lines have proprietary mobile apps designed for use during the cruise, without having to pay for shipboard Wi-Fi. Check your app store for apps from Carnival Cruise Lines, Disney Cruise Lines, Holland America, Norwegian Cruise Lines, and Royal Caribbean.

Book Cruises Using Mobile Apps

Several mobile apps are available that allow you to find and book your cruises with any of the popular cruise lines: Cruise Deals, Cruise.com, and iCruise.com. To read reviews of cruise ships, consider using the Cruise Critic mobile app or visit www.cruisecritic.com.

You can also use several of the travel services featured in this chapter, including Expedia.com, Priceline.com, and Travelocity.com, to find and book cruises at a discount.

Expedia

Expedia is both an online travel service and a mobile app that lets travelers shop for and book flights, hotels, rental cars, cruises, travel packages, and activities from a single service. As a result, if you book some combination of travel arrangements, such as flights, hotels, and/or a rental car at the same time, you automatically receive an additional discount. Plus, by becoming an Expedia member (which is free), you're entitled to an additional 10 percent discount on hotels.

AARP Travel Center Powered by Expedia and AARP

The AARP Travel Center powered by Expedia is the booking engine within AARP Travel's website. It provides special savings and offers to AARP members. To take advantage of them, visit travel.aarp.org to find and book your flight, hotel, rental car, cruise, or activities.

In addition to the benefit of being able to find and book most aspects of a trip from a single service, Expedia offers a Best Price Guarantee and does not charge to cancel or change any reservations. Based on what you book, however, the individual travel providers might have a no changes or cancellation policy, or they might charge a hefty fee to change or cancel a reservation.

Earn Points for Free Travel

Like most airlines and hotel chains, Expedia has its own point-based frequent traveler program, called Expedia+. The more bookings you do with this service, the more points you earn. You can redeem points for free travel. To join Expedia+, visit the website or use the mobile app, and select the Rewards option and then click or tap on the Join Now and Get Rewards button.

When you launch the Expedia.com website or use the mobile app, click the appropriate button for the type of travel you're looking for. Your options include Flights, Hotels, Bundle Deals, Cars, Cruises, Things to Do, or Vacation Rentals. You can also choose among Fight + Hotel, Flight + Hotel + Car, Flight + Car, or Hotel + Car to save additional money.

Based on the option(s) you select, you'll be prompted to enter pertinent information about what you're looking for. For example, if you select Flight + Hotel, you'll be asked for your departure city, destination, departing date, return date, number of rooms requested, and the number of adults and children you'll be traveling with. You'll also be prompted to choose between flight classes (First class, Business class, Economy/Coach class, or Premium Economy class).

Click the Search button to have Expedia seek out the best deals and travel options for you. The service works with more than 282,000 hotel and motel properties, 475 airlines, 15,000 activities, and dozens of rental car companies around the world, and quickly searches among all its travel provider partners to find and display your options.

Hotel listings

The results related to your search criteria are displayed as individual listings. Click any listing to view the details and book your reservation. Alternatively, narrow your search results by using the Filter Results tool to choose specific neighborhoods for your hotel, a preferred star-based hotel ratings, and/or hotel amenities you want or need. You can also sort search results based on price or rating.

When booking a flight, for example, you're able to choose between nonstop and multi-stop flights, compare prices between nearby airports, check alternative travel dates for lower fares, and click the Flight Details and Baggage Fees option to discover additional charges you'll likely incur.

Special Needs Requests Are Easy

You can indicate special needs requests as you make your reservation. When booking a hotel, for example, you can use the Filter Results menu to choose various accessibility options, such as Accessible Bathroom, In-Room Accessibility, or Roll-In Shower.

Select Nonstop Flight Options

When available, many of the online services, including Expedia, allow you to seek out nonstop flights or choose flights with one or more stops. Although nonstop flights are more convenient, they tend to cost more, when available. Nonstop flights also typically sell out first, so if you're booking last minute, these more convenient flights might no longer be available. This is the case even if you book your flights directly with an airline.

From a convenience standpoint, when you book all your travel-related needs through a single service, like Expedia.com, you can keep track of your entire itinerary through that website. In Expedia, you simply click the My Trips menu. Keep in mind that by using multiple websites to book various aspects of your trip separately, you can sometimes save more money (even though Expedia offers bundle deals and packages). It's then possible to use a third-party service, like TripIt.com, to manage your itinerary.

FlightTrack 5

Your mobile device's app store offers many apps to manage your travel itinerary in one location and share aspects of your travel plans with specific people via email, text message, or social media.

FlightTrack 5 automatically tracks your flight itinerary and issues reminders and alarms for check-in times and locations for your upcoming flights and connecting flights. In addition, after you enter your flight information in the app, it automatically alerts you of flight delays, cancellations, gate changes, weather issues, and potential other problems that could affect your travel.

During the flight, the app can display real-time location, speed, and altitude information for many flights, as well as radar weather imagery, when your mobile device has Internet access (via an aircraft's onboard Wi-Fi service).

The app has information about more than 3,000 airports and 1,400 airlines, so you can receive help navigating your way around airports, finding your gate, and determining where to pick up your checked baggage. If you need to find a last-minute alternative flight, the app can also be helpful.

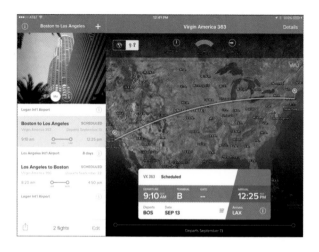

As you receive reservation confirmation emails from airlines, you can forward those emails to a specific email address that the app provides, and all your travel details for each trip are imported into the app without any data entry on your part. You can also manually add or change flight itinerary details as needed from within the app.

Another useful feature of FlightTrack 5 is that it can store and manage multiple itineraries. You can view details about all upcoming trips or only specific trips. If you use the iPhone edition of FlightTrack 5, Apple Watch integration is included.

The FlightTrack 5 app costs $4.99. For frequent travelers, being able to manage and quickly access details about all aspects of your upcoming flights is a useful tool. This particular app offers a stunning user interface, detailed maps, and a comprehensive collection of useful features.

Similar Apps Are Available

Other apps that offer similar functionality include FlightAware, Flight Tracker, mi Flight Tracker, and the TripIt mobile app.

Hotels.com

Hotels.com and the Hotels.com mobile app help you research, find, and book hotels around the world, typically at a discounted price. After you set up a free account with this service, booking a hotel reservation takes just minutes, and for every 10 hotel nights you book (with any hotel), you receive an award of one free night. Plus, Hotel.com Rewards subscribers are eligible for "Secret Price" deals through the service.

What makes Hotels.com so popular is that it's easy to use. Once you launch the website or mobile app, you simply need to enter a destination, hotel name, landmark, or address in the app's main search field, provide your check-in and check-out dates, select the reason for your travel (business or leisure), and then select the number of rooms required (based on the number of people you're traveling with).

Click the Search (or Show Deals) button to view detailed listings for participating hotels, motels, and other accommodations. You see applicable listings that are based on the information you provide. Special offers are displayed in a "Deal of the Day" frame. Each listing includes the hotel's name, address, average star-based rating, and nightly rate. You'll also see the rate for that hotel that's being offered by completing online services, such as Expedia, Orbitz, and Travelocity, when applicable.

To modify your search and narrow your options, use the Narrow Results tools to search for a specific hotel chain, hotels with a specific star-based rating, accommodations that fall within a defined price range, or accommodations that have specific amenities that you select.

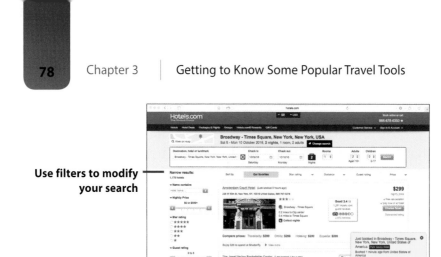

Use filters to modify your search

Hotels.com does not charge a reservation change or cancellation fee. Once a reservation is booked, however, you must abide by the policies of the hotel you've made your reservation with, so change or cancellation fees may apply.

Find Money-Saving Deals Fast

To quickly find hotel deals throughout the world, select the Hotel Deals option on the Hotels.com website or in the app. Here, you'll find last-minute deals, as well as information about other sales and online promotions being offered by the service.

Hotwire

Hotwire is available via its website (www.hotwire.com) as well as its mobile app. You can use this service to find and book flights, hotels, rental cars, or vacation packages, and extra discounts are offered when you book multiple aspects of your trip at the same time, such as flights and hotel; flights, hotel and rental car; or hotel and rental car.

It's Not All Good

Limitations of the Hotwire Mobile App

Currently, the Hotwire mobile app allows travelers to find and book hotels and rental cars but not airfares or vacation packages.

In addition to being easy to use, Hotwire has relationships with many airlines, hotels, rental car companies, and other travel providers, so the website can offer deeply discounted rates, whether you book well in advance or make your reservations at the last minute. For example, Hotwire.com advertises that travelers can save up to 60 percent on published hotel rates.

Comparing Prices Across Multiple Travel Sites

Instead of visiting Hotwire.com's website directly, you can visit the Booking Buddy website (www.bookingbuddy.com) and quickly perform the same search for flight and/or hotel discounts across multiple services, including CheapOAir.com, Expedia.com, Hotwire.com, Orbitz.com, Priceline.com, and Travelocity.com. Only listings for applicable online travel service options, based on your search criteria, will be displayed.

Sign Up for Price Alerts

Prices for travel change daily. If there's a destination you're interested in visiting, and you want to be notified by email when airfares or hotel rates drop, sign up for Hotwire.com's free Price Alert feature. After you sign up, you'll also receive periodic emails outlining special deals for travel throughout the world.

Sign in to the service using your account information, and then perform a search for a flight or hotel. Access the My Account option, click Settings, add a check mark to the Price Alert option, and click Update. You will then receive automatic alerts when the price of the flight or hotel you recently searched for drops.

Kayak

Unlike other travel services that you use to shop for flights, hotels, rental cars, travel packages, or activities, and then book that travel directly with the service, Kayak.com and the Kayak mobile app compile prices from many travel sites so you can search in one location to quickly find prices from many travel sites and online travel agencies, as well as individual airline, hotel, and rental car websites.

When you visit the Kayak.com website or launch the mobile app, click the Hotels, Flights, Cars, Packages, Activities, or Trips option, provide the requested information, and allow Kayak to access many different services to display the best available deals. When your search results are displayed, click any listing to view more detail. If you want to book that deal, click the View Deal button to be transferred to the travel service or travel website that's offering it.

As you're looking at search results, click or tap the Top Filters or More tab to narrow and customize your search. For example, if you're looking for a hotel, you can choose an average rating or overall review score, select a price range, seek out a hotel by name, or narrow down the geographic location where you'd like to stay (when applicable). You can view maps to help you better choose a location. It's then possible to sort the listings based on criteria you select, such as price, stars, or distance from your desired location.

Search results

When searching for a flight, for example, choose between one-way, round trip, or multi-city, select your departure and destination cities, enter your travel dates, as well as the number of people you're traveling with. As you enter your departure and destination city, click or tap on the Include Nearby option to have Kayak.com see whether lower airfares are available if you travel to alternative airports.

After you get your search results, you can set up free price alerts and be notified if prices for properties drop in the future. (Click the Create a Price Alert button to do this.) You're also able to search for nonstop flights or flights that make one or two (or more) stops, narrow your departure times, and adjust your search to include only specific airlines.

Click the More Filters option to display additional flight-related options. For example, you can select between First Class, Business Class, Premium Economy, or Economy seating, show only flights that offer in-flight Wi-Fi, or choose nondirect flights with a specific length layover.

Priceline

Priceline is another online service that allows you to shop for flights, hotels, rental cars, travel packages, or cruises from a single website or mobile app. The service is best known for its television commercials featuring William Shatner (Captain Kirk from *Star Trek*), and it boasts savings of up to 60 percent off hotels, 40 percent off flights, and 40 percent off rental cars.

You can use this service just like any other by entering information about what you're looking for and then viewing a selection of deals being offered by the service's travel provider partners. What sets Priceline apart from its competition, however, is that the service also offers its proprietary Name Your Own Price feature. Using this feature offers some definite money-saving advantages, but it also has a few drawbacks. It's important to understand that after you make a reservation using this feature, you can't make changes or cancellations.

Before you use the Name Your Own Price feature, use at least two other services to shop for the best deals you can find for the airfare, hotel, and/or rental car you're looking for. Then access Priceline's website or mobile app and enter the same travel details. When asked to make an offer and name your own price, enter a price between 10 and 40 percent lower than the lowest price you found elsewhere.

If your offer is accepted, your reservation will be made, your credit or debit card will be charged, and you'll receive confirmation information within minutes. If your offer isn't accepted, you have the opportunity to place a new bid or book your desired travel at a price that's quoted by the Priceline service.

It's Not All Good

Be Careful Using Priceline's Name Your Own Price Feature

Yes, you can save money using Priceline's Name Your Own Price feature, but you must understand a few things before using this option. For one thing, after you enter your travel details, you are not offered a list of specific travel options or details to choose from.

For example, if you request a flight—either one way or round trip—you can choose your departure and destination city and travel dates but you won't discover your flight times, any connections, or airline until *after* you've made an offer that gets accepted and have booked and paid for your reservation.

Likewise, if you choose to book a hotel using the Name Your Own Price feature, you can specify an approximate location (geographic region), check-in and check-out dates, star-based rating, and the number of rooms needed. You're then required to make an offer. If your offer is accepted, the hotel will have the star-based rating you requested (or higher) and be within the geographic region you chose, but you won't know the hotel name or exact location until after your non-changeable and non-cancellable reservation is booked and paid for. It's extremely important to carefully choose the region where your hotel will be located, or you could wind up far away from your desired location.

Use Priceline to Make a Booking

Whether you access Priceline's website or use the service's mobile app, the steps to use Priceline's Name Your Own Price feature to make a booking are pretty much the same. This example demonstrates booking a hotel. If you opt to book a rental car or flight, the steps and the information you're required to provide varies slightly, but the process is basically the same as what's given here.

(1) Launch your computer's web browser and visit www.Priceline.com. (Not shown.)

(2) Scroll down to the heading For Deeper Discounts - Name Your Own Price, and click the Save Up To 60% on Hotels option.

(3) Enter your destination city in the pop-up window.

(4) Fill in your check-in and check-out dates by clicking on the dates. Double-check the dates you select to make sure they're correct.

(5) Use the pull-down menu to select the number of rooms.

(6) Click the Bid Now button.

(7) Define your desired location. To increase the chance of your bid being accepted, choose multiple regions, but pay attention to the map so you don't wind up too far away from where you'd ultimately like to stay.

(8) Choose the quality of hotel you want to stay at, based on its average star-based rating. You can choose between one and five stars. Always select one star rating higher than you'd normally choose. So if you want to stay at a three-star hotel, choose the 3 1/2 and/or 4 star option.

Picking Your Rating Level

Keep in mind that Priceline uses its own star-based rating system for hotels, so what Priceline calls a four-star hotel might be considered only a three-star hotel by other travel services.

9 Enter your bid price. Whatever price you bid will not include taxes, service fees, resort fees, and other charges, so the final price will be higher than the bid you enter. Enter an amount that is between 10 and 40 percent lower than the lowest price you found for a hotel in the region where you want to stay and that has the same or similar star-based rating.

Buyer Beware

Remember, once your bid is accepted, your credit or debit card is charged immediately, and the reservation cannot be changed or refunded.

10 Fill in the name under which the reservation should be made. Keep in mind that a photo ID and a major credit card are required to check in to the hotel, even though the reservation is prepaid.

11 Click the Preview Offer button to continue.

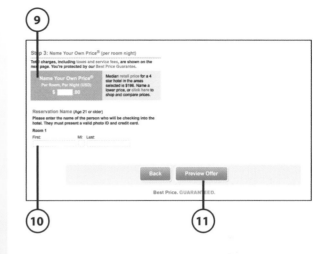

12 You see a summary of your reservation request and bid, and also the total cost of the reservation after taxes, service fees, hotel fees, and other required charges have been added. This price includes the hotel's mandatory "resort fee," if applicable.

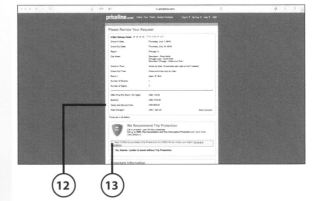

13 If you choose, purchase the optional Trip Protection insurance that's offered by adding a check mark to the appropriate check box. Add a check mark to the check box that indicates you agree to Priceline.com's terms and conditions. Click the Continue button. (Not shown.)

Independent Travel Insurance Can Be Useful

Any time you purchase an airline ticket or hotel, the travel service you use may offer you optional trip protection insurance. This insurance covers only the airline ticket or hotel booked through that service. It's often a good idea to invest in more comprehensive and independent travel insurance, from a company like Travel Guide or Travelex, that covers all aspects of your trip.

Chapter 12, "Finding and Purchasing Travel Insurance," offers more information on the benefits of travel insurance, especially when traveling abroad, or if there's a chance you'll need to change or cancel a trip that includes nonchangeable and nonrefundable reservations.

14 Choose and enter your credit or debit card details, or opt to pay using PayPal. You're also prompted to enter your billing address and contact details. If you haven't already done so, from this screen, set up a free Priceline account so your information is saved and the process for using the service in the future will be quicker.

15 Click on the Buy My Hotel Now button to finalize your request. If your offer is accepted, your reservation is automatically booked, you receive a confirmation email, and you see a message on the website telling you the name and address of the hotel and your confirmation number. It typically takes between 30 seconds and several minutes for an offer to be accepted or rejected. (Not shown.)

What If My Request Is Rejected?

If your request is rejected, you have the opportunity to refine your responses in steps 7 through 9 and resubmit your bid.

Travelocity

Travelocity.com and the Travelocity mobile app can also serve as a one-stop-shop for seeking out and booking flights, hotels, rental cars, cruises, activities, and travel bundles. In fact, when you book your flight and hotel; flight, hotel and rental car; or hotel and rental car together, you're guaranteed extra savings.

Travelcity.com offers a price match guarantee, does not charge for cancellations or changes made to reservations, and works with more than 400 airlines and 282,000 hotels to offer deeply discounted deals. (Your ability to change or cancel a reservation, as well as the extra cost, is based on the policy of the travel provider.)

The Travelocity service and mobile app work very much like its competitors, including Expedia.com, Hotwire.com, and Orbitz.com. You select what you're looking for, provide basic travel details, and then see search results that include a variety of deals from participating travel partners (airlines, hotels, rental car companies, and so on).

Click the Vacation Packages option to find and compare all-inclusive vacations (or travel bundles/packages) that include airfare, hotel, and in some cases, transportation, meals, and activities. This is a feature that only some online travel services offer. Click the Travel Deals option to see the daily listing of money-saving deals based on where and when you want to travel, or click Things to Do to learn about tours, attractions, and activities in or near a particular destination.

With the Get Inspired option you can read timely travel-related articles about different destinations and discover useful travel tips when visiting those places.

Book a flight by clicking the Flights button, or click the Hotels or Cars button to book a hotel or car, respectively.

Click the Cruises button to find and book a cruise, or click on the Fight + Hotel button and choose a travel bundle you're interested in. Provide the requested information to seek out travel opportunities and book your reservations.

TripIt

TripIt's website and mobile app offer a set of comprehensive and easy-to-use tools for keeping track of your entire travel itinerary in one convenient place. This includes your flight, hotel, and rental car information. When you sign up for a free TripIt account, you're able to simultaneously manage multiple itineraries for multiple trips, and you can share travel-related information with specific people via email, text message, or social media.

You can set TripIt to automatically sync with the calendar app you use on your computer or mobile device, and the service lets you import information directly from the confirmation emails you receive from airlines, hotels, and rental car companies. In other words, you typically don't have to manually enter your travel-related information on your calendar.

For an annual fee of $49.00, the TripIt Pro service offers a handful of additional features, including automatic alerts to inform you of flight delays, gate changes, or flight cancellations. You can also keep track of your frequent flyer and hotel accounts and use a tool that helps you find the perfect seat on a flight. If you're a frequent traveler who uses your computer and a mobile device to manage your travels, TripIt will quickly become an indispensable tool, and the annual fee for the TripIt Pro service will prove to be a worthwhile investment.

TripIt Pro Helps You Discover Refunds

Many airlines advertise that they offer the lowest airfares, and they will match a competing airline if you find a lower rate. After you book your reservation, the TripIt Pro service automatically tracks flight prices and alerts you if you become entitled to a refund from the airline where you have your flight booked. Even if this feature works just once or twice per year, you can often recover the cost of the TripIt Pro membership.

Trivago.com

Similar to Booking.com and Hotels.com, Trivago.com and the Trivago mobile app offer powerful, easy-to-use tools for finding and booking hotel accommodations almost anywhere in the world (in more than 190 countries). What sets this service apart is the simplicity of the website and app's user interface and the way that information is conveyed to users in a colorful, graphic format.

The opening screen of the website and mobile app includes the Find Your Ideal Hotel for the Best Price field. Enter your desired destination in this field and click Search.

You're prompted to enter your check-in and check-out dates and the type of room you're looking for. Adjusting the optional filters to easily narrow your hotel search by seeking out hotels with a specific star-based rating, hotels that offer rooms within a price range you select, or hotels that offer specific amenities.

Optional filters

As you become more acquainted with the site, you can fine-tune up to 100 different filters to find the exact hotel to meet your budget and expectations. For example, you can seek out a pet-friendly hotel, find rooms that are wheelchair accessible, or find rooms (where applicable) that allow smokers.

In addition to working with its own hotel partners around the world to offer the best online deals, Trivago allows you to access more than 250 hotel booking sites and hotel chains simultaneously so you can see the search results in one place on the Trivago website or mobile app. This gives you the ability to access information about more than 1 million hotels around the world and save money on your bookings.

Social Media Can Help You Save Money

To find additional money saving offers directly from travel providers, follow your favorite airlines, hotels, rental car companies, and restaurants on social media. Many of these companies offer online-only sales and promotions that are available only via their respective Facebook pages or Twitter feeds.

Other Travel Services

In addition to the travel services described in this chapter, many others offer similar functionality. For example, there's Orbitz.com (www.orbitz.com). Whether you visit the service's website or use the Orbitz mobile app, it allows you to shop for discounted rates on flights, hotels, rental cars, cruises, vacation packages, and destination-specific activities, all from one service.

When you set up a free Orbitz account, you're entitled to Insider Pricing, which will often save you an additional 10 percent off of whatever you book.

If you're just looking for last-minute discounts on flights, a service called AirTkt.com helps you find deeply discounted deals from the major airlines, and LastMinuteTravel.com offers last-minute deals on flights, hotels, rental cars, cruises, and destination-specific activities.

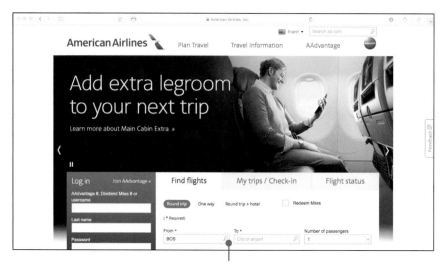

Use the website or mobile app from your favorite airline to
create, book, and manage your flight itinerary.

This chapter explains some of the advantages of using the websites and mobile apps operated by specific travel providers to book your flights, hotels, and rental cars. Topics include

→ How to find and make reservations using a specific airline, hotel, or rental car company's website or mobile app
→ How to check in for your flights and generate boarding passes in advance
→ How to handle other travel-related tasks

4

Using Travel Provider Websites and Mobile Apps

Many travel service websites and mobile apps let you search for the lowest prices among many airlines, hotels, and rental car companies. AARP Travel (travel.aarp.org), Hotwire.com, Orbitz.com, Priceline.com, and Travelocity.com are examples. In addition, each airline, hotel chain, and rental car company, as well as other travel providers (including resorts, cruise lines, and timeshare companies), have their own proprietary websites and mobiles apps that can also be extremely useful.

Airline Websites and Mobile Apps

Every major airline operates its own website and mobile app that let travelers handle a wide range of trip-related tasks without needing to call the airline's toll-free reservations or customer assistance phone number. Although what's offered by each airline's website and mobile app varies, some of the more common tasks you can handle include the following:

- Find and purchase flights on that airline

- Manage flights, change flights, select airplane seats, or upgrade from Economy class

- Find and book a hotel and/or rental car through one of the airline's partners

- Manage your frequent flier account for the airline, including the ability to redeem award miles

- Check in for the flight up to 24 hours prior to departure and either print your boarding pass or generate a digital boarding pass that gets stored in your smartphone

- Check the status of a flight you already have a reservation for

- Prepay for checked luggage and then track your bags

- Access maps that help you navigate the airports through which you'll be traveling

When you know which airline you'll be traveling with, you can find the official website for that airline by launching your web browser, going to your favorite search engine, typing the name of the airline, and selecting the airline's official website from the listed search results. The following are the websites for a handful of popular major airlines based in the United States:

- Alaska Airlines (www.alaskaair.com)

- American Airlines (www.aa.com)

- Delta Airlines (www.delta.com)

- Hawaiian Airlines (www.hawaiianair.com)

- JetBlue (www.jetblue.com)

- Southwest (www.southwest.com)

- Spirit Airlines (www.spirit.com)

- United (www.united.com)

- Virgin America (www.virginamerica.com)

To find the official mobile app for an airline, launch your app store app on your mobile device, and in the Search field type the name of the airline. Select the official airline app from the search results, and tap the button that allows you to acquire the app.

Check International Airlines Too

If you're traveling abroad, you might find lower airfares to and from another country if you travel with a non-U.S.-based airline. For example, if you're traveling from the U.S. to Europe, British Airways (www.britishairways.com), Iceland Air (www.icelandair.us), Lufthansa (www.lufthansa.com), Swiss Air (www.swiss.com), or Virgin Atlantic (www.virgin-atlantic.com) may be viable options.

In addition to selling airline seats at the "published prices," the airlines offer online sales and promotions, which sometimes allow you to find fares that are the same or even lower than fares from the travel websites or online services.

You Can Still Book Your Flights Elsewhere

Even if you opt to book your flights using a travel service other than the airline's website or mobile app, it's still possible to use the features and functions of an airline's website or app after you've made your reservation. Your confirmation will contain a confirmation number or eTicket number from the airline. Enter this information into the airline's website or app to find and manage your reservation.

Finding and Making an Airline Reservation

There are a few advantages to booking your flights via the airline's website or mobile app, especially if you're a member of that airline's frequent flier program. For example, at the time you make your reservation, you can add your frequent flier account number to the reservation and automatically receive any perks you're entitled to based on your status with the frequent flier program. You'll also receive maximum benefits if you use your airline credit card to pay for the reservation using the airline's website or mobile app.

It's Not All Good

Earning Frequent Flier Miles

When you make a flight reservation using one of the popular travel services or websites, you often must contact the airlines separately to provide your frequent flyer accounts and earn points.

In addition, your ability to use frequent flier miles to upgrade from one class to another (such as from Economy to Business class) may be hindered if you've made your initial booking using one of the discounted online travel services or websites. Each airline's policy differs. You need to call the customer service phone number for the airline's frequent flier program to determine your favorite airline's policies.

Redeeming Frequent Flier Miles

If you want to redeem frequent flier miles for airline tickets, you need to book your airline tickets using that airline's website or mobile app, or you need to call the airline's toll-free phone number. You can't purchase a ticket using frequent flier miles when you use other travel service apps or websites, such as the AARP Travel Center, Hotwire.com, Orbitz.com, Priceline.com, or Travelocity.com.

The appearance of each airline's website differs, yet all offer many of the same features and functions. What's possible using each airline's mobile app varies a lot; some airlines stay on the cutting edge of what's possible using smartphones and tablets, whereas others do not.

Make an Airline Reservation Using an Airline's Website

All the official airline websites allow you to shop for and compare flights offered by that airline and its airline partners. This example shows you how to use Southwest Airlines' website.

You Can Also Use An Airline's Mobile App

From your Internet-enabled smartphone or tablet, it's possible to find and book airline reservations using an airline's proprietary mobile app. While the screens shown in the airline's mobile app on your mobile device will look different than when visiting the airline's website on your computer, the information that's requested and ultimately displayed is the same.

(1) From your computer, launch your favorite web browser, and in the address field, enter the website address for the desired airline. For this example, type **www.southwest.com**.

Sign In to Your Account

If you have an account set up with an airline's website, be sure to sign in to the site using your username and password. By storing your name, address, payment details, phone number, email address, and flight preferences in your account, you'll save time when you make reservations online using that website. If you don't already have an account, click the Join option the first time you visit an airline's home page.

(2) To find flights, and potentially book a new reservation, click the Flight option.

>>>Go Further
SELECT ADDITIONAL AIRLINE-SPECIFIC OPTIONS

Some airline websites allow you to immediately choose between paying for an airline reservation using a credit or debit card or allowing you to redeem miles you've earned as a member of the airline's frequent flier program.

Also, when entering your departure and arrival city, you might be given the opportunity to check alternative nearby airports, where you might find lower airfares.

As you're entering your departure and return dates into the airline's website, some offer the opportunity to automatically check alternative dates for lower fares. If you have flexible travel dates, this feature can potentially save you money.

(3) Choose between booking a one-way or round-trip flight. In some cases, a multi-city option may also be available. The differences between these types of flights are explained in the next chapter.

(4) Fill in the fields for your desired departure city and arrival city. To save time, you can use airport codes, such as BOS for Boston Logan International Airport or LAX for Los Angeles International Airport. (For a complete list of airport codes, visit www.world-airport-codes.com.)

(5) Fill in the fields for your desired departure date and return date.

(6) Use the appropriate pull-down menu or field to select the number of adults and children you'll be traveling with. Some airlines, including Southwest, offer lower rates for passengers over the age of 65, so if applicable, look for the Senior fare option when selecting the number of travelers.

(7) Click the Search button to have the website seek out flight options for you on that airline (and with partner airlines, if applicable).

Many Airlines Have Partners

Many airlines have partner airlines. This means that the airline works with specific other airlines to let passengers book tickets to more destinations than it actually flies to. For example, United Airlines is part of Star Alliance, which allows United Airlines customers to fly globally on more than a dozen airlines but book their tickets through United Airlines and earn MileagePlus frequent flier points.

Many airlines also have partnerships with one or more popular hotel chains and rental car companies, allowing some airlines to offer discounted travel bundles.

(8) Some airlines, like JetBlue and Southwest, allow you to select each segment of the flight itinerary separately. You can first choose the flight(s) from your departure city to your destination and then select your return flight(s), if applicable. The price for each flight segment is displayed, along with the flight's date and times. Each flight listing indicates whether it's a direct flight or whether a connecting flight is required. Flights with stops that include gate or plane changes are also indicated.

Choose the Class You Want

Southwest allows you to choose between Business Select, Anytime, Senior, and Wanna Get Away fares (based on availability).

(9) Select the departing flight(s) you desire, and if applicable, scroll down the screen and select your return flight(s). Click the Continue button to proceed.

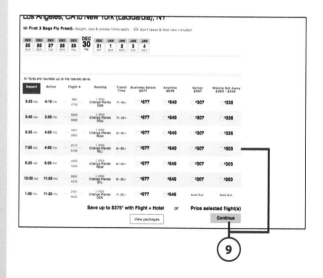

10 You see a screen of your selected flight itinerary and total cost of the airfares, including taxes and fees. At this point, it's possible to return to the previous screen to alter your flight options. Otherwise, click the Checkout button to continue booking the reservation.

11 Enter the first, middle, and last name of each passenger as prompted, as well as each passenger's date of birth and gender. If you'll be taking an international flight, you also need to provide your passport information. Remember, this information must match the information displayed on each passenger's driver's license or passport, whichever will be used to check in and go through airport security.

12 Enter each traveler's frequent flier account number, as well as their Redress Number and/or Known Traveler ID number, if applicable.

13 Scroll down on the screen and provide the passenger's email address or cell phone number, which the airline can use to send the confirmation and flight updates. (Not shown.)

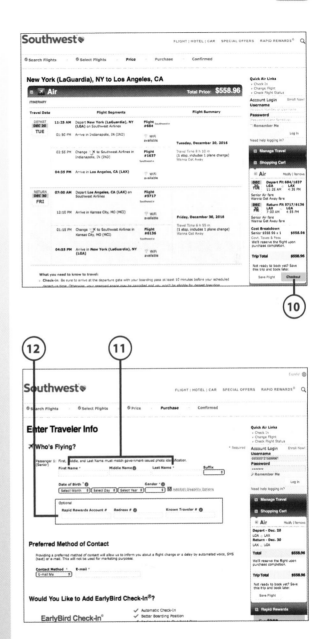

14 Each airline offers optional upgrades or the ability to prepay for checked luggage. Provide the required information as prompted by the airline. For example, Southwest offers an EarlyBird Check-In option for an additional fee. (Not shown.)

15 Scroll down, as needed, to provide your payment information, along with the billing address for the credit card or debit card you'll be using. Be sure to fill in all the required fields with the requested information. As needed, answer the additional questions asked by the website to finish processing the reservation. Remember, if you signed in to the website using your account details, many of the fields will automatically be filled in for you.

16 Click the Purchase button to complete the reservation booking process. Your selected method of payment will immediately be charged, and a confirmation email (containing your reservation confirmation number or booking number) will be sent to you within a few minutes. You're now ready to travel, so start packing. (Not shown.)

15

What Payment Method Would You Prefer?

Payment Preference *
- Credit Card
- PayPal (Available for your air fare only) *PayPal* More Info

Card Type * Select Your Card
Card Number *
Expiration Date * Select Month Select Year
Security Code *

First Name *
Last Name *
Billing Street Address *

City *
State * Select State
Zip Code *
Country * UNITED STATES OF AMERICA - (US)
Billing Phone Number * ( ) --
Address Type * Home Business Other

Where Should We Send Your Receipt?

Send my confirmation receipt via... *

- Email

Additional Options Might Be Available

As you're making your flight reservations, unless the airline has an open boarding policy, like Southwest, you'll be prompted to select your airplane seat for each leg of the flight. Certain seats will have a premium price associated with them. Reserve your seats as far in advance as possible so that you have the best selection. Based on availability, it's typically possible to choose between a window, aisle, or center seat at the time you book your reservation.

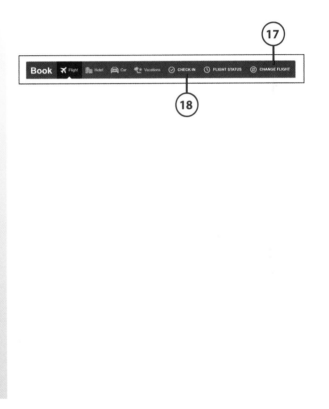

(17) At any time in the future, you can return to the airline's website and use your reservation confirmation number to manage or change your reservation (although you'll likely pay additional fees to make changes). From the web page's main menu, select the Change Flight (or Manage Reservation or equivalent) option.

(18) Within 24 hours prior to your flight's departure, check in for your flight via the airline's website or mobile app. Click the Check In option from the main menu. See the next section for more information.

Make Additional Arrangements in Advance

You'll need to make special arrangements in advance if you require wheelchair assistance at the airport, need help boarding the airplane, want assistance traveling between gates to make a connecting flight, or are traveling with a service animal or pet, or want to request a specific type of meal (diabetic, Kosher, vegetarian, and so on). Immediately after you've booked your reservation and have a confirmation number, call the airline directly to request the additional services.

Check In for Your Flight and Create Boarding Passes

Regardless of how you've booked your airline tickets, you'll probably want to access an airline's website or mobile app to check in for the flight (within 24 hours prior to your departure) and generate your boarding passes. At this time, you can also modify your seat assignments, prepay for checked luggage (if applicable), and handle additional tasks that will potentially speed up your check-in process when you arrive at the airport.

(1) Make sure you have the confirmation number that's associated with your flight reservation. (Not shown.)

(2) Access your airline's website. For demonstration purposes, the United Airlines website (www.united.com) is shown here. However, the steps are similar, regardless of which airline you've booked your air travel with.

(3) From the airline website's main web page, click the Check In button or option.

(4) Enter your reservation confirmation number or eTicket number, as well as your first and/or last name (based on the prompts provided).

(5) Follow the on-screen prompts to check in for your flight, prepay for checked luggage, if applicable, and generate your boarding passes, which you can print. If you're using an airline's mobile app, you'll typically be given the option to save a digital version of your boarding passes in your smartphone. You'd then show the appropriate information displayed on your smartphone screen when you get to the airport and visit the airline's ticket counter or baggage drop-off counter, as well as when passing through TSA security checkpoints. (Not shown.)

(4)

Check-in ⊘

Enter the following

| Confirmation number or eTicket number* |

| Last name* |

Check in with your MileagePlus number

Continue

Check-in is available starting 24 hours before your scheduled departure. See our Check-In and Airport Processing Times page for details

>>>Go Further
CHECK IN AHEAD OF TIME

If you're checking in for a flight from a computer, you can print your boarding passes in advance. If you're checking in via your smartphone, you can easily generate a digital boarding pass that you can store in your mobile device access from the airline's mobile app (as well as from the Wallet app if you're using an iPhone).

You can also check in up to 24 hours prior to your flight, at the airport, at either the airline's ticket counter or one of the airline's automated check-in kiosks. At that time, you can, if you have not already done so, select seat assignments, pay for checked luggage, add your airline frequent flier account number to the reservation (so you earn miles for taking the flight), and generate your boarding passes.

Checking in at the airport adds a few extra minutes and your seating options might be limited. You're better off handling as many check-in related tasks as possible in advance from the airline's website or mobile app.

It's Not All Good

Make Sure Your Smartphone's Battery Is Charged

Just a reminder that if you opt to use an airline's mobile app to create and store your boarding passes on your smartphone, it's important that your phone have ample battery power so you can access and display the boarding pass when you first check in at the airport, when you pass through TSA security, when you board your aircraft at the gate, and when you board any connecting flights. In any case, you might want to take the precaution of printing out your boarding pass ahead of time or request paper boarding passes at the airport.

Managing Your Itinerary from an Airline's Website

From an airline's website, you can manage reservations for all airline tickets purchased from that airline. Click the My Trips (or equivalent) option. You also can manage your frequent flier account, track the status of any of that airline's flights, and access information about all of the airline's various rules and policies.

Many airlines also have partnerships with other airlines, as well as hotels and rental car companies, and are able to offer discounted vacation packages or allow you to find and book a hotel and/or rental car from the same airline website used to make your flight reservations. One benefit to doing this is that you can earn extra frequent flier miles and potentially become eligible for extra discounts by booking other aspects of your travel directly with the airline.

**Flight, hotel, rental car, and
vacation package options**

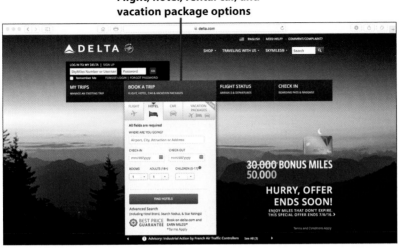

You'll definitely want to shop around using other travel websites to find the lowest price possible for travel bundles or travel packages. Although the airline may be able to offer you a discounted rate on an Avis or Hertz rental car, for example, that rate may or may not be competitive with rates you can find with competing rental car companies by shopping online using other services, like Hotwire, Kayak, Orbitz, Priceline, or Travelocity.

Accommodation Websites and Mobile Apps

Every major hotel and motel chain has its own website that allows you to pinpoint specific hotel locations anywhere you're traveling and then select a room type and book your reservations. In addition, many independently owned and operated hotels and motels, as well as bed and breakfasts, have their own websites that you can use to make reservations.

Typically, when you make a reservation directly with a hotel (using its website or via its mobile app), the reservation can be cancelled or changed, but restrictions typically apply. Prepayment using a major credit card or debit card might be required, but to check in, you often need a major credit card in the guest's name, even if the reservation is prepaid.

Many hotels offer online discounts and promotions that are competitive with the discounts offered by online-based booking services, but this is not always the case. So, in addition to shopping for hotel reservations directly from a hotel's website (or mobile app), also check with at least two other services, such as Booking.com, Hotels.com, HotelTonight.com, Kayak.com, or Trivago.com, to see if better room rates for your travel dates are available.

If you collect loyalty points from a specific hotel chain, keep in mind that you might not earn points for your stay if you make your reservation using an online travel service that offers deep discounts. You will, however, potentially save a lot of money.

Where to Find the Best Hotel Rates

Typically, when you visit the website or mobile app for a hotel, you'll get the best rates if you make your reservation 7 to 14 days (or more) in advance. When using a hotel's website or mobile app, look for the opportunity to request a special Senior rate (for people over the age of 65), or request a discount if you're a member of AAA, AARP, or USAA, or qualify for government/military discounts.

Keep in mind that as you get closer to the check-in date rates typically increase, especially if the hotel is booked near capacity. (Hotel prices change constantly, based on demand and occupancy rates.) However, when you use other online travel websites, you can find discounted room rates pretty much anytime. In fact, certain services, like Booking.com, GetARoom.com, or HotelTonight.com, offer last-minute deals that the hotels don't offer.

In addition to making and managing reservations, you can use a hotel's website or mobile app to manage your guest loyalty program membership, and you can often access tourist information about the area where the hotel is located.

Many hotel chains are part of corporate partnerships with other hotel chains, so by visiting one website you can find information about and manage reservations for several different hotel chains. For example, from the Hilton.com website, you can access information about Hilton hotels worldwide, as well as Canopy, Conrad, Curio, DoubleTree, Embassy Suites, Hampton, Hilton Garden Inn, Home2Suites, Homewood Suites, and Waldorf Astoria branded hotels. It's also possible to book Hilton Grand Vacation timeshare locations as traditional hotel rooms, even if you're not a timeshare owner.

Save Money When Booking a Hotel

There are many strategies you can use to save money when shopping for and booking a hotel. For more information, be sure to read Chapter 7, "Finding and Booking Accommodations."

If you plan to stay at hotels operated by the same chain, or you visit the same hotel often, set up a free online account with that hotel chain's website or mobile app. This lets you store all of your key information so you don't have to reenter it when making each future reservation. An account also makes it easier to earn, track, and later redeem your hotel loyalty program points.

Make a Reservation Using a Hotel's Website

The steps for using a hotel chain's website versus using a hotel chain's mobile app are similar. The menus and screens look different, but the same information will be requested from you.

1. Launch your favorite web browser and visit a hotel or hotel chain's website. The Hilton website (www.hilton.com) is shown here for demonstration purposes.

2. Click the Sign In button if you already have an account set up for the website. If you need to set up a free account, click the Join button and complete the registration.

(3) Enter your destination city. Here, you can include a city; city, state, and country; or a region within a city. For example, you could enter **New York, New York**, **New York City**, **Manhattan's Upper East Side**, or **Times Square, New York**.

(4) Click the Check-In Date field and select your desired check-in date.

(5) Click the Check Out field and select your desired check-out date.

(6) Click the Go or Search button to continue.

(7) You see a list of hotels within that chain (or that have a partnership agreement with that chain). Each listing includes details about the hotel, the nightly rate, and a Book a Room button (or equivalent). Click a listing to continue. You can also view photos, read a more detailed description of a hotel, and, in some cases, read guest reviews of the hotel by clicking on the appropriate option.

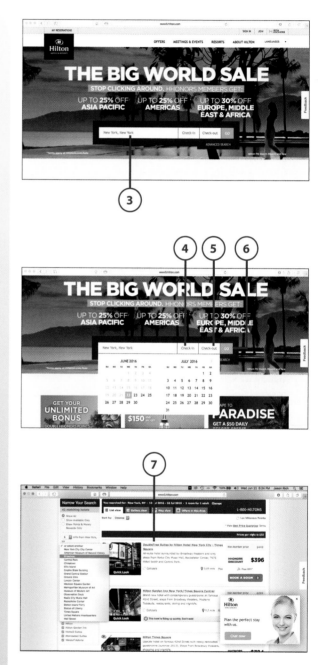

(8) Alternatively, use the Narrow Your Search options to fine-tune your hotel request preferences. For example, you can narrow down the region within the selected city where you want to stay (shown), or choose specific hotel amenities that you want or need, such as Wi-Fi or wheelchair accessibility.

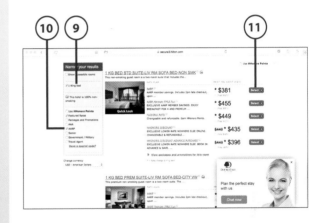

(9) Make a selection from the available room types and bed configurations (if applicable). The option you select may alter the room rate.

(10) If applicable, click the option that allows you to choose between a smoking and nonsmoking room or that entitle you to a specific discount (such as AARP or AAA).

(11) Click the Select button to choose your room type and continue booking a reservation.

Resort Fees Not Included

In many cases, the room rates displayed on a hotel's website do not include taxes, booking fees, or a mandatory "resort fee" sometimes charged by hotels. Read the fine print before booking a hotel to determine what additional fees you'll be responsible for upon checkout.

12 Enter your name, address, phone number, email address, and other requested information. If you signed in to the website using your account information, you don't need to enter your details again.

13 Check all the information carefully to make sure it's correct. When prompted, enter your credit or debit card payment information, as well as your billing address. Once again, if you signed in to the website using your account information, you don't have to manually enter this information again.

14 Scroll down to the bottom of the page, be sure to click on the check box that requires you to agree to the hotel's Booking Terms and Conditions, and then click the Book Reservation button.

15 Your reservation will be made, and in a few minutes you'll receive a confirmation email. (Not shown.)

12

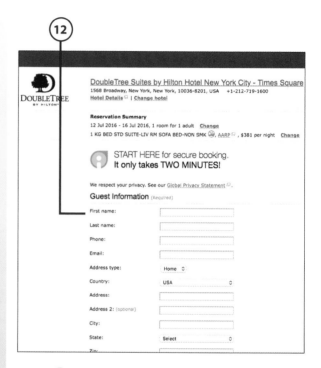

13

14

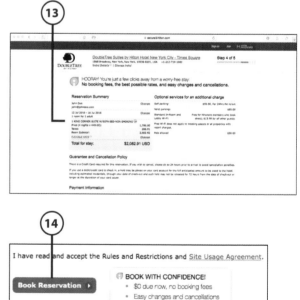

>>>*Go Further*
ADVANTAGES OF USING A HOTEL'S MOBILE APP

With hotel chain–specific mobile apps, you can find hotels, make reservations, and then manage your reservations, all from your Internet-enabled smartphone or tablet. In addition, some hotel chains have built additional functionality into their proprietary mobile apps. For example, the SPG hotel mobile app allows you to remotely check in to your hotel room upon arriving and then use your smartphone or Apple Watch as your electronic room key.

Using a Rental Car Company's Website or Mobile App

You can compare rates among many rental car companies for a destination city using websites like the AARP TravelCenter powered by Expedia, Hotwire.com, Kayak.com, Priceline.com, or Travelocity.com, or you can handle a wide range of tasks related to a specific rental car company by accessing that company's website or mobile app.

If you're a member of a rental car company's customer loyalty program, it's possible to earn, manage, and redeem points related to that program from the rental car company's website or mobile app. You can also read about the types of cars in the company's rental fleet, learn about insurance options, and make your rental car reservations.

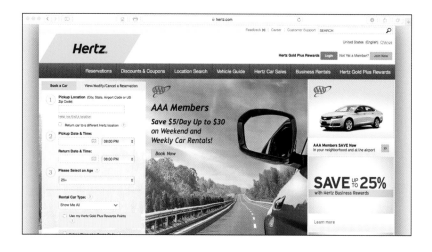

If you first set up a free account and store your contact and billing information, you can complete the reservation process a lot faster. So, if you don't already have an account, when you visit a rental car company's website, click the Join Now button. However, if you already have an account, click the Sign In button and log in using your account information.

After you visit the website for a rental car company, such as Avis, Budget, Hertz or National, you'll be prompted to enter your desired pickup location. Here, you can enter a city; city, state, and country; or the name of a major airport.

Next, you're prompted to provide your desired pick-up date and time, as well as your drop-off date and time. You're also asked for your age and asked to choose the car type (or vehicle size) that you want to rent. Rental car companies classify car sizes using terms like economy, mid-size, full-size, luxury, or SUV.

As you proceed through the reservation process, you're ultimately asked to provide information from your driver's license and to choose the type of optional insurance coverage you'd like to add to the rental car agreement.

Choose a car type

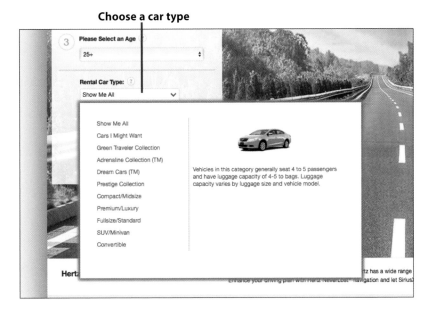

Saving Money When Renting a Car

There are many strategies you can use to save money when shopping for and booking a rental car. For more information, be sure to read Chapter 6, "Finding Ground Transportation."

Especially if you're loyal to a specific rental car company, using that company's website or mobile app to book and manage your reservations will save you time and allow you to earn the maximum reward points with its loyalty program. If you don't care which rental car company you use and want to pay the lowest price possible, you'll typically find the best deals using a travel website or online service rather than a specific rental car company's website or mobile app.

Discover Websites and Mobile Apps Operated by Cruise Lines

All the popular cruise lines offer websites that allow you to find, compare, and book cruises online. Meanwhile, each cruise line's mobile app is focused more on enhancing your experience after you're actually aboard the cruise ship.

If you're interested in cruising, be sure to read Chapter 8, "Finding and Booking a Cruise."

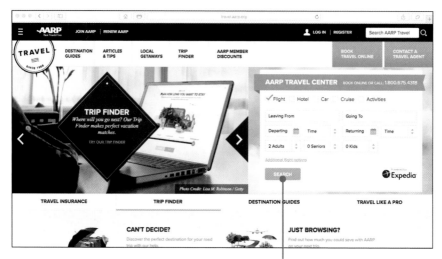

Shopping for low-cost flights is easy using a service like
Hotwire.com, Kayak.com, Orbitz, Priceline, or Travelocity.com.

In this chapter, you discover how to shop for, find, and book the lowest airfares possible using your Internet-enabled computer, smartphone, or tablet. You'll learn

→ How to calculate all the added costs associated with air travel
→ How to determine what kind of ticket you want
→ Five tips for finding the lowest airfares possible
→ What to consider when you're preparing for international travel

Finding and Booking the Best Airfares

As mentioned in earlier chapters, if you want to find the lowest possible airfare by quickly comparing prices among multiple airlines, you should use an online travel service, website, or mobile app, such as Hotwire.com, Kayak.com, Priceline.com, or Travelocity.com.

When you use one or more of these services, you can find a low airfare but your reservation typically can't be changed or cancelled. If you are able to change or cancel your flight reservations, there's usually a high change fee (up to $150 per ticket), plus the price difference between your existing airline ticket and the new one. A few airlines, like JetBlue and Southwest, still offer much more flexibility for changing or cancelling flights.

It's Not All Good

Some "Discount" Airlines Don't Always Offer the Best Deals

Some discount airlines, such as Spirit Airlines, promote themselves as offering extremely low-cost flights. Although it's true the base airfare might be less than its competitors, once you add in all the extra fees, such as a ticketing fee, seat assignment fee, check-in fee, carry-on baggage fees, checked luggage fees, onboard beverage fees, and onboard snack fees, the price of the one-way or round-trip airline ticket will often be much higher than its competitors. Plus, many discounted airlines serve only smaller airports located outside popular cities, so the ground transportation fees (taxi or Uber, for example) getting to and from the airport will be higher.

Before purchasing an airline ticket with a discount airline, make sure you understand all the additional fees you'll be responsible for, and compare the final price to what other airlines are charging.

Calculating Added Costs Associated with Air Travel

As you're researching online, bear in mind that the airline ticket price that's initially displayed might *not* include all the charges that can be applicable. You don't see all these fees added to your total until you're further along in the booking process.

In addition to the airline ticket–related fees you're required to pay at the same time you book your reservation, other fees might come up prior to or during your travels. These fees may include the following:

- **Cancellations or flight changes:** If you've purchased your ticket at a deep discount from one of the popular online travel services, it's often not possible to cancel or change one or more of your flights. If you booked with an airline that does allow flight changes or cancellations, you usually have to pay a fee to make the change. For example, to change a flight, many airlines charge a $150.00 change fee, plus the difference in price between your existing ticket and the new ticket. Check with the airline before you book the ticket to determine its policy for canceling or changing a flight. In some cases, travel insurance could offset the cost of cancelling or changing your flight, if the reason for the cancellation or itinerary change is covered by your policy. A travel insurance policy with a Cancel for Any Reason option from AIG's Travel

Guard (www.travelguard.com), Allianz (www.allianztravelinsurance.com), or Travelex (www.travelexinsurance.com), for example, offers the most coverage and flexibility in this situation (see Chapter 12, "Finding and Purchasing Travel Insurance").

- **Food and drinks:** Although most international flights still include a complimentary meal or snack, you will find that the majority of airlines now charge for meals or snacks on domestic flights. Most airlines still offer complimentary soda, juice, coffee, and tea during a flight but charge for alcoholic beverages and premium beverages, such as energy drinks.

Bringing Food with You

No drinks can be brought through TSA airport security checkpoints. You're limited as to the types of foods that can be carried through security as well—for example, no yogurt or soups. Many people now buy meals or snacks after passing through TSA security at the airport and carry their food purchases onto the airplane.

To read current regulations for foods that can't be brought through airport security, visit the Transportation Security Administration's website (www.tsa.gov/travel/security-screening/prohibited-items) and click the Food tab.

- **In-flight entertainment:** Some airlines offer TV shows and movies you can watch for free, using headsets and the monitor that's built in to the seatback in front of you. Other airlines charge passengers a per-flight or per-program fee to watch in-flight entertainment.

>>>Go Further

TAKE YOUR OWN IN-FLIGHT ENTERTAINMENT

Although many aircrafts offer onboard Wi-Fi to access the Internet, in most cases, access to streaming video or music services, such as Amazon Prime Video, Apple Music, Hulu, the iTunes Store, Netflix, Pandora, or Spotify, is blocked. Thus, you'll want to download this type of content to your mobile device.

Before leaving home, download movies, TV show episodes, music, audiobooks, eBooks, and digital editions of magazines to your notebook computer, smartphone, tablet, or eBook reader to enjoy on demand during your flight. This approach allows you to customize your in-flight entertainment experience with content that's of interest to you.

To learn more about how to access and enjoy all forms of digital entertainment using your computer or mobile device, pick up a copy of the book *My Digital Entertainment for Seniors* (Que, 2016). It's available from bookstores, Amazon.com, BN.com, and QuePublishing.com, where AARP members get 40 percent off.

- **In-flight Wi-Fi:** More and more aircrafts operated by major airlines are offering in-flight Wi-Fi, but they charge a fee. Using the in-flight Wi-Fi costs between $8.00 and $30.00 per day (or per flight, depending on the service). You can use in-flight Wi-Fi to access the Internet to send and receive emails or text messages or use social media, but your web surfing experience will be slow, and services that allow you to make and receive Internet calls (such as FaceTime or Skype), as well as stream music or video, are often blocked. A few airlines offer free Wi-Fi to all passengers, or just to their frequent fliers who have reached a certain level.

- **Luggage fees:** When it comes to luggage, there are two types as far as airlines are concerned—carry-on baggage or checked baggage. Each airline has different luggage policies and prices for carry-on and checked baggage.

- **Pillows and blankets:** A few airlines still offer complimentary pillows and blankets for long domestic flights or international flights, but don't count on this. Some airlines now charge for pillows and blankets, or you can purchase them at any airport, but you'll pay a premium price. Consider bringing your own travel pillow and travel blanket (or a jacket) when you're taking a long flight.

- **Preferred seating:** When it comes to Economy class seats aboard most airplanes, you can plan on your seat being narrow, with little legroom. If the person sitting in front of you reclines their seat during the flight, you'll become even more cramped. Instead of upgrading to Business class or First class, some airlines now offer what they call Preferred Seating, Economy Plus, or Premier Economy seats. You pay more for these seats, but they're typically slightly larger or offer more legroom.

- **Priority boarding:** If you want to be one of the first passengers to board an aircraft (after First Class and Business Class passengers), you can often purchase a priority boarding pass. Doing this is useful if the airline, like Southwest, has an open seating policy or if the flight is fully booked and overhead storage space will be limited. By boarding early, you can store your carry-on bag in the overhead storage space while it's still available, which helps you avoid the possibility of having to gate check your bag if the storage compartments become full. People with physical disabilities or who need assistance boarding an aircraft can receive priority boarding for free upon request.

Airline Credit Cards Have Special Perks

By applying in advance for the credit card that's available for your specific airline, you're entitled to special perks whenever you travel with that airline. For example, in addition to earning bonus frequent flier miles when you pay for your airline tickets using an airline's credit card, the airline typically waives the charge for a passenger's first checked bag and offers priority boarding to the credit-card holder.

To learn more about airline credit cards, visit www.creditcards.com/airline-miles.php. Virtually all the major airlines have teamed up with banks or financial institutions to offer a branded major credit card.

Each credit card has its own set of perks and typically has an annual fee associated with it. Credit-card applicants are often offered bonus frequent flier miles ticket upon being approved for the credit card or after a certain dollar value of purchases has been made on the card. Refer to the card's terms and usage guidelines for specifics.

Understanding Baggage Allowances

For Economy class passengers, most airlines allow you to carry onto the aircraft, for free, one piece of carry-on luggage that meets specific size requirements. This carry-on bag can be stored either under the seat in front of you or in the overhead storage compartment above your seat.

You're also allowed to carry on one personal item, such as a purse, backpack, messenger bag, briefcase, or laptop computer case.

As for checked luggage, for domestic flights, airlines require each bag to weight less than 50 pounds. For international flights, some airlines have a higher per-bag weight limit for checked luggage. If your bag is overweight, you must pay a hefty fee, between $50.00 and $100.00. Airlines also have restrictions on the dimensions of bags. If your bag is oversized, a similar oversize bag fee will apply.

Some airlines allow you to check one bag for free but charge for additional checked bags. The additional bag fee is typically between $50.00 and $100.00 per bag. A growing number of domestic airlines also charge between $15.00 and $35.00 for each passenger's first checked bag. Keep in mind that all of these fees are one way, so if you have a round-trip ticket booked with an airline, your luggage fees will ultimately be doubled.

Based on the airline, the price of each ticket could increase by $100.00 (or more) based on the number of bags and the size and weight of the bags you're checking. Prior to booking your airline tickets, check with the airline to learn about their luggage fees.

What Each Airline Charges for Checked Baggage

To access a listing of the baggage-related fees charged by each airline, visit www.tripadvisor.com/AirlineFees.

Airline baggage fees are charged when you book your flights, or when you check in for each flight, either online or at the airport. Most airlines have become very strict in terms of enforcing their luggage policies. So, if you're trying to check a bag that weights 55 pounds and the limit is 50, for example, to avoid the additional "overweight bag fee," remove at least five pounds of content from your bag prior to check in.

To avoid the hassle of having to repack your luggage after it's weighed at the airport, weigh your bags before leaving home.

An Easy Way to Weigh Your Luggage

If you don't have a luggage scale but do have access to a home scale, first step on the scale to see how much you weigh. Next, pick up your luggage and step on the scale while holding the luggage. Deduct your weight from the total weight. The result is your luggage's weight.

Save Money on Luggage Fees by Flying with Southwest

Southwest Airlines is currently the only U.S.-based airline that allows passengers to check two pieces of luggage (up to 50 pounds each), plus have one carry-on bag and one personal item, for no extra charge.

Some of the major airlines waive the charge for the first checked bag after you reach a certain level in its frequent flier program, or if you possess and use the airline's credit card. The baggage fees for Business class or First class passengers tend to be lower, although the price of these airline tickets is significantly higher than an Economy class ticket, so paying a baggage fee might be less costly than paying the higher price for the overall ticket.

Minimizing Your Packing

If you're planning to embark on a long trip, consider packing one week's worth of clothing, and plan on doing laundry or sending your dirty clothing to a dry cleaner or full-service Laundromat during your trip. Most hotels and cruise ships offer laundry and dry cleaning services for a premium fee.

On a cruise ship, during longer cruises (more than seven nights), many ships allow you to fill a supplied bag and have that laundry done for a flat fee, as opposed to the à la carte, per-piece laundry service that's typically offered. Some ships, hotels, and resorts also offer self-service washers and dryers, so you can save money by doing your own laundry (but this will take time out of your vacation).

When traveling to cities within the U.S., it's possible to save money by finding a local dry cleaner that offers drop-off laundry service. Look for discounted offers from local dry cleaning and laundry services using Groupon or Living Social, for example.

Determining the Type of Airline Ticket You Want

When you set out to find and make an airline reservation, there are a handful of decisions you need to make beyond which airport you'll leave from and which city or country you want to travel to. You need to decide what type of airline ticket you want to purchase. The various options are explained in this section.

Most airlines allow you to choose between booking a one-way, round-trip, or multi-city ticket and also allow you to choose between Economy, Premium Economy, Business, or First class travel. In some cases, a nonstop flight is available, although in many cases you'll need to use connecting flights (two or more flight segments or legs) to reach your desired destination.

The One-Way Ticket Option

A *one-way ticket* can be from one city to another (with no return flight), whereas a *round-trip ticket* provides both flights from your departure city to your destination city and flights to get you back to your original departure city on the dates you specify.

Sometimes, you can find lower round-trip airfares if you shop for and book two separate one-way tickets. Airlines like JetBlue and Southwest require you to book one-way flights to create your travel itinerary. With most major airlines, though, round-trip tickets are considerably more affordable than a one-way ticket.

The Multi-City Ticket Option

A multi-city ticket allows you to go from your departure city to another city, and from that city to a third city, and then potentially go back to your originating departure city. In other words, there are several legs to the trip, with extended layovers (one or more days) in each city.

For example, you might go from LaGuardia Airport in New York City to O'Hare Airport in Chicago, spend a few days in Chicago, and then travel to Los Angeles International Airport in Los Angeles, California, where you'll spend a few additional days. The multi-city ticket enables you to fly from Los Angeles back to New York. Depending on the airline, you can typically add multiple optional legs to the trip, allowing you to visit several cities by making a single airline reservation.

The more stops you add to your itinerary, the higher the cost of the ticket, although booking a multi-city ticket is typically far less expensive than separately booking a series of one-way tickets for the same itinerary.

Choosing Your Travel Class

The least-expensive travel class on any airline is Economy class. Especially for large people, think sardine can with wings. These seats offer the least amount of space, legroom, storage space for your belongings, and comfort. For an additional fee, many airlines now offer a class called *Premium Economy* or *Economy Plus*, which offer seats with more legroom and a higher ticket price.

A *Business class* seat is more expensive than an Economy seat, but it's wider and has much more legroom; it also comes with more in-flight amenities. Traveling Business class on long international flights or overnight (red-eye) flights is certainly a better way to go, if you can afford it. In some cases, you can use frequent flier miles to receive a free upgrade from Economy to Premium Economy, Business, or First class.

A *First class* airline ticket is the premium and most comfortable way to fly. In many cases, the seats turn into beds and fully recline, plus you're enclosed in a small cubicle that offers an added level of privacy. First class travel typically includes gourmet meals, free alcoholic beverages, priority boarding, better in-flight entertainment, and a variety of other travel amenities.

Choosing Your Flight

Regardless of which travel class you choose, a flight between your departure city and destination city can be nonstop, or it could require you to take one or more connecting flights along the way. A connecting flight means you land in another city, and, in some cases, you will need to change airplanes before proceeding to your final destination. The layover time between flights is typically between one and three hours.

Nondirect flights typically cost less than nonstop flights. For convenience purposes, you're better off sticking to flights that are nonstop or that make just one stop. If you have physical limitations, be sure to request wheelchair support or assistance to help you go from one airplane to another in your connecting city, as the walk between gates and terminals is sometimes long and the available time to make a connecting flight is sometimes limited.

Five Tips for Finding the Lowest Possible Airfares

Before flights could easily be booked online, the airlines often offered the lowest rates if you made your reservations 21 days in advance, but you could still find discounts if you booked 14 days or 7 days in advance and stayed in your destination city over a Saturday night. These rules no longer apply.

Using the various online travel services, as well as the websites operated by specific airlines, you can now find low fares any time, whether you book months, weeks, or even one day in advance.

Airfares, which are based on demand, constantly fluctuate. As flights get close to being fully booked, prices for those flights tend to go up (sometimes significantly). So, if you wait until the last minute to book your airline tickets for travel during a peak travel time, such as around a holiday, or on a Friday, Saturday, or Monday, you'll tend to find higher airfares.

You'll also discover that if you were to ask 10 people on any flight how much they paid for their ticket, you'll typically get 10 different answers. This is because each person made their reservation at a different time prior to the flight and also potentially used a different service to make their reservation.

When it comes to using your computer or mobile device to shop for the lowest airfares available, use the following five tips to help you maximize your savings.

Research the "Discount" Airlines Separately

While the popular travel services allow you to compare flight prices across multiple airlines, many of these service do not work with the "discount" airlines, such as JetBlue, Southwest, or Spirit, so when researching low airfares, you might need to separately check the websites for these airlines.

Check Three or More Services

Each of the popular travel services and websites has an agreement with the various airlines and is able to offer discounts based on that agreement. This is why it's always a good idea to check with at least three services, including one or more websites operated by specific airlines, before finalizing and booking your reservation.

Find Flights as an AARP Member

You can book flights through the AARP Travel Center, powered by Expedia.

(**1**) Visit the AARP Travel website (travel.aarp.org) from your computer (using any web browser).

(**2**) If you already have a free account, click Log In and enter your username and password. To register for a free account for the first time, click Register. (Note that an AARP Travel Center account is separate from your AARP membership and the AARP website, so you have to create an account that's specific to the AARP Travel Center.)

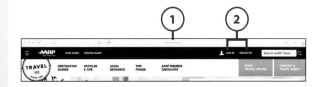

Set Up a Free AARP Travel Center Account

Having an account on the AARP Travel Center helps you save time when you're booking travel because your name, address, phone number, email address, AARP membership number, and credit card details will already be securely stored in your account. Thus, you won't have to manually reenter this information each time you make a travel reservation using the service.

(3) Click Flight. To shop for a travel bundle, including flights, hotel, rental car, and/or activities, add checkmarks to the appropriate check boxes. Booking travel as a bundle almost always saves you more money.

(4) Enter your departure city in the Leaving From field. As you type, applicable city options are displayed. Select an appropriate option, or keep typing.

(5) Enter your destination (city or city and country) in the Going To field.

(6) Click Departing, and then choose your desired date of departure. Optionally, click Time to select a desired departure time.

(7) Click Returning, and then choose your desired return date if you're looking for a round-trip ticket. Optionally, click Time to select a desired time for your return flight. Leave both of these fields blank if you're looking for a one-way ticket.

(8) Select the number of adults, seniors, and kids you'll be traveling with.

(9) Click Search. The site generates a list of flight options.

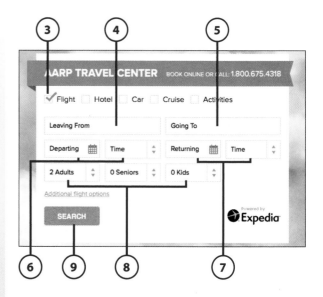

10 Click the Flight By Flight tab to choose one leg of your itinerary at a time, or click the Complete Trip tab for flight itineraries covering all legs of your trip. To help you find the lowest fares possible, AARP Travel Center might recommend booking flights with multiple airlines.

11 Narrow your flight selection by clicking check boxes below the Filter Your Results By heading.

Flight options

12 Click the Price drop-down menu to sort the results by Price (lowest to highest) or Price (highest to lowest), or choose different sort criteria from the displayed menu.

13 Each flight listing displays the name of the airline, flight times, the duration of the flight, number of stops, and other pertinent information. Click Flight Details and Baggage Fees to learn more about the flight and see a list of additional fees you might be responsible for.

14 See how prices for your desired itinerary have fluctuated recently by clicking the See Price Trends button.

15 When you find a specific flight or entire itinerary that you want, click the Select button for its listing.

16 Review your selected flight details, including the total cost of the airfares you've selected for all of the passengers you're booking for.

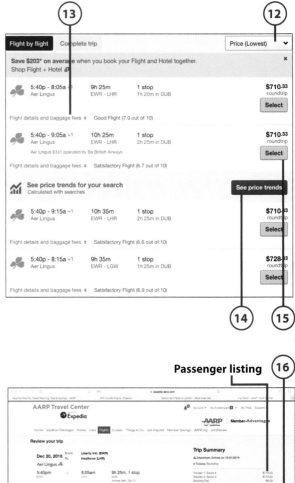

Finding the Price per Ticket

Click a passenger listing to see the airline ticket price breakdown for a particular passenger.

17 Click the Continue Booking button to proceed. (Not shown.)

Safety Net

When you book most airline tickets through the AARP Travel Center, you can cancel your reservation at no charge if you do it within 24 hours. This is an option not offered by most other travel services. If you want to edit your itinerary and choose other flights or airlines, click the Change Flights option instead of the Continue Booking button.

AARP Member Information

Join AARP / Renew Membership

AARP Member Number *

AARP Member Number

Please check your AARP Member Number.

Need to look up your AARP Member Number? ⌄

18   21

18. Enter your AARP membership number when prompted.

19. Scroll down, and enter the requested information for each traveler, including his or her name, phone number, gender, and date of birth. If the passenger has an airline frequent flier number, Redress Number, or Known Traveler ID, click the link to add this information in the appropriate fields. (Not shown.)

20. Click the Continue Booking button to proceed. (Not shown.)

21. From the Payment screen, it's possible to acquire optional trip protection (for an additional fee). After you scroll down, enter your credit card information and billing address in the appropriate fields to pay for your flight reservation.

How would you like to pay?

VISA

Cardholder name *

John Doe

Debit/Credit card number *

Expiration date *

Month ⌄   Year ⌄

Security code * ❓

Country *

United States of America ⌄

Billing address 1 *

(ex. 123 Main)

Billing address 2

(ex. Suite 400, Apt. 4B)

Trip Protection

What's covered by the trip protection you purchase from an online travel service or airline varies greatly, but it almost always covers less than buying standalone travel insurance for your trip from a company like Travel Guard or Travelex. Read the coverage information carefully before purchasing any trip protection.

(22) Enter your email address (or the email address for the person who should receive the email that will contain your flight confirmation number) in the Where Should We Send Your Confirmation? field.

(23) Click the Complete Booking button to finalize and pay for your reservation. In a few minutes, you'll receive a confirmation email. (Not shown.)

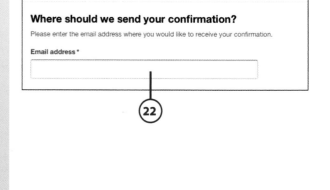

Using Other Membership Discounts

If you're a AAA member, visit www.aaa.com and click the Travel option near the top of the screen. Click the Hotels, Flights, Cars, Cruise, or Vacations button to begin looking for the flight deals.

As with other travel services, you can save money by taking advantage of bundled travel offers (such as by booking your flights and hotel at the same time).

Active or retired members of the U.S. Military (as well as their family members) are also entitled to discounted travel from some airlines, hotels, rental car companies, cruise lines, and resorts. Some of the travel-related websites worth exploring to find these discounts include

- Armed Forces Vacation Club (www.afvclub.com)
- Military Fares (www.militaryfares.com)
- Military.com (www.military.com/Travel/Home)
- MilitaryTravel.com (http://militarytravel.com)

Look for Package Deals or Travel Bundles

Regardless of which service or website you use to book trips, it's almost always possible to save additional money when you book your flights, hotel, and/or rental car at the same time.

Some travel services have package deals that include flights, hotel, and, in some cases, rental car, a meal plan, and/or admission to various attractions or activities. Other services allow you to create your own travel bundles. In this case, how many different aspects of your trip you book at the same time determines how much extra discount you receive.

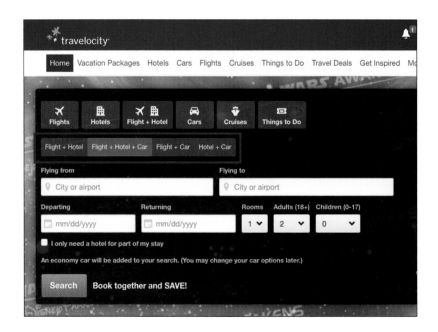

It's Not All Good

Always Read the Fine Print

When booking any type of travel package or travel bundle online or through a mobile app, always read the fine print so you understand exactly what's included and what's not. Otherwise, you might get an unpleasant surprise when you discover you're responsible for a bunch of additional fees.

Set Up Free Price Alerts and Take Advantage of Price Match Guarantees

If your travel dates are flexible and you're planning a trip weeks or months in advance, visit several of the websites and seek out the lowest prices you can find, but don't make your reservations right away. Instead, sign up for free Price Alerts, which automatically send you an email when there's a drop in airfares, hotel rates, rental car prices, or cruise prices that you've previously searched.

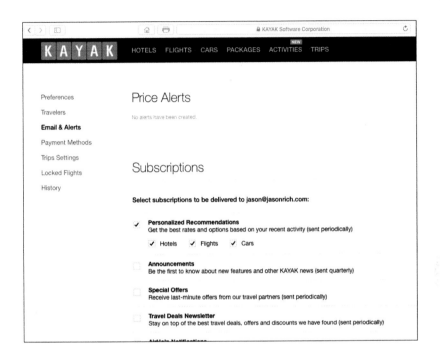

Wait a few days to see if you receive any Price Alerts, and then book your travel with a service that offers a price match guarantee (sometimes called a best price guarantee). Then, if you discover a lower price for one or more aspects of your travel before you depart, the travel service you used will refund the price difference, allowing you to benefit from that lower price.

Price match guarantee

Taking advantage of price alerts and low price guarantees requires some extra work on your part because you need to continue seeking out lower prices from various online travel services and then contact the travel service you used so you can request the price match and receive your refund.

AARP Travel Center's Best Price Guarantee

To learn how to take advantage of the Best Price Guarantee offered by AARP Travel Center when you book flights or other travel using this service, visit www.expedia-aarp.com/p/info-other/guarantees.htm. When you find a qualifying lower price on travel you've booked through the AARP Travel Center within 24 hours, click the Best Price Guarantee Application to apply for a refund.

Additional Considerations for International Travel

When traveling by air anywhere within the United States, you need a valid driver's license, state-issued identification card, or valid military ID to check in for your flight and pass through TSA security checkpoints.

Take a Photo of Your ID and Passport

Before leaving home, use the camera that's built in to your smartphone and take a digital photo of your identification (driver's license) and passport. Store this photo in your smartphone or tablet, but also email it to yourself so you have a copy in your email account's inbox. Alternatively, save a backup of the image file in the cloud using iCloud Drive, Microsoft OneDrive, or Dropbox.

If you lose your identification when traveling, or your wallet/passport gets stolen, you can more easily check in with your airline and get through TSA security. If you lose your ID, contact your airline, explain the situation, tell them you have a digital copy of your driver's license and/or passport, and follow their directions. For your trip home, make sure you arrive at the airport at least one or two extra hours early, so the authorities can verify your identity.

If you're a U.S. citizen traveling abroad (including to Mexico or Canada), you must have a valid U.S. passport. A U.S. passport remains valid for 10 years. At least a few months prior to a planned overseas trip, check your passport's expiration date to make sure it will remain valid throughout your upcoming travels and, if you're traveling abroad, for an additional three to six months, depending on the country.

The process of applying for a new passport, renewing a passport, or replacing a lost or stolen passport takes three to six weeks using normal methods. However, if you live in or near a city that has a Department of State Passport Agency office, you can call to make an in-person appointment, pay an extra rush fee, and obtain a same-day or next day passport.

Another alternative is to use an independent third-party agency to help you fill out and process your passport applications. These services charge up to $200.00 more than the fees charged by the U.S. Department of State, which issues U.S. passports. However, these companies can often arrange to have your passport application completed and processed within 48 hours.

To find this type of independent (for profit) service, type **Expedited Passport Application Processing** in any Internet search engine. Following are some websites for these services:

- G3Passports.com (www.g3passports.com)

- PassportsandVisas.com (www.passportsandvisas.com)

- RushMyPassort.com (www.rushmypassport.com)

- U.S. Passport Now (www.uspassportnow.com)

U.S. Customs and Immigration Global Entry

If you travel abroad often, consider joining the Global Entry program, which can speed up your reentry into America as you go through U.S. Customs and Immigration at the airport. The application fee is $100.00, and the application process involves a background check and in-person interview conducted by someone from the U.S. Customs and Border Protection agency.

To learn more about Global Entry, visit www.cbp.gov/travel/trusted-traveler-programs/global-entry.

Applying For or Renewing Your U.S. Passport

When filling out the application to apply for a new passport, passport renewal, or passport replacement, original versions of specific documentation must accompany your application. The documentation that's required varies, based on your personal circumstances. Also, be sure to follow the guidelines carefully when having your passport photo taken. For passport photo guidelines, visit https://travel.state.gov/content/passports/en/passports/photos/photos.html.

Where to Go for Help

When you have passport-related questions, call (877) 487-2778 from within the United States. To speak with a representative from the National Passport Information Center, call Monday through Friday, between 8:00 a.m. and 10:00 p.m. (Eastern Time), or on Saturday between 10:00 a.m. and 3 p.m. (Eastern Time). During all other times, this phone number offers an interactive automated information service.

If you are experiencing a passport-related emergency outside of normal business hours, call (202) 647-4000.

For a listing of U.S. embassies and consulates around the world, visit www.usembassy.gov.

It's Not All Good

Make Sure Your Passport Is Not About to Expire

Some foreign countries will not accept a U.S. passport that is slated to expire within three to six months of your travel date, or if the passport has fewer than two blank pages in it. So, if your passport is approaching its expiration date or is already almost filled with stamps, consider renewing your passport early to avoid potential problems.

Check country-specific information on the U.S. Department of State site (travel.state.gov/content/passports/en/country.html) for the country or countries you plan to visit.

Applying or Renewing Online

To begin the application process and determine what documentation you need, visit https://travel.state.gov/content/passports/en/passports/apply.html. Fill out the online questionnaire to determine your eligibility, and then complete the online questionnaire related to the passport application or renewal.

If you're not in a hurry, another option is to handle your passport-related application through your local U.S. Post Office. For more information on how to do this, visit www.usps.com/international/passports.htm.

To determine the fees associated with a new passport application, passport renewal, or passport replacement, visit https://travel.state.gov/content/passports/en/passports/information/fees.html. At the bottom of the page there is an automated passport fee calculator (see figure).

Handling Passport-Related Applications and Issues in Person

If you choose to handle your passport needs in person and will be traveling internationally within the next two weeks, set up an appointment with a nearby Department of State Passport Agency office. To do this, visit https://travel.state.gov/content/passports/en/passports/information/where-to-apply/agencies.html, or call (877) 487-2778. Make sure you fill out all the necessary forms (available online), and bring all the appropriate documentation and copies of your passport photo to the scheduled meeting to avoid delays and complications.

To download the various forms required to apply for, renew, or replace a U.S. passport, visit https://travel.state.gov/content/passports/en/passports/forms.html.

Understanding Travel Visas and Travel Warnings

The world is not always a safe and calm place. To help ensure you're fully prepared to travel abroad, the U.S. Department of State and the Bureau of Consular Affairs offers a free and informative website that alerts you of various health issues and travel warnings that are in effect in specific countries throughout the world.

After you've decided what countries you'll be visiting (including countries that may be ports of call during a cruise), point your web browser to https://travel.state.gov/content/passports/en/go.html and then click the Your Destination tab. Click the Learn More option to continue. This website will also provide you with emergency contact information for U.S. embassies in the countries you'll be visiting.

Depending on which countries you plan to visit, you might need a travel visa in addition to your passport. In many cases, obtaining a travel visa is a straightforward process that involves visiting the website for the country's embassy where you'll be traveling, filling out an online form, and paying a small fee (using your credit or debit card). Within 24 to 48 hours, the appropriate visa will be sent to you electronically via email, and you can print it on your computer's printer.

To determine whether a travel visa is required for a country you'll be visiting, and to discover how to apply for and obtain the required visa, contact the embassy for that country as far in advance of your trip as possible. You can find contact information for each country's embassy at www.state.gov/s/cpr/rls/dpl/32122.htm.

>>>*Go Further*

TIPS FOR MANAGING AIRPORT SECURITY

After checking in for a flight and checking your luggage with an airline at any U.S. airport, you're required to pass through a Transportation Security Administration (TSA) security checkpoint before proceeding to your airplane's gate.

At a TSA security checkpoint, each passenger's ID and boarding pass is verified and their carry-on items are passed through an X-ray machine. At the same time, each passenger passes through some type of metal detector or security scanner and is subject to an additional search by a TSA officer. Typically, adults about to pass through a TSA security checkpoint must remove all metal that they're wearing, as well as their hat, jacket, belt, and shoes. Passengers with medical implants or who are carrying medical devices must notify a TSA security officer and undergo a separate screening procedure. These procedures are outlined at www.tsa.gov/travel/special-procedures.

TSA security checkpoint lines at major airports can sometimes be long and take up to an hour to get through, so be sure to arrive at the airport at least two hours before a domestic flight or three hours prior to an international flight. (Allow even more time if you're traveling during a busy holiday period or need more time to get around the airport on foot or via wheelchair, for example.)

If you're over the age of 75, most U.S. airports allow you to go through an expedited screening procedure that allows you to leave your shoes, belt, and light jacket on. Children under 12 can also leave their shoes, light jackets, and headwear on. In some airports, older passengers are permitted to use the TSA Precheck line, which allows them to avoid long waits at the airport's TSA security checkpoint. When checking in at your airline's ticket or baggage drop off counter, ask if this is possible. If you're under the age of 75 and a U.S. citizen, for a fee of $85 you can apply for the TSA Precheck program. When you're approved for the program, you receive a Known Traveler ID number, which you can submit to an airline whenever you make a new reservation. For more information about TSA Precheck, visit https://www.tsa.gov/precheck.

TSA security requirements and rules change often, so it's important that you understand the latest rules and adhere to them. To read the latest TSA security guidelines, visit www.tsa.gov/travel/security-screening.

Use the Hotwire mobile app (shown here on an iPad) to find
and reserve a rental car almost anywhere in the world.

In this chapter, you discover strategies for finding the best deals on rental cars and other ground transportation. You learn

→ How and where to find the best rental car deals

→ How to avoid the extra fees often imposed by the rental car companies

→ How to make sure you choose the best protection options (insurance) for the rental car

→ What alternative ground transportation options are available, such as Lyft, Uber, or a private limo service

→ How to use your mobile device to navigate while you travel

Finding Ground Transportation

Renting a car at your travel destination offers convenience, but it comes with a lot of extra expenses. Based on where you're going and what you plan to do when you get there, you might discover that using local public transit, relying on taxis, or using services such as Lyft or Uber is just as convenient but far more economical. With the various services and mobile apps covered in this book, such as AARP Travel (travel.aarp.org), Hotwire, Kayak, Orbitz, or Travelocity, it takes just minutes to provide your rental car pick-up location, the dates and times you need the car, and the type of vehicle you want to rent, so that you can quickly compare rates among a handful of rental car companies that are available in your destination city.

Beyond these websites and mobile apps, there are online services that focus exclusively on car rentals, such as AAA Travel's Rezserver (www.rezserver.com/AAA-Travel), Carrentals.com, or Rentalcars.com.

Minimum Age Requirements

In the United States, most rental car companies require all drivers to be over the age of 25. Pay attention to this minimum age requirement if you're planning to have your kids or grandchildren added to the car rental agreement as a driver.

Renting a Car Abroad?

It is illegal to drive without a valid license and insurance in most countries. You should check with the embassy of the country you plan to visit or live in to find specific driver's license requirements. Many countries do not recognize a U.S. driver's license, but most accept an International Driving Permit (IDP), which may be valid only with a U.S. or local license. Holders of a valid U.S. driver's license can acquire an IDP from AAA for $20.00 (www.aaa.com/vacation/IDPApplication20.pdf) or from the National Automobile Club (www.nacroadservice.com/#!international-driving-permit/c2eg) for $25.00.

You can also acquire an IDP (while you wait) by visiting any AAA office in person. (To find the closest location, visit www.aaa.com/locations.) If you'll be applying for an IDP by mail, send in your application at least several weeks prior to your departure, or you'll need to pay an expedited service fee.

When driving in another country, you must adhere to all local traffic and driving laws and follow all road signs, even if they're not displayed in English.

Yet another option is to go directly to the website or mobile app for a specific rental car company. This option lets you explore your vehicle options and rates with just one rental car company at a time. If you're a member of a rental car company's loyalty program, you might receive additional perks for working directly with that rental car company.

The Avis.com website

Here are some websites for popular car rental companies:

- Alamo (www.alamo.com)
- Avis (www.avis.com)
- Budget (www.budget.com)
- Dollar (www.dollar.com)
- Enterprise (www.enterprise.com)
- Hertz (www.hertz.com)
- National (www.nationalcar.com)
- Payless (www.paylesscar.com)
- SilverCar (www.silvercar.com)
- Sixt (www.sixt.com)

Rental Car Companies Also Have Mobile Apps

The majority of these companies have websites as well as mobile apps, so you can just as easily use your smartphone or tablet to find and reserve a rental car pretty much anywhere in the world. To download these apps, visit the app store associated with your mobile device.

Considerations for Selecting a Rental Car Company

When you start shopping for the best deal on a rental car, you'll discover several things. First, the daily or weekly rental rates you're quoted vary dramatically between companies, even if you're comparing rates for the same dates and similar vehicles with pickup at the same location.

Second, some rental car companies have pick-up and drop-off locations located in the major airports, typically very close to the baggage claim areas. Others require you to collect your baggage at the airport and lug it to a complimentary shuttle bus to the rental car location.

Many of the smaller rental car companies have off-site locations located far outside the airport, so you have to take a free shuttle bus (or paid taxi) to that location, which could save you money but add an extra 20 to 30 minutes (or more) to the time it takes to pick up your vehicle.

The larger rental car companies with locations near airport pick-up and drop-off locations often have offices in major cities or rental counters at popular hotels, resorts, or tourist attractions.

The Advantage of Using a Travel Service to Find a Rental Car

One advantage to using a travel service to find a rental car is that these services have partnerships with both the largest and most popular rental car companies and the smaller companies. Thus, depending on where you're traveling, you may discover a smaller, highly competitive rental car company that services your travel destination—one that you might not have otherwise heard of.

It's Not All Good

The Hidden Agenda

Most rental car companies don't want you to rent the least expensive vehicle they have available. Instead, the customer service agents are trained to strongly encourage you to upgrade to a higher priced vehicle, agree to vehicle upgrades, and sell you the most extensive and costly vehicle protection (insurance coverage) possible, regardless of whether you need any of these extras.

Although the customer service people you deal with at the rental car pick-up location may be friendly and professional, their goal is to up-sell you in as many ways as possible and to generate the highest profits possible for their company. Beware of these sales tactics and avoid getting caught up in them.

Select the type (size) of vehicle you want to rent at the time you make the reservation, and make sure that this vehicle type and its daily or weekly rental fee are clearly displayed in the confirmation you receive. Print out a copy of this confirmation and have it with you when you pick up the vehicle.

Also, before you pick up the rental car, research your insurance coverage options and know exactly what additional coverage you need, if any. Determine the most economical way to acquire that coverage (which is seldom directly from the rental car company).

If you have reserved a specific type of rental car at a specific rate, don't allow the customer service agent to pull a bait-and-switch routine or tell you that your requested vehicle is unavailable and that the only vehicles that are available will cost more per day or week. If the representative tries this tactic and you have a confirmed (or prepaid) reservation, ask to speak with a manager. Demand that the company provide you with a vehicle that's equal to or better than the one you reserved at the same rate that you were originally quoted in your confirmed reservation.

Planning for Extra Charges

In addition to the daily or weekly rate you're quoted to rent a car, there are many additional costs you need to consider:

- **Add-on options:** The daily rate you're quoted for a rental car includes the basic vehicle. Rental car companies charge extra for options such as a GPS, car seat, ski rack, or other equipment that you request.

- **Additional driver fees:** The only person allowed to drive a rental car is the person whose name appears on the rental agreement. Many rental car companies charge an additional driver fee to have more than one name added to the agreement. Each person whose name is added to the agreement must have a valid driver's license.

- **Cleaning fee:** Most rental car companies have strict policies for no smoking and no pets in the vehicle. If you violate this rule or create a serious mess in the vehicle, you'll be charged an added cleaning fee.

- **Drop-off charge:** The typical arrangement for rental vehicles is that you drop it off at the same location where you picked it up. However, if you want to drop off the vehicle at another location—across town, at a different airport, or in another state, for example—expect to pay an extra drop-off fee.

- **Gas:** When you pick up a rental car, most often its gas tank is full. Based on your rental agreement, you're required to return the vehicle with the same amount of gas as when you picked it up, or the rental car company will charge you up to $6.00 per gallon (in the U.S.) to replace the gas. Another option is to prepay for gas and return the gas tank on empty (or at any level). Based on which option you choose, it's essential that you adhere to the arrangement so you avoid financial penalties.

Save Money on Gas

Wherever you are, use a free smartphone mobile app, such as Fuelzee, Gas Around Me, or GasBuddy, to help you find gas stations offering the lowest gas prices in the area.

- **Insurance:** Each time you rent a car, you are responsible for any damage to that vehicle, unless you acquire an optional vehicle protection plan (insurance coverage). For this, you have multiple options, which are covered later in this chapter. It's essential that you have some type of protection plan for a rental vehicle in case the car is damaged or stolen while it's in your possession. Check your own car insurance and any coverage your credit card provides. Keep in mind that when you use your own insurance, if you need to file a claim, your standard deducible (if applicable) will apply, whereas if you have travel insurance or rental car insurance, there is no deductible if you need to make a claim.

- **Late drop-off penalty:** The drop-off date and time is part of your rental agreement. If you're late returning the vehicle and haven't called the rental car company to extend your rental period, you'll be billed a high hourly rate for any time beyond the established drop-off time, which could wind up being much higher than the daily rate.

- **Parking:** You might have to pay parking fees both at the hotel where you stay and at the various locations you travel throughout the day. Keep in mind that parking fees, especially in major cities and at hotels, can add up quickly. In New York City, for example, expect to pay $40.00 or more to park in a parking lot for just a few hours, and between $50.00 to $75.00 per night for overnight parking at or near your hotel.

Save Money on Parking

To help you save money on parking, especially in a major city, use a free mobile app, like BestParking, Parking Panda, ParkMe Parking, or SpotHero. These apps allow you to quickly compare rates between nearby public parking lots and, in some cases, reserve a discounted parking space in advance. These apps are particularly useful in cities like New York, where hourly, daily, or overnight parking is very expensive.

On-property airport parking is typically costly. Most airports offer short-term parking (where you pay an hourly rate), as well as a long-term parking lot (where you pay a discounted daily or weekly rate). These lots are often located close to the airport terminals, so you'll pay a premium to park there.

Some airports also offer less expensive satellite parking options, which are located farther away from the terminals, but a free shuttle service is provided. This option is ideal if you're going away for a week or longer and want to park your vehicle near the airport.

Also located near most major airports are privately owned parking lots that offer a less expensive parking option compared to airport parking rates. These lots typically offer a free shuttle service to the airport. Many hotels that are located near airports also offer long-term parking options, even for nonguests.

When you know which airport you're flying out of, if you plan to park your car at or near that airport during your trip, use any search engine to discover your parking options, and potentially find online coupons that offer additional parking discounts. For example, in your favorite search engine, type **Boston Logan Airport Parking**, or **Chicago O'Hare Airport Parking Options**.

- **Taxes and government-imposed fees:** In addition to taxes, many local governments and airports impose local fees for renting a car. The taxes and fees are automatically added to your bill.

- **Tolls and tickets:** While driving a rental car, you are responsible for paying all tolls, parking tickets, speeding tickets, and moving violation tickets that you receive. If you fail to pay a toll or ticket and the local law enforcement needs to track you down through your rental car company, hefty fines will be imposed by both the law enforcement agency (for late fees) and the car rental company.

Finding and Renting a Car

One of the fastest ways to see which rental car companies offer the most competitive rates in the city where you'll be traveling to is to use one of the services that allow you to compare rates among a handful of rental car companies. Some of these travel services include (but are not limited to) AAA Travel, the AARP Travel Center (travel.aarp.org), Expedia, Hotwire, Kayak, Orbitz, Priceline, or Travelocity, as well as those that focus exclusively on rental cars.

>>>Go Further

SIZE MATTERS!

Rental cars come in all sizes and colors, just like regular cars. As you reserve the vehicle, you're asked to select a vehicle size. You need to take the number of passengers and how much luggage you'll be transporting into account.

Rental car companies use terms like compact, economy, mid-size, full-size/standard, SUV/minivan, convertible, or luxury to categorize their offerings. More and more rental car companies now also offer "green" hybrid options.

Each rental car company defines the types of cars it offers slightly differently, so determine your needs and reserve the smallest and most efficient car that will meet those needs. Larger vehicles typically cost more to rent and consume more gas. The most expensive vehicles to rent are typically the SUVs, minivans, and cars in the company's premium or luxury collection, but the rates fluctuate constantly based on local demand at the pick-up location.

It's Not All Good

Prepayment May Be Required

Some of the popular travel services require full payment in advance for the rental car you reserve. Others require you provide a credit or debit card to hold the reservation, but payment isn't made until you present a major credit card (in the driver's name) when you pick up the vehicle. Other services guarantee the reservation and the rate without a credit card or payment.

Before booking a rental car reservation, pay careful attention to the company's policy for making changes to or cancelling the reservation. Some cannot be changed or cancelled at all.

Use a Travel Service's Website

To comparison shop and then make a reservation, choose which travel service you'd like to use and visit its website. (You can also handle this task with the mobile app offered by any of the services.) You'll discover these services are most helpful if you plan to pick up and drop off the vehicle at an airport location.

For demonstration purposes, Hotwire is shown here. The steps are similar among all the services.

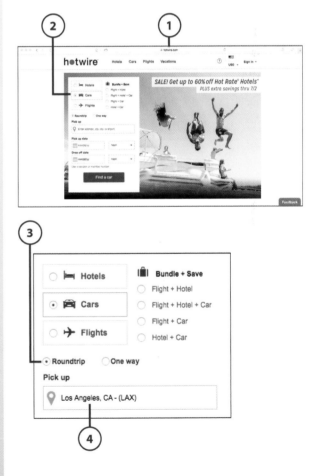

1. Launch your computer's web browser, and visit the website for the online travel service you want to use. To follow along with this example, enter **www.hotwire.com** into the web browser's address bar.

2. Click the Cars menu option or button, which is typically located near the top of the browser window.

3. Choose between round-trip or one-way. Round-trip means you'll pick up and drop off the vehicle at the same location (which is always the least expensive option). A one-way rental means you'll pick up the vehicle at one location and drop it off at another.

4. Type where you'd like to pick up the rental car. Use the name of an airport (or an airport code), enter a city name (or city, state, and country), or include a complete address to find the closest location to where you plan to stay.

5 Select a date in the Pick Up Date field.

6 Select an approximate pick-up time in the Time field that's related to the Pick Up Date field. Try to be as accurate as possible. If you'll be flying in to an airport, check your flight itinerary and then add one hour to the arrival time of your flight.

7 Select a date in the Drop Off Date field.

8 Select a drop-off time in the Time field that corresponds with the Drop Off Date field.

Calculate Your Drop-Off Time Accurately

If you'll be dropping off the vehicle at an airport (before your outgoing flight), allow one extra hour to drop off the vehicle and get from the vehicle drop-off location to the appropriate airport terminal. So, for a domestic flight, plan to drop off the vehicle three to four hours before your flight's scheduled departure. For an international flight, plan to drop off the vehicle four to five hours before the flight's scheduled departure time.

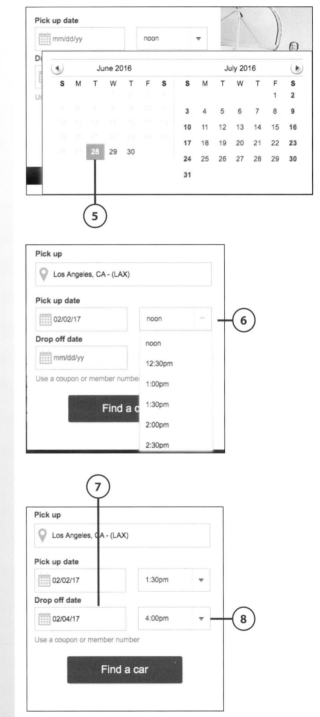

It's Not All Good

Every Hour Counts

Most rental car companies quote you a rate based on the number of days you plan to rent the vehicle. Typically, a weekly rate kicks in if you plan to keep the vehicle for more than five (or in some cases seven) days. The pick-up and drop-off dates and times you provide are used to calculate how many weeks, days, and/or hours you'll have possession of the car, which directly affects your rate, so be as accurate as possible.

Be sure to return the car within one hour of your scheduled drop-off date and time, or the rental car company will begin charging you a hefty per-hour surcharge. If you will be delayed dropping off the vehicle, or you opt to keep it for extra time, be sure to call the phone number in your rental agreement to request an extension at no charge so that you can keep your existing daily or weekly rate. Otherwise, expect to pay a late drop-off penalty.

9 Click the Use a Coupon or Member Number link if you have a coupon code or a loyalty program membership number with one or more rental car companies. If you already have an account set up with the online service you're using, all of your personal information should already be saved and will not need to be reentered as long as you sign in to the website.

10 Click the Find a Car button.

Pick up

Los Angeles, CA - (LAX)

Pick up date

02/02/17   1:30pm

Drop off date

02/04/17   4:00pm

Use a coupon or member number

Find a car

11 You see the results the online service has prepared based on the information you entered.

12 Click the Favorite, Lowest Price, Small to Large, or Large to Small button to re-sort the search results. Remember, the vehicle size you select could affect your quoted rate.

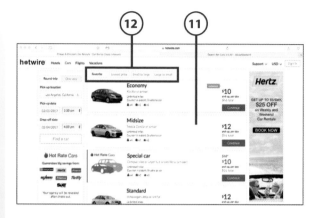

Sort Your Options

When the available rental cars are displayed after a search, based on the service you use, the rate quoted may be per day or for the entire length of your rental. In most cases, this rate does not include taxes, fees, or insurance coverage.

13 Use the Filter Your Search tools on the left side of the screen to narrow the results.

Easy Comparison Shopping

Hotwire enables you to check the rates quoted by other travel services. (Not all services provide this competitive information.) Under the Run This Search heading, click the option buttons for the other services you'd like to check, and then click Go. The search results for each service are displayed in a separate web browser window.

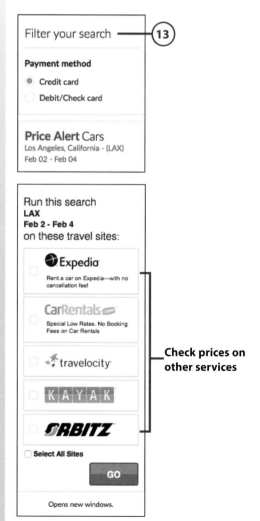

Check prices on other services

14 When you find an offer you like in the search results, click on the Continue button associated with that listing. Otherwise, you can change your search parameters by clicking the appropriate on-screen option or clicking your web browser's Back button.

15 You see additional information about the vehicle, the offer, and the rental car company. Check the dates and times, type of vehicle, and quoted rate. Notice that the appropriate taxes and fees have been added. Additional fees for a vehicle protection plan (insurance) and other extras may be added later.

16 Scroll down and provide the requested information for the driver. Be sure to confirm that the driver is over the age of 25. If you plan to add an additional driver to the rental agreement, click the Need to Add an Additional Driver option.

17 Scroll down and choose whether you want to pay the extra fee for the protection plan (insurance) offered by the rental car company. Before making this decision, be sure to read the "Understanding Your Rental Car Insurance Options" section later in this chapter.

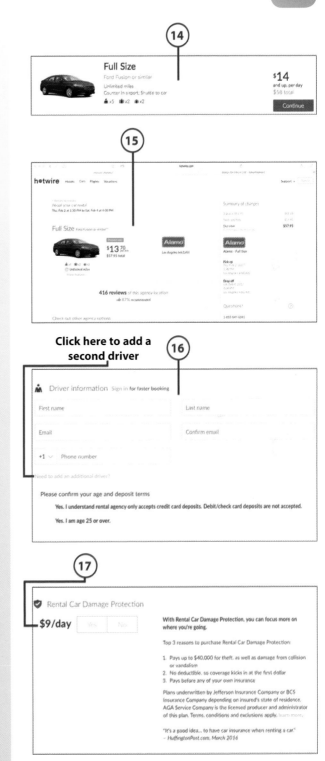

Click here to add a second driver

18 Enter your credit card payment options.

19 Accept the company's policies by clicking the appropriate check box.

20 Click the Book Now button to make your reservation.

The Fine Print

The Car Booking Rules and Regulations portion of the page explain that Hotwire does not require prepayment for rental car reservations, and you can cancel or change the reservations at any time.

21 You see the Success! Your Trip Is Booked screen (assuming you've provided all the necessary information). The screen includes your reservation's confirmation number and your quoted daily or weekly rate. You need the confirmation number to change or cancel your reservation and also to pick up the vehicle. Be sure to print this screen by clicking the Print Confirmation option. You also receive a confirmation email. (Not shown.)

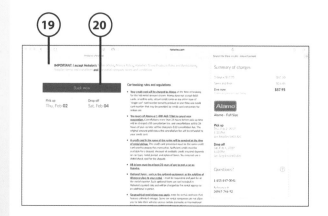

Using a Specific Rental Car Company Website

If you opt to use the website or mobile app from a specific rental car company to check rates or make your reservation, the process is more streamlined. However, you see rates quoted by only that rental car company.

Using a company's website is extremely convenient if you have an account set up and you're a member of that company's loyalty program, because all your personal details and preferences are already saved with the site. In addition, rental car companies typically offer the best rates and perks to their loyalty program members.

Always Sign In to Your Account First

If you already have an account with a rental car company, sign in to that account when you first access the website or use the mobile app. Click the Login button. If you're not yet a member, click the button to join and create an account. In some cases, having a website account is separate from being a member of the rental car company's loyalty program.

To be offered the best rates, join the loyalty program before booking your reservation. When creating your account profile, be sure to include your AAA, AARP, and/or airline frequent flier membership numbers if they're applicable so that you're automatically offered special discounts from participating rental car companies.

Sign in

To get a rate quote or make a reservation with a specific rental car company, visit that company's website or use the company's mobile app. When prompted, sign in to your account and provide your desired pick-up location, pick-up date and time, drop-off date and time, and desired vehicle type (size). You see a list of available cars and their corresponding rates. Follow the on-screen prompts to complete your reservation.

Tips for Saving Money on Rental Cars

The following tips will help you save money when you book your rental car, no matter what method you use to make the reservation.

Avoid Unnecessary Upgrades

At the time you pick up your rental car, the customer service specialist will offer you several upgrade options, each of which has an additional daily fee associated with it. When you add up these daily fees, your car rental cost could go up by several hundred dollars.

To save money, don't pay the extra $10.00 to $25.00 per day to rent a GPS from the rental car company. Instead, bring your own GPS unit or rely on the maps app on your mobile device for navigation assistance.

Unless you absolutely need the additional space in the vehicle for passengers or luggage, don't agree to a vehicle upgrade (unless you're getting it for free). Also, only purchase insurance (vehicle protection coverage) from the car rental agency if you actually need it. (You need to base this decision on your personal situation, the coverage you get through your existing automobile insurance, and the insurance offered by your credit card, if applicable.)

Choose the Right Type of Insurance Coverage

Unless you pre-purchase vehicle protection coverage, you are responsible for 100% of the costs associated with damage you cause to the vehicle. The sum you owe can include lost revenue for the rental car company if the vehicle winds up in the shop for repairs for an extended period of time. Remember, without insurance or vehicle protection coverage, you are 100% financially responsible for the vehicle if it gets stolen or damaged.

Read the "Understanding Your Rental Car Insurance Options" section later in this chapter before purchasing the optional protection plans offered by your rental car company.

Select the Correct Pick-Up and Drop-Off Dates and Times

When making your car reservation, it's important to provide the company with the correct pick-up and drop-off dates and times. If you are going to be very late picking up the vehicle—for example, because of a flight delay—call the rental car company and have them hold your reservation. If you show up several hours late, especially during a peak travel time, you might discover that your reserved vehicle has already been rented to someone else.

If you wind up needing to return your rental car early, you could be penalized as well. For example, if you were receiving a discounted weekly rate for a seven-day rental, but you return the vehicle after just four days, the rental car company will often switch you to the higher-priced daily rate.

Likewise, to avoid excessive late charges, drop off your vehicle at the drop-off time listed in your rental agreement. You can always drop off the vehicle early, but if you drop off the vehicle late (without calling first), you'll be charged a high hourly rate for each hour (or fraction of an hour) past your designated drop-off time.

Providing the correct pick-up and drop-off date and time when making your reservation also helps you qualify for the lowest daily or weekly rate that's offered.

Take Advantage of Discounts

Beyond being quoted a lower rate as a member of a particular rental car company's loyalty program, many airlines, hotels, and organizations (such as AAA, AARP, and USAA, as well as government/military) offer additional discounts when you book with specific rental car companies.

Look for special offers from frequent flier or hotel loyalty programs you're a member of, and see if AAA, AARP, USAA, your employer, or your alma mater offers any promotional codes or offers for one or more rental car companies. Many credit card issuers also offer discounts with specific rental car companies.

Another option is to do an Internet search for [*rental company name*] **Discount Code**. You might discover discount codes you can enter at checkout that will save you additional money on your rental. For example, Coupons.com, Dealsplus.com, Groupon.com, Offers.com, and Travelzoo.com often offer discount codes for popular rental car companies.

After you acquire a discount code, be sure to enter it in the appropriate field on the rental company's website as you're making your reservation.

When you use an online travel service, you typically receive an additional discount if you book your flight and rental car (or flight, hotel, and rental car) at the same time, with the same service.

>>>Go Further

ADDITIONAL CAR RENTAL ADVANTAGES FOR AARP MEMBERS

As an AARP member, you're entitled to extra discounts and prenegotiated rates when you rent from Avis, Budget, or Payless, so be sure to provide your AARP membership number or present your membership card. When making a reservation, ask for details on these special offers (offers subject to change):

- Free upgrade, Garmin GPS for $6.99/day, and unlimited mileage on most rentals.

- One Additional Driver fee waived.

- In the event of damage to a rental vehicle, as an AARP member, your liability is limited to the first $5,000 of damage without purchase of a Loss Damage Waiver. You can always purchase a Loss Damage Waiver (LDW) for the remaining $5,000 if you choose.

- Frequent traveler miles/points and 24-hour roadside assistance.

Understanding Your Rental Car Insurance Options

Every car rental company will offer you protection coverage for your rental vehicle at a per-day rate. In some cases, you'll be offered several levels of coverage: the company might have multiple coverage options that cover just the vehicle (lost/damage waiver); cover the occupants of the vehicle and their belongings; and/or cover everyone involved in an accident.

Sometimes adding the optional protection could double or triple the cost of your rental car. What the rental car companies typically don't tell you is that some or all of the coverage you're acquiring from them might already be provided by your own car insurance company or by the major credit card you're using to pay for the rental.

There are also third-party insurance companies that offer the same coverage as the rental car policies but at a fraction of what the rental car companies charge. The following are some third-party insurance companies:

- Allianz (www.allianztravelinsurance.com/find-a-plan/quote#/RentalCar)
- Insure My Rental Car (www.insuremyrentalcar.com)
- Travel Guard (www.travelguard.com/travelinsurance/carrental.asp)
- Travelex (www.travelexinsurance.com/travel-insurance/plans/rental-car-insurance)

Before acquiring any rental car–related coverage or insurance, contact your existing car insurance provider and determine what coverage you already have when renting a car. Coverage varies based on whether you'll be renting a car in the United States or abroad.

After you understand what coverage you already have, determine what additional coverage and protection you want, and then shop for the best way to acquire it. For example, if you're an American Express credit card holder, you can acquire premium rental car protection for a flat fee of between $19.95 and $24.95 for a rental period of up to 42 consecutive days. This is a total rate, not a per-day rate, which is what the rental car companies charge.

American Express Coverage

For more information about rental car insurance through American Express, call 1 (866) 518-0259, or visit www.americanexpress.com/carrental.

Exploring Ground Transportation Alternatives

Instead of using your computer or mobile device to find and reserve a rental car, you can use this same technology to help you identify other ground transportation options that could wind up being far less costly during your trip.

Here are some alternatives to renting a vehicle:

- **Hop-on/hop-off bus tours:** If you're visiting a major city anywhere in the world and want to visit the most popular attractions or landmarks in one to three days, one of the most cost-effective transportation options is to purchase a ticket to ride a hop-on/hop-off bus. These privately operated buses operate continuously during specific hours, and they offer narrated tours. The buses stop at each of the city's most popular landmarks and tourist attractions. During a one-, two-, or three-day period (depending on your ticket), you're able to freely get off the bus as often as you like to visit each attraction, and then you can pick up a later bus and continue your city tour. To find these tours, enter **hop on, hop off bus tour, [*the city you're visiting*]** in any Internet search engine, or use Viator.com (www.viator.com).

- **Hourly car rentals:** In some cities there are local services that rent cars by the hour. Two examples in the United States are GetAround.com (www.getaround.com) and ZipCar (www.zipcar.com).

- **Lyft or Uber:** You can use the Lyft or Uber app on your mobile device to call for a ride almost anywhere in the world. With these services, you pay about half of what you'd pay a taxi. After you set up a free account using the mobile app, the app determines your location, calls for a ride, and then allows you to pay for that ride (from an independent driver) using the credit card that's linked to your account. Unlike when using a taxi or limo, you are not expected to tip a Lyft or Uber driver. For more information, visit www.lyft.com or www.uber.com, respectively, or download the mobile app for the services.

- **Peer-to-peer car sharing:** Some services allow you to rent cars from private owners. FlightCar (www.flightcar.com), Getaround (www.getaround.com), and Turo (turo.com) are services in the United States that offer this option. Similar companies operate throughout the world. To find them, enter **peer-to-peer car sharing, [*insert the country you'll be visiting*]** in your search engine. If you opt to use one of these services, be sure you acquire ample insurance.

- **Public transportation:** With the help of your mobile device, it's easy to navigate around almost any city in the world using public transportation (buses, trains, and/or subways). Determine whether the Maps app that comes preinstalled with your iPhone or iPad or the Google Maps app that comes preinstalled on your Android device offers public transportation information for the city you'll be visiting. If not, visit the app store to find an appropriate app by searching for **public transportation [*insert city*]**.

- **Taxi or limo service:** In any major city around the world, you can hail a cab on the street, pick up a taxi at a nearby taxi stand, or make advance arrangements for a pickup. The concierge at any hotel will also call a taxi for you. Taxi rates vary, but depending on how far you need to go or how many rides you need to take during a trip, it could be a more convenient and cost-effective way to get around than renting a car. Many taxi companies around the world now have their own mobile apps that you can download and use to call for a taxi whenever and wherever you need one in the city where the taxi company operates. The mobile app pinpoints your location and informs the taxi driver where to pick you up. You can then pay the taxi fare via the app (using a credit or debit card).

Navigating Using Your Mobile Device

Whether you opt to drive, walk, or take public transportation where you visit, chances are you'll have no trouble navigating if you rely on the map app that comes preinstalled on your mobile device. If you're using an iPhone or iPad, this app is called Maps. On Android mobile devices, the app is called Google Maps.

The information in this section includes details about the iOS 9 and iOS 10.1 editions of the Maps app, and version 9.27.2 of Google Maps for the Android mobile devices. The apps are updated when new versions of the operating systems are released, so additional features and functions may be available in your version, and some menu options, command icons, or the appearance of some screens might look slightly different based on which version of the app you're using.

Install an Alternative Navigation App

Other navigational apps available for iOS and Android mobile devices include CityMaps, CoPolit GPS, Here Maps, MapQuest, Maps.me, Maps+, Scout GPS Navigation, and Waze. Most of these apps offer real-time, turn-by-turn navigation and include their own unique set of features and functions. You can also download the Google Maps app for free from the App Store for use on your iPhone or iPad.

Using Maps and Google Maps

The following are some things you can do with Maps and Google Maps:

- Display a detailed map for any region of the world. Simply enter a specific address, city, state, or country.

- Look up a specific business or point of interest.

- Seek out detailed directions between two locations.

- Obtain real-time, turn-by-turn driving directions (that include current traffic conditions) between two locations.

- Access real-time, turn-by-turn walking directions between two locations.

- Look up real-time public transit directions (available for a growing number of cities around the world).

It's Not All Good

Internet Connectivity Is Required for Navigation

All the various navigation apps available for smartphones and tablets require a continuous cellular Internet to provide real-time, turn-by-turn directions when you're on the go. These apps consume a lot of wireless data, so be mindful of that if you're on a limited data plan. In addition, when you're traveling abroad, cellular data usage can be costly, especially if you haven't prepaid for an international cellular plan.

You can use the navigation app while you're connected to a free Wi-Fi hotspot to plan your routes in advance of heading out on the streets. As you move, though, the app will not be able to determine your exact location or provide real-time turn-by-turn directions when you leave the Wi-Fi signal's radius.

See Chapter 14, "Connecting Your Computer, Smartphone, or Tablet While Traveling," to read about your options for cellular data roaming when traveling overseas.

The Maps Apps Offer Multiple Viewing Perspectives

As you're using the Maps app for iOS, tap on the Info icon to access the Info menu. Then, switch between viewing perspectives by tapping the various options. It's possible to superimpose real-time traffic information over both traditional and satellite map views. Google Maps and other navigational apps for smartphones and tablets offer similar functionality. Google Maps also offers a street view option, which lets you see what a specific address or area looks like.

Shown here are examples of the various viewing modes offered by the Maps app. Depicted is a map of New York City, which is centered on the Empire State Building.

Traditional
2D view

Satellite 2D
view

Traditional
3D view

Satellite 3D
view

Use the iOS 9 Edition of the Maps App

This example shows you how to obtain turn-by-turn walking directions between two locations in London using the iOS 9 edition of the Maps app running on an iPhone.

1 Launch the Maps app.

2 Tap the arrow icon to have the app zero in on your current location. A pulsating blue dot displays on the map in the center portion of the screen.

3 Tap the Directions icon.

The Maps App and Siri

On your iPhone or iPad, the Maps app works nicely with Siri, so from wherever you happen to be, it's possible to activate Siri and say, "How do I get to [*destination*] from here?" Your device determines your location and then provides turn-by-turn directions to that destination without you having to manually type anything into the mobile device.

Recent Searches

When you begin typing in the Start or End fields, recent locations you've used in the Maps app are displayed below the field under a Recents heading. Tap any of the options to use that location.

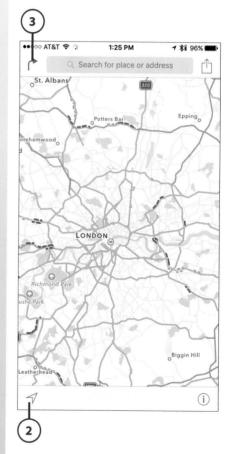

4 Type the address of your starting location in the Start field; state the name of your location (for example, **Four Seasons Hotel, London**); enter the name of a contact that's stored in the Contacts app; or leave the default Current Location option in place. If you state a location, the Maps app automatically looks up and displays the address. Tap the correct listing.

5 Type your intended destination in the End field.

6 Tap Route.

7 Tap the Walk tab for walking directions. Alternatively, tap the Drive tab for driving directions or the Transit tab for public transportation directions.

8 The map displays up to three different routes, with the recommended route indicated by a dark blue line. (Only one route is shown here.)

9 Tap Start to access Navigation mode and receive real-time directions to your destination.

10 Tap the Info icon to display the app's Info menu.

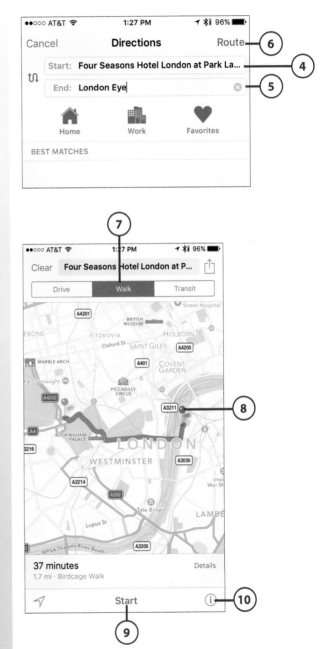

Mass Transit Information

If the Transit option is available in the city you're visiting, tap the Transit tab to see step-by-step directions for getting to the closest bus, subway, or train station (whichever is applicable). You also get detailed instructions for using the necessary form(s) of mass transit to reach your destination. For example, the Maps app tells you when to get off one bus or train and where and when to catch the next one. Real-time schedules are provided for buses, trains, and subways.

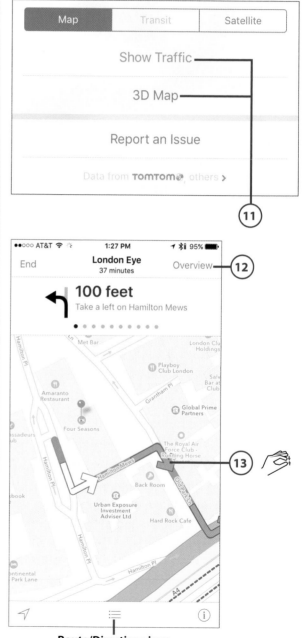

(11) Tap Show Traffic to see real-time traffic information on the map (or tap Hide Traffic to hide it). Tap the viewing perspective (3D Map is shown here) to see the map displayed in that format.

(12) Tap Overview to zoom out and see an overview map that shows your entire route.

(13) Use a reverse-pinch or pinch gesture to zoom in or out on the map at any time. Tap the Route/Directions icon to view a summary route screen that can be helpful if you lose Internet access while en route.

Route/Directions icon

Navigating in Satellite View

When you're in Satellite view, after zooming, place two slightly separated fingers on the screen simultaneously, and then drag or rotate them to rotate and reposition the map display. Swipe your finger horizontally from right to left across the current direction directive to preview upcoming turns and navigational instructions.

(14) Follow the directions provided to reach your destination, keeping in mind that a continuous cellular Internet connection is required. If you make a wrong turn or deviate from your route, the Maps app automatically compensates and provides updated directions to your intended destination. (Not shown.)

(15) To exit out of navigation mode before reaching your destination, tap anywhere on the screen to make the on-screen options appear, and then tap End.

(15)

•●○○○ AT&T 🛜   1:30 PM   ⬆ ⁎ℹ 94% ▬

End   **London Eye**   Overview
            37 minutes

➡ **900 feet**
Take a right

Using Other Apps with Maps Running

While using Maps, you can launch and use other apps at the same time. Press the Home button once to return to the Home screen and then launch a different app, or quickly press the Home button twice to access the App Switcher and switch between apps. While you're using the other app, Maps continues running in the background and alerts you of upcoming turns. Tap the banner along the top of the screen to quickly return to the Maps app.

Maps and Your Apple Watch

If you have an Apple Watch wirelessly linked with your iPhone, as navigation information is displayed on the smartphone's screen, similar information is displayed on the watch's screen.

Use the iOS 10.1 Edition of the Maps App

In September 2016, Apple offered a free update to its iOS operating system for the iPhone and iPad. Included with this update is a revamped and vastly improved edition of the Maps app. It offers a plethora of powerful new features and functions, including more accurate and detailed turn-by-turn navigational directions between two locations, as well as more detailed information about businesses, landmarks, services, and points of interest.

This example shows you how to obtain turn-by-turn driving directions between two locations in Boston, Massachusetts, using the iOS 10.1 edition of the Maps app running on an iPhone.

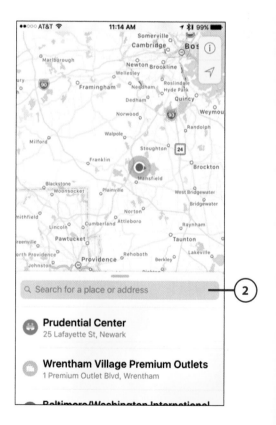

①   Launch the Maps app.

②   A map of your current location is displayed automatically. In the Search for a Place or Address field, enter your destination, and tap the Search key to continue. Notice that below this field are recently found addresses, businesses, or locations. Tap any of these options to revisit that destination.

3 After the app finds the address, tap the large blue-and-white Directions icon.

4 By default, the Maps app calculates driving directions between your current location and your destination. To change the starting location, tap the From My Location option that's displayed immediately below the destination you just entered, and then enter your starting location. (Not shown.)

There Are Several Ways to Enter Your Starting Location and Destination

When entering your destination and starting location, you have several options. For example, you can enter the name of a person or business that's stored in your Contacts app database. You can also enter the name of a popular landmark, tourist attraction, or point of interest, such as the name of an airport. Alternatively, you can enter a complete address (street, city, and state).

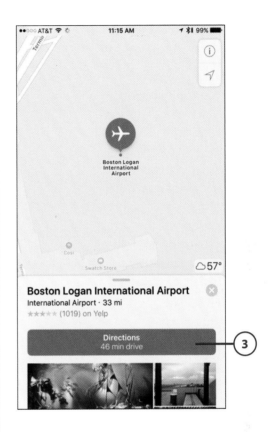

(5) After you fill in the From and To fields, tap the Route button. (Not shown.)

(6) By default, multiple driving routes are calculated. The recommended route is displayed using a dark blue line on the map. If you want to switch to an alternative route, tap it in the map that's displayed in the top portion of the screen. Alternatively, to switch transportation methods, tap the Walk, Transit, or Ride option displayed along the bottom of the screen.

(7) Tap the green-and-white Go button to begin receiving real-time turn-by-turn directions. Follow the onscreen prompts and listen to the navigation voice to reach your destination.

Based on traffic conditions, your travel speed, and other factors, your estimated time of arrival, remaining travel time, and current distance from your destination are displayed along the bottom of the screen. The next turn or driving direction you'll need to make is displayed along the top of the screen, while your current location is displayed and continuously updated in the map that's displayed in the center of the screen.

Choose an Alternative Transportation Method

When you tap the Walk icon, you're provided with detailed, real-time walking directions to your destination. By tapping the Transit icon, you're provided with detailed directions for using the region's subways, trains, buses, or ferries to reach your destination. Tap the Ride option to request a ride via Lyft or Uber. To use this feature, you must have an established account with the service you choose, and the official mobile app must be installed on your iPhone or iPad.

Make Stops Along the Way

While using the iOS 10 edition of the Maps app for real-time navigation directions, if you want to make a stop along the way—at a nearby gas station, restaurant, or coffee shop, for example—tap the button area of the screen (anywhere but on the End button). Tap the type of business or service you're looking for, and then select one of the nearby options. The Maps app adjusts your route to the closest location you searched for, and then when you're ready to continue to your original destination, it provides updated navigation directions.

Maps Offers Real-Time Traffic Information

The iOS 10 edition of the Maps app now more accurately displays real-time traffic conditions along your route and warns you in advance of traffic, detours, accidents, or road construction that could cause a delay. When this happens, you'll be given the option to recalculate your route to avoid the problematic areas.

Heavy traffic is displayed using a red line on the map, while icons are used to showcase accidents or road construction.

Use the Google Maps App

This example shows you how to obtain turn-by-turn walking directions between two locations in New York City using the Google Maps app running on an Android smartphone.

(1) Launch the Google Maps app from the Home screen.

(2) Tap on the Target icon to have the app pinpoint your current location and display it on a map.

(3) To obtain directions between two locations, tap on the Navigation icon.

Recent Searches

Recent addresses you've accessed using Google Maps are displayed when you start to type a location in the To or From fields. Tap any listing to insert it into the field.

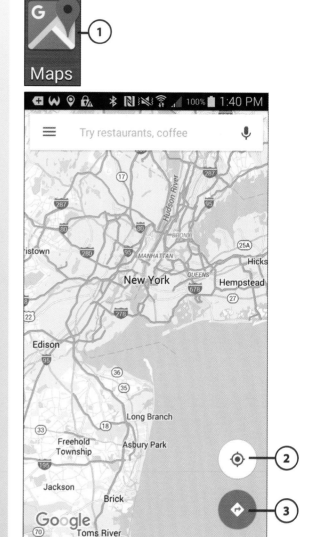

4. Enter your starting location in the From field. You can type the name of a landmark or point of interest or enter a specific address.

5. Type your destination in the To field.

6. Tap the Car icon for driving directions, the Bus icon for mass transit directions, the Person icon for walking directions, or the Bike icon for cycling directions. Tap the Taxi icon to compare rates between taxi and other ride services, such as Uber. (Only available options are displayed.) Notice that the approximate travel time is listed next to each option. This example uses the Person icon.

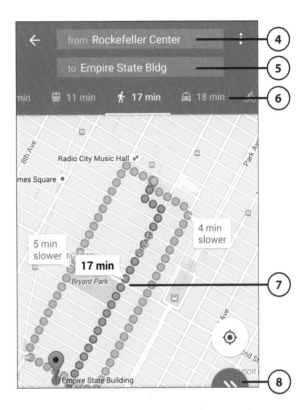

7. You see up to three different routes on the map. The route depicted with dark blue dots is the recommended route. The approximate travel times are displayed in banners near each route.

8. Tap on the Start icon when you're ready to begin your journey.

Capitalization Isn't Required

You do not need to capitalize the names of locations, streets, cities, states, countries, or landmarks when entering information. You should, however, separate pieces of information with a comma or space. For example, type, "Empire State Building, NY" or "30 Rockefeller Plaza, NY."

(9) Follow the directions displayed on the screen and that you hear. The map updates as you move.

(10) Tap on one of the arrow icons to jump through each navigational instruction along your route, or tap Route Preview at the top of the screen to see a summary of your route.

(11) Tap the More icon to switch between satellite and terrain map views.

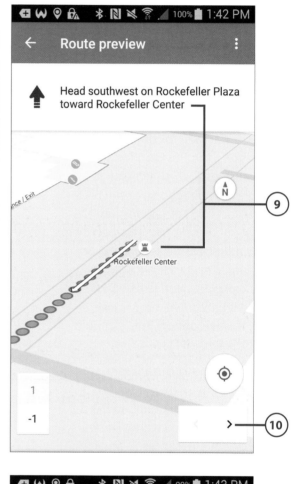

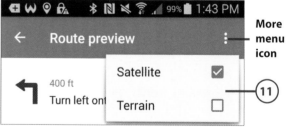

More menu icon

(12) Use a pinch or reverse-pinch figure gesture to zoom out or in. Place two fingers (slightly separated) and rotate them on the screen to change your map viewing perspective. (Satellite view now shown.)

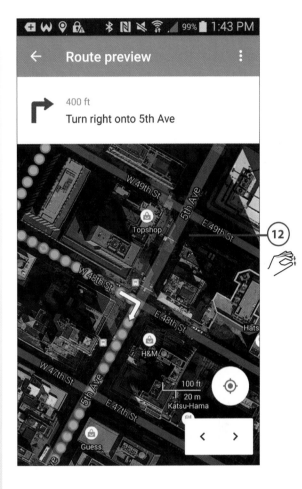

13 Follow the provided directions until you reach your destination. Tap the left-pointing arrow at any time to exit out of the Google Maps app's navigation mode.

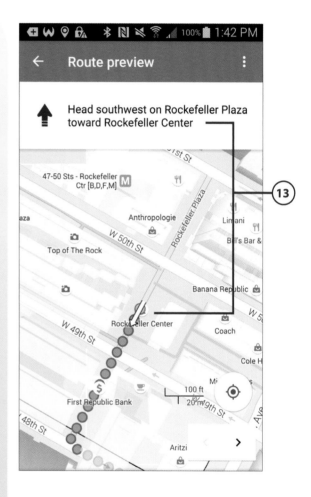

Finding great accommodations takes just minutes using a travel service or a lodging's website.

In this chapter, you'll discover how to use the various websites and mobile apps to find and book accommodations almost anywhere in the world. You'll learn

→ How to determine your accommodation wants and needs
→ Where to find and book accommodations using a travel service's website or mobile app
→ Strategies for saving money on accommodations when you travel
→ Pitfalls to avoid when booking accommodations online

Finding and Booking Accommodations

You have more options than ever before when it comes to choosing accommodations. In most places, you're no longer limited to staying at a traditional hotel or motel. Some of your other options include

- Airbnb (or a similar option) rentals
- Bed & breakfasts (B&Bs) or inns
- Boutique or independently owned hotels
- Timeshare properties (even if you're not a timeshare owner)
- Vacation home rentals

Regardless of which option you choose, you can use your Internet-enabled computer, smartphone, or tablet to quickly find the perfect accommodations. However, based on your decision, you'll want to use the appropriate tools to ensure you're able to find what you need at a price you can afford.

Many services, including AAA Travel (www.aaa.com), AARP Travel (travel.aarp.org), Expedia, Kayak, Orbitz, Priceline, and Travelocity, let you compare rates across many hotel and motel chains. These tools enable you to see what traditional accommodation options are available during the dates of your travel and compare their offerings based on things like quality, price, location, and amenities. You can also use specialty online travel services such as Booking.com, GetARoom.com, Hotels.com, and Trivago.

Airbnb

For a change from a traditional hotel, motel, or B&B, try Airbnb, which includes properties throughout the world. Refer to Chapter 3, "Getting to Know Some Popular Travel Tools," for more information about this service.

Define Your Accommodation Wants, Needs, and Budget

After you decide where you're going, you need to decide where you'll stay. For most people, the default option is to find a traditional hotel and book a basic room. However, if you're willing to put in some time to research options, you can book much more unique, comfortable, and memorable accommodations to fit your budget.

Considering the Extra Fees

When you're shopping around to find and book accommodations and comparing rates among options, you'll probably notice the low prices. These rates you find online and in apps are often up to 60 percent off the rates published by the actual hotels or motels. To be able to offer these low prices and appear competitive, many hotels, motels, and other types of accommodations offer a lower nightly rate but charge a mandatory fee—sometimes called a resort, per-guest, or per-night fee—that is not part of the displayed rate.

Regardless of which service you use, determine whether one or both of these extra fees will be added to your bill. Then, take into account the state and local taxes that will be applied to your final bill. Depending on how you make your reservation, you might also be charged a booking fee.

The following are some other charges you may incur:

- Cleaning fee (for example, if you smoke in a nonsmoking room or bring a pet to the hotel)
- Extra cot fee
- Late-checkout fee
- Parking fees
- Pay-per-view/on-demand movie fees
- Telephone local and long-distance charges
- Room service dining fees
- Reservation change or cancellation fees
- Wi-Fi Internet charges

Understanding Payment Terms

With some travel services, the compromise for receiving a deeply discounted rate is that prepayment in full is sometimes required when you book your accommodations, and your reservation can't be changed or refunded. Resort fees, per-guest fees, and other charges might be added to your bill later; you pay for these charges upon checkout.

Before booking accommodations, make sure you understand and agree to the policies related to changing or cancelling your reservation, and understand that regardless of how you prepay for the reservation, you typically need a major credit card (in your name) to check in to the hotel.

Hotel Credit Cards

Most hotel chains have their own credit card that allows you to earn points toward free accommodations for every dollar you spend using that card, whether for everyday or travel-related purposes. Using one of these cards to make hotel reservations also often entitles you to special perks, a room upgrade, or some type of discount. So, if you enjoy staying at hotels or motels operated by a specific chain, such as Hilton, Marriott, or Sheraton, consider applying for that hotel chain's credit card.

Understanding the Accommodation Ratings

Accommodations are often rated using a star-based system of between one and five stars. However, not all hotels, motels, and travel-related services rely on the same system. Thus, if you look up a hotel on one service, it might be referred to as a three-star hotel, but on another service that same hotel could be referred to as a four-star hotel. Make sure you know whose rating system is being used, and understand the rating system's guidelines for what constitutes a three-, four-, or five-star hotel.

In general, unless you're looking for ultra-low-cost, no-frills accommodations, avoid staying anywhere that's earned only one or two stars, regardless of which rating system is being used.

The AAA Rating System

For more than 80 years, AAA has been using professionally trained inspectors to review hotels, motels, and B&Bs throughout the United States, Canada, Mexico, and the Caribbean and then award each inspected property a diamond-based rating. Every year, more than 28,000 hotels, motels, and B&Bs are rated, and fewer than 0.4 percent receive the much-coveted five-diamond rating.

You can view these ratings using the AAA Mobile app for smartphones and tablets, or using the TripTik Travel Planner website (http://ttp.aaa.com/TripTik). The ratings also appear in all of AAA's printed and online travel guides. For a current list of all AAA four- and five-diamond rated hotels, visit www.aaa.com/Diamonds.

Using the Reviews

Although you can rely solely on star- or diamond-based ratings for a location, another tool available to travelers are customer reviews. Many travel services publish ratings and reviews from travelers, and several services, like TripAdvisor. com, focus on providing extensive traveler reviews.

Read detailed reviews from past guests who have stayed at a property by looking up that property on TripAdvisor, using its website or mobile app.

By investing a few minutes to read a handful of reviews for a hotel, motel, or B&B before making your reservation, you can learn about the experiences past travelers have had and get a good idea about whether the hotel offers a clean, safe, comfortable, accessible, and friendly environment that's worth the nightly fee.

Selecting the Right Location

One of the more important decisions you need to make related to accommodations is about the location and accessibility to transportation. After all, you want to be close to your intended destination(s)—not several miles or more away from it.

Especially when you're using an online travel site that saves you 30 to 60 percent on accommodations but has a no-changes-or-cancellations policy, make sure the location works for you prior to booking.

>>>*Go Further*

CONSIDERING TRANSPORTATION OPTIONS

If you'll have a rental car during your trip, make sure your selected accommodations offer on-site or nearby parking and determine in advance the daily parking fee for them. Also find out whether unlimited in-and-out privileges are offered. Parking for a rental car could add between $25.00 and $75.00 per night to your hotel bill.

If you'll be relying on public transportation, determine how far the hotel is from the closest bus, train, or subway station. Or, if you'll be relying on taxis or a service like Lyft or Uber, figure out how much the average fare will be each time you need to go somewhere from the hotel (and then need to get back).

Most travel services allow you to view the location of available accommodations on a map when you're making the reservation. If the service doesn't offer this feature, use a free mapping service on your computer or mobile device to determine the exact location of the accommodations you're interested in.

When you figure in parking and transportation costs, a low-cost hotel that's far away from where you want or need to be could cost you much more than a slightly more expensive hotel that's exactly where you want or need to be.

Choosing Amenities

The list of popular amenities offered at hotels, motels, inns, and B&Bs is often extensive, but some amenities are more useful than others. Determine in advance which amenities are the most important to you, and seek out accommodations that offer them. When you're shopping for accommodations, check the detailed listings for properties to find a summary of offered amenities.

Amenities offered are listed in a hotel's listing on Hotels.com.

For no additional fee, most accommodations offer handicap-accessible rooms as well as rooms with bathrooms that are wheelchair accessible. It's often possible to contact a hotel (after making a reservation) to request a room on a low or high floor. In some locations, you can also request smoking or nonsmoking rooms or special rooms for people with allergies or chemical sensitivity.

The following are some other amenities that might be available, free or for an additional fee:

- In-room Wi-Fi
- A flat-screen television with cable programming
- A gym/workout facility
- Premium bed linens and towels
- An in-room mini bar
- Iron and ironing board
- Free on-site parking
- Continental breakfast
- A bathroom that includes a bathtub or whirlpool (instead of a walk-in shower)

Four- and five-star hotels tend to offer higher-end amenities, such as complimentary bathrobes. A three-star hotel typically offers basic soap and shampoo in the bathroom, whereas a four- or five-star hotel will upgrade these amenities to luxury name brand products.

The Resort Fee Covers Additional Amenities

Even though you might not be staying at a full-service resort, many hotels and motels now charge a daily resort fee, which is mandatory. This fee typically gives you access to additional amenities at the hotel, such as a daily newspaper delivered to your room, free local calls, free Wi-Fi Internet access, and admission to the hotel's gym.

Understanding Vacation Home Rentals

Several online travel services allow you to seek out and book hotels, motels, or vacation home rentals. Unlike a hotel or motel, with a vacation home rental you get an entire house, condo, or apartment that is fully furnished and typically is equipped with a full kitchen, multiple bedrooms, multiple bathrooms, laundry facilities, and a separate living room.

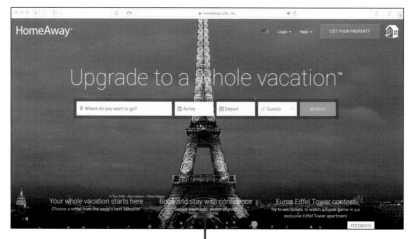

HomeAway.com is one service that enables you to find and book a vacation home rental.

An Ideal Accommodation Solution for Families

If you're traveling with your entire family or your extended family, a vacation home rental is often a more economically viable and comfortable solution than booking one or more traditional hotel or motel rooms.

Not only do vacation homes give you and the people you're traveling with much more living space and privacy, they also allow families or extended families to stay together while saving money by preparing meals instead of eating out and doing laundry so you pay less in airline baggage fees.

With a vacation home rental, travelers can have their own bedrooms and bathrooms—whereas they have to share bedrooms and bathrooms in a hotel— which gives them more personal space, comfort, and privacy. These things can ultimately make traveling with family members more enjoyable and less stressful.

You can typically rent vacation homes by the week, although some can be rented for a minimum of three to five nights. Depending on the number of people you're traveling with, a multi-bedroom vacation home will often cost less than booking one or two separate or adjoining hotel rooms.

Vacation rental homes are listed in some of the travel services previously discussed, but there are also online services and mobile apps dedicated only to this type of accommodations, such as the following:

- FlipKey (www.flipkey.com)
- HomeAway (www.homeaway.com)
- Homes for Vacation Rental (www.hometogo.com)
- Tripping.com (www.tripping.com)
- VacationHomeRentals.com (www.vacationhomerentals.com)
- VRBO (www.vrbo.com)

Considering Renting a Timeshare Unit

When you're planning a trip with your entire family or extended family, another way to save money on accommodations is to book a unit with a timeshare resort. Most timeshares resorts, including those operated by major hotel chains, allow you to book a timeshare unit even if you're not a timeshare owner. Often, the rates are more competitive than rates for hotel rooms that offer less space and fewer amenities.

Most timeshare resorts require a minimum of a three-, five-, or seven-night stay, but the nightly cost for the timeshare unit is typically equivalent to a three- or four-star hotel in that same area. However, unlike a traditional hotel, a timeshare offers a handful of advantages:

- A typical timeshare unit is located close to popular tourist attractions or vacation destinations. For example, you'll discover dozens of timeshare resorts within a 10-mile radius of the Walt Disney World Resort in Orlando, Florida.

- Most timeshare units offer multiple bedrooms and bathrooms to accommodate four, six, or even eight (or more) guests.

- Timeshare units include a full kitchen (or kitchenette), so you can save money by preparing one or two of your meals each day rather than dining out.

- Timeshare properties typically have resort amenities, including a swimming pool, tennis courts, on-property restaurants, and other activities.

- Most timeshare units contain a washer and dryer, so you can conveniently do laundry and ultimately pack less (to save money on airline baggage fees).

- Timeshare units tend to be much more spacious than traditional hotel or motel rooms because they include a separate living room, dining room, and patio or porch.

- If you book a timeshare through a major hotel chain and you're a member of that hotel chain's loyalty program, you earn points for your stay, or you can redeem points to stay at the timeshare resort for free.

- Timeshare resorts are often updated and refurbished more often than hotels, so you're more apt to have more modern or more recently renovated accommodations.

The best way to find and book a timeshare property (if you're not a timeshare owner) is to call the resort directly or visit the company's website. The following websites help you find and book units within timeshare resorts throughout the world:

- Disney Vacation Club (www.DisneyVacationClub.disney.go.com)

- Hilton Grand Vacations (www.hiltongrandvaations.com)

- Marriott Vacation Club (www.marriottvacationclub.com)

- RCI (www.rci.com/resort-directory)

- Sheraton Vacation Club (http://sheratonvacationclub.com/timeshare)

- Timeshare Adventures (www.timeshareadventures.com)

- Wyndham Vacation Club (www.wyndhamvacationrentals.com)

Remember, you do not need to be a timeshare owner to stay at a timeshare resort. Also, during your stay, you are *not* required to participate in a sales pitch to become a timeshare owner. However, if you opt to participate in an optional sales presentation (which typically lasts about one hour), you'll be awarded with something like an additional discount for your stay, a free meal, or free tickets to a local theater or tourist attraction.

Find and Book a Marriott Vacation Club Timeshare Unit

This example demonstrates how to book a timeshare unit at a Marriott Vacation Club in Orlando, Florida. The steps for booking a timeshare unit are pretty similar on any other service you use.

(1) Using your computer, launch your favorite web browser. Enter **www.marriottvacationclub. com** in the address field.

(2) Click the MVC Rentals option, and then select Find and Reserve.

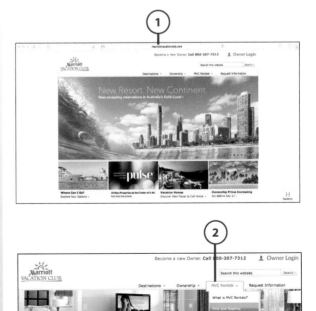

3 Click the pull-down menu to select your desired destination (Country, State, City).

Manual Entry

On some sites, you're asked to type the location rather than choose a destination from a menu.

4 Select which property you want to stay at from the Property Name field.

5 Select your check-in date.

6 Select your check-out date.

7 Choose the number of bedrooms required. Your options are typically one, two, or three.

8 Choose the number of guests per room.

9 Provide your email address in the Email field. (Not shown.)

10 Click the Search button to continue. (Not shown.) You see a list of available timeshare units.

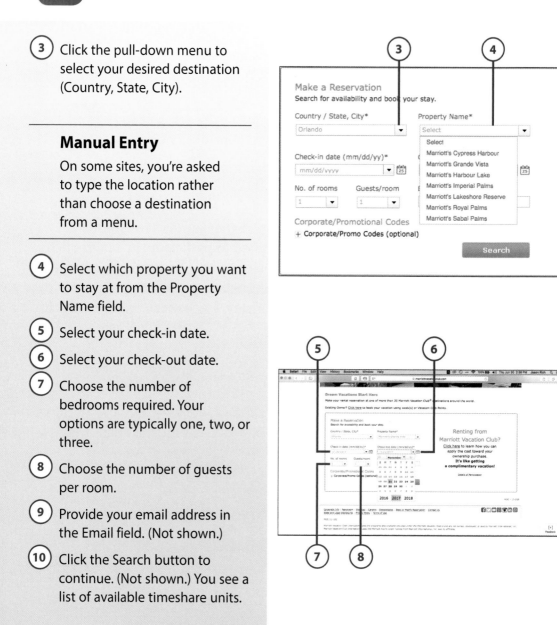

11 Click the Rate Details or Room Details option to view additional information about what's being offered.

12 Click the Special Rates option to determine whether you qualify for a discount. For example, from Marriott Vacation Club, people over the age of 62 or AAA members qualify for a 15 percent discount.

13 If you're a member of Marriott's loyalty program, enter your membership number in the Rewards Number field to earn points for your stay.

14 Click the Select button associated with the listing you want to book. Alternatively, use the Edit Your Search options to select a different timeshare resort property or unit configuration. It's also possible to modify your Check In or Check Out dates.

15 Make specific requests and review your reservation details on the Review Reservation Details screen. Be sure to read the reservation cancellation policy that's displayed on this screen. Click the Continue button to proceed.

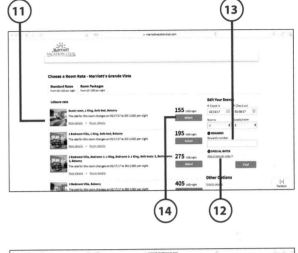

(16) Fill in the appropriate fields with your name, address, email address, phone number, rewards program membership number, and credit/debit card payment details.

(17) Click the Book Now button to complete your reservation. You see a confirmation screen and receive a confirmation email almost immediately. (Not shown.)

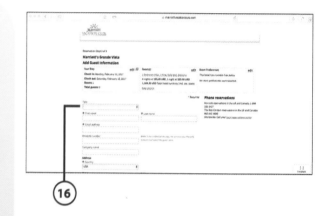

(16)

Considering B&Bs

For a romantic getaway or a quiet retreat for solo travelers or couples, another alternative is a bed & breakfast (B&B). Some services, like Booking.com (www.booking.com/bed-and-breakfast/index.html), allow you to include B&B establishments in your accommodation search or narrow down your search for this type of accommodation.

A typical B&B offers only a handful of guestrooms, and the owner(s) of the establishment serve as your host. Breakfast is included. What's nice about these accommodations is that each guestroom is often uniquely furnished and decorated, so the experience is very different (more home-like and comfortable) than staying at a chain hotel.

What's an Inn?

An inn is similar to a B&B, but it offers more guestrooms and may or may not include breakfast.

No Kids Allowed

Some people prefer staying at a B&B because children and pets are often not allowed, so the accommodations tend to be more peaceful.

There are online services and mobile apps that focus exclusively on B&Bs around the world:

- B&B Finder (www.bnbfinder.com)
- Bed and Breakfast Directory (www.napopo.com)
- BedandBreakfast.com (www.bedandbreakfast.com)
- iLoveInns.com (www.iloveinns.com)
- The Bed and Breakfast Directory (www.thebedandbreakfastdirectory.com)

B&B Ratings and Reviews

Unlike hotel and motel chains, B&Bs tend to be independently owned and operated. From the various directories and websites that help you find and book B&Bs, you can typically read ratings and reviews from past guests to help you choose the best place to stay.

Finding and Booking Traditional Hotel or Motel Accommodations

When it comes to finding and booking a traditional hotel or motel room, you can compare rates between many different hotel and motel chains (as well as independently operated hotels and motels, and boutique hotels) using a general travel service or one of the online services that focus exclusively on booking hotel reservations. Another option is to visit the website or use the mobile app for a specific hotel or motel chain, which allows you to find available rooms only with that specific chain. This option typically allows you to qualify for senior, AARP, AAA, corporate, or loyalty program discounts as you make the reservation, plus you can take advantage of online-only promotions or sales from that hotel or motel chain.

Whichever option you choose, it's a good strategy to create a free account with the website or mobile app and then create a profile that includes your name, address, phone number, loyalty program membership number(s), email address, and credit/debit card information. When this information is entered and stored, booking reservations in the future is much faster and more convenient.

Find and Book Accommodations

The process of finding and booking a hotel room using one of the online travel services that specializes in hotels is similar, regardless of which service you use. There are many online services you can use to shop for and book hotel accommodations, such as GetARoom.com, Hotels.com, Hotwire.com, Orbitz.com, Priceline.com, or Travelocity.com. Here are the steps to find and book a hotel using the Hotels.com online service (via a computer):

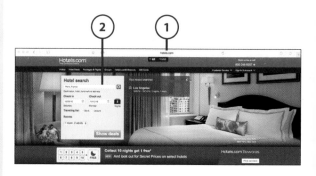

(1) From your computer, launch your favorite web browser and enter **www.hotels.com** in the address field.

(2) Enter your destination information in the Search field. You can include a city; city and state; city, state, and country; a specific address; the name and location of a particular hotel/motel (such as the Ritz-Carlton, New York, New York); or the name of your favorite hotel/motel chain and location information.

(3) Click the Check In field and provide your desired check-in date.

(4) Click the Check Out field and provide your desired check-out date. The number of nights you require accommodations for is automatically calculated.

5 Choose either Work or Leisure in the Traveling For section. (Not shown.)

6 Click the pull-down menu displayed below the Rooms heading and choose your desired room configuration.

7 Click the Show Deals button.

8 You see a comprehensive listing of available rooms at various hotels/motels that meet your search criteria. Click the hotel name to view more information about that property.

Property Ratings

Hotels.com offers a star-based rating for each listing and sometimes gives an average TripAdvisor rating.

9 Fine-tune your search by adjusting any of the options listed below the Narrow Results heading. For example, choose to view only hotels with a specific rating or that are within a specific distance from a nearby attraction or landmark.

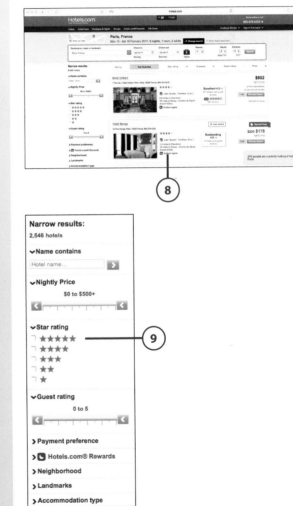

(10) Scroll down to view additional search filters, such as Accommodations Type, Amenities, Themes/Types, and Accessibility Features. Click any of these options to further narrow your search. As you change sort filter options, the listing of available accommodations updates automatically.

(11) Click the Choose Room button that's associated with a specific listing to book your reservation.

(12) You see a detailed description of the hotel/motel, including a listing of amenities offered and ratings and reviews of that property. A summary of your quoted nightly rate and overall reservation cost is also displayed.

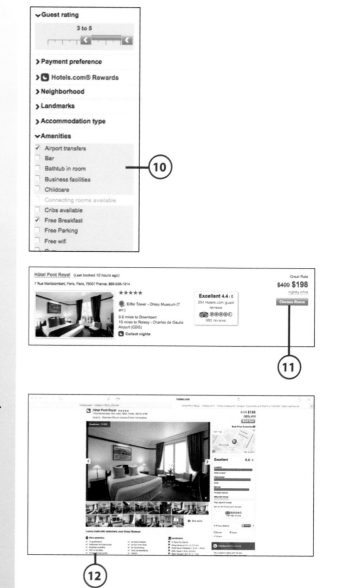

(13) Scroll down to view specific room configuration options available for the selected hotel. Select the room type you want, and click on the Book button to continue.

Nightly Rates

Which room configuration you choose affects the quoted nightly rate. *Room configuration* refers to the number and size of the beds in the room. For example, some rooms have one king-sized bed, two queen-sized beds, or two twin beds. Also, remember that the displayed rate does not include the hotel's daily resort fee, if applicable, or taxes.

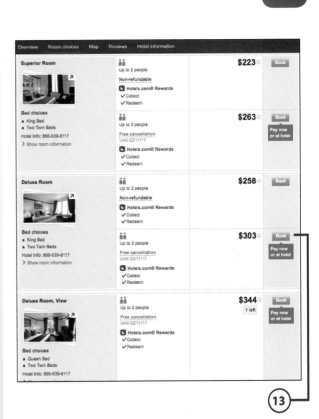

(14) Fill in the First and Last Name fields, and then scroll down to enter payment details for the reservation.

(15) Scroll down to enter your billing address. If you want, register for the Hotels.com Rewards program, which allows you to earn one free night of accommodations after booking 10 nights with Hotels.com. (Not shown.)

16 Review the Reservation Terms and Cancellation Policy, which varies based on which hotel/motel you are booking with.

17 Click the Book button to finalize your reservation. You receive a confirmation number and a confirmation email for the reservation.

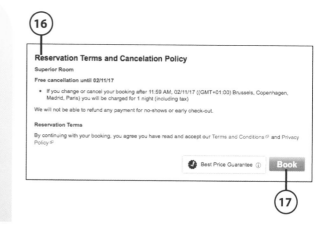

Prepare for Check-In

When you arrive at your hotel, be mindful of the posted check-in time (which is often after 3:00 p.m.). If you're early, you can request early check-in, although your guestroom might not be available.

Even if a reservation is prepaid, be prepared to present your driver's license (domestically) or passport (for accommodations abroad), as well as a credit card in your name. It's a good idea to have your reservation confirmation available, either in printed form or accessible from your mobile device's screen.

>>>Go Further
USING THE HOTELS.COM APP

If you want to use the Hotels.com mobile app, the process is similar to using the website and the same information will be required of you, but the various menu screens will look slightly different. Shown here is a sampling of what the Hotels.com mobile app on an iPhone looks like.

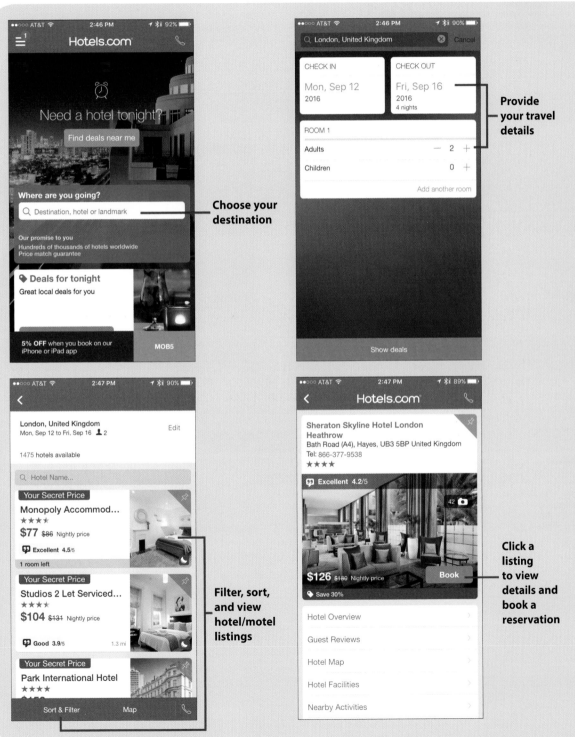

Choose your destination

Provide your travel details

Filter, sort, and view hotel/motel listings

Click a listing to view details and book a reservation

Get free help choosing the perfect cruise using the
CruiseCritic.com website.

In this chapter, you'll discover how to plan, book, and ultimately experience a fun and memorable cruise vacation using tools available for your computer and mobile apps for your smartphone or tablet. You'll learn

→ How to choose the best cruise opportunity
→ Where to find and book the best cruise deals
→ How to plan your cruise experience in advance
→ How to get the most out of your cruise experience and shore excursions during your cruise

Finding and Booking a Cruise

Experiencing a vacation aboard a cruise ship continues to become more and more popular around the world for a variety of reasons. For example, cruises allow you to unpack once and get comfortable in your cabin (which typically offers the same or nicer amenities than a hotel room, including twice daily housekeeping), but over the duration of the cruise, you get to experience multiple countries or ports of call. Dining is also included in the cruise experience, as are many shipboard activities.

In fact, the larger cruise ships offer countless onboard activities designed to appeal to a much broader audience than ever before. For example, in addition to swimming pools, Jacuzzis, a luxury spa, casino, bingo, art auctions, trivia contests, and nightly shows, many cruise ships now offer activities like rock climbing walls, miniature golf, water slides, ice skating, surfing, indoor sky diving, bumper cars, zip lines, and even trapeze lessons. Many cruises also offer onboard classes, enrichment lectures, cooking demonstrations, plus a choice of bars and restaurants.

With dozens of popular cruises lines offering exotic, unique, and exciting cruises throughout the world, there are more decisions than ever that go into finding and booking the right cruise, including

- Finding the best cruise line that caters to your interests and lifestyle.

- Choosing a ship within a specific cruise line's fleet that offers the size, onboard activities, and amenities you'll appreciate.

- Planning an itinerary that will allow you to experience the ports of call you'll most enjoy visiting.

- Selecting a cabin size and layout that offers space and amenities you want. A typical cruise ship offers more than a dozen cabin layouts, some with balconies and some without.

- Picking the location of your cabin.

- Selecting onboard dining options, entertainment options, and activities that will make your time aboard the ship memorable.

- Planning optional shore excursions, tours, or activities that will allow you to experience each place you visit.

Each cruise offers its own unique experience. From riverboat cruises that hold just a few hundred passengers to mega-ships that hold more than 5,000 passengers and 2,000 crew members, the specific ship you select will affect your onboard experience.

Some people book cruises based exclusively on the cruise line itself, or even a specific ship, and pay little attention to the itinerary and which ports of call will be visited. Others choose a cruise based heavily on the itinerary and begin by choosing the ports (cities, islands, and/or countries) they want to visit.

There are Caribbean cruises, Hawaiian cruises, Mediterranean cruises, Alaskan cruises, Panama Canal cruises, European cruises, Australian/New Zealand cruises, Asian cruises, transatlantic cruises, and transpacific cruises, to name just a few options. Each offers a vastly different experience that allows passengers to see and visit different countries, and experience a wide range of cultures and activities.

Cruise Ships Can Accommodate Almost Anyone

One of the great things about cruise ships is that they can accommodate all types of passengers, including of all ages, so they're great for intergenerational travel. They can also accommodate people with physical limitations, dietary restrictions, or various medical conditions. Most cruise ships are entirely handicap accessible and offer a state-of-the-art medical facility onboard that's staffed by doctors and nurses. With advance notice, the dining rooms and restaurants aboard the ships are able to prepare meals to meet any dietary needs.

If you have specific requirements, it's best to contact a cruise line directly, before making your reservation, to ensure the most appropriate cabin type, dining options, and other services will be available to you.

All Ships Offer Adults-Only Areas

Even if you choose a family-friendly cruise ship, you can still enjoy adults-only pool areas and decks, as well as bars, nightclubs, casinos, lounge areas, and other locations of the ship where children aren't allowed.

Getting to Know the Popular Cruise Lines

Each individual cruise line caters to a slightly different audience. Some focus on offering lower prices or shorter cruise options, whereas others cater to those looking for luxury or longer cruises. Some cruise lines are family friendly; others appeal more to solo travelers, honeymooners, or people who are retired. Some ships offer a quieter, more relaxing environment; others host nonstop activities throughout the day and late into the night.

Throughout the world, dozens of cruise lines operate hundreds of cruise ships that continuously offer 3-, 5-, 7-, 10-, 12-, and 14-day (or longer) cruise experiences. In alphabetical order, here are some of the more popular cruise lines:

- Azamara Cruises (www.azamaraclubcruises.com)
- Carnival Cruise Lines (www.carnival.com)
- Celebrity Cruises (www.celebritycruises.com)
- Cunard (www.cunard.com)

- Disney Cruise Lines (www.disneycruise.com)
- Holland America (www.hollandamerica.com)
- MSC Cruises (www.msccruisesusa.com)
- Norwegian Cruise Lines (www.ncl.com)
- Oceania Cruises (www.oceaniacruises.com)
- P&O Cruises (www.pocruises.com)
- Princess Cruise Lines (www.princess.com)
- Regent Seven Seas Cruises (www.rssc.com)
- Royal Caribbean (www.royalcaribbean.com)
- Viking River Cruises (www.vikingcruises.com)
- Windstar Cruises (www.windstarcruises.com)

You can visit the website for a particular cruise line to discover more about what it offers and become familiar with the ships in its fleet and the available itineraries.

New Ships Are Always Being Launched

A new mega-size cruise ship costs in excess of $1.5 billion to build. To stay competitive, all the major cruise lines are continuously introducing state-of-the-art ships (or refurbishing older ships) to offer new types of onboard activities, amenities, and experiences.

For example, the latest Royal Caribbean ships offer full productions of popular Broadway shows, such as *Chicago*, *Mama Mia!*, *We Will Rock You*, or *Grease* (as well as original production shows). Admission to these shows is included in the cruise price.

Ships offer more than a dozen restaurant choices, or adventurous activities, such as ice skating, bumper cars, or indoor sky diving. Keep in mind that the newest mega-ships are extremely large, and a lot of walking is required to get around.

Many travel services, such as travel.aarp.org, Expedia.com, Priceline.com, and Travelocity.com, and specialty online services that focus exclusively on cruises allow you to discover what's offered by a wide range of cruise lines at once. You can compare travel dates, itineraries, ships, and prices. Try checking out some of these cruise-specific sites:

- Cruise Cheap (www.cruisecheap.com)
- Cruise Direct (www.cruisedirect.com)
- Cruise.com (www.cruise.com)
- CruiseCritic (www.cruisecritic.com)
- Cruises Only (www.cruisesonly.com)

The advantage to using a cruise-specific service is that most are able to offer online sales and promotions you won't find elsewhere. Most also offer customizable package deals that include upgrades and perks that will save you additional money.

Understanding Cruise Pricing

When you start researching cruise opportunities, one of the things you'll notice is that prices vary dramatically based on where you book your cruise, the season, and what discounts you take advantage of.

Each year, all the cruise lines publish their individual ship itineraries for the upcoming year, as well as the published prices for each cruise, based on cabin type. However, very few passengers actually pay this published price.

Throughout the year, all the cruise lines have sales during which they discount prices up to 30 or 40 percent. Beyond that, the cruise lines offer a range of discounts that many passengers qualify for. For example, if you're a repeat cruiser with a particular cruise line, over the age of 65, serve (or have served) in the military, or have a membership with AAA or AARP, chances are you quality for an additional discount.

Prices vary based on how far in advance you book your trip. Plus, if you're aboard a cruise and opt to book another cruise for the future, you receive even greater discounts and perks. Like airlines and hotels, cruise lines have loyalty programs, so the more you travel with an individual cruise line, the bigger the discounts and the more perks you'll receive.

Many of the travel-related services offer deeper discounts on cruises whether you book months in advance or just days before a ship's scheduled departure. In fact, some of these services offer discounts between of 60 to 80 percent off of published rates.

Research the Best Deals

To get the biggest discounts when booking a cruise, do your own research. Use at least three or four online services to compare prices.

Compare prices and offers among multiple cruise lines. When you decide on a cruise line and ship, shop online for the best deal you can find for a specific sailing.

For example, after you select a cruise line, cruise ship, itinerary, and travel dates, visit at least two online travel services, such as AARP Travel Center (travel.aarp.org) and Travelocity.com (www.travelocity.com), as well as the website for that particular cruise line. Also, check rates being promoted by online services that specialize in cruises.

If your travel schedule is flexible and not during holidays or school vacation times, you'll almost always find the best deals if you book a cruise within two weeks prior to departure.

The advertised price for most cruise experiences includes a cabin, meals, most onboard activities, and onboard entertainment for the length of the cruise. But you're responsible for many additional charges that can add up quickly, such as the following:

- Airfares and ground transportation to and from the ship.

- Parking during the cruise.

- Artwork acquired from onboard art auctions and sales.

- Casino.

- Certain fitness center services and classes (such as yoga or Pilates classes or personal training sessions).

- Gratuities for your cabin attendant and waiters, for example (although some cruise lines will allow you to add a set amount of gratuity to your cruise package that is paid up front). The amount of recommended gratuity can vary dramatically from one cruise line to another; check with the cruise line for specific recommended gratuity.

- Lodging before and after the cruise (people often arrive a day early to avoid the chance of missing the ship due to flight delays).

- Laundry or dry-cleaning services.

- Onboard phone charges.

- Onboard shopping (at the duty-free stores aboard the ship).

- Onboard Wi-Fi Internet service.

- Optional shore excursions and tours.

- Pay-per-view/on-demand movies.

- Photos taken by the ship's professional photographers.

- Premium dining experiences at specialty restaurants aboard the ship.

- Premium drinks, soda, gourmet coffees and teas, bottled water, and all alcoholic beverages.

- Premium onboard activities (such as Bingo that offers cash prices).

- Salon and spa services.

Some cruise packages include round-trip airfare between your home city and the ship's port, as well as ground transportation between the airport and the ship. This is not always included, so you might need to pay extra to get yourself to and from your home to the ship.

Pay Attention to What's Included

You can often book and pay for just a cruise, or you can acquire a cruise package, that includes all flights and ground transportation to and from the ship, premium dining experiences, and/or a drink package.

If the cruise line does not include airfare with your preferred cruise, consider booking with a popular travel service, like AARP Travel Center (travel.aarp.org), Orbitz.com, Priceline.com, or Travelocity.com, that offer discounted travel packages that you can put build yourself (and save additional money in the process).

Pay close attention to the cabin type that a package includes and determine whether you'll want or need an upgrade.

>>>*Go Further*
CABIN TYPES

Every cruise ship, regardless of the cruise line, offers a selection of cabin types of various criteria: room size, bed configuration, location within the ship, and amenities. For solo travelers, some of the larger and newer ships offer solo cabins, whereas others require solo passengers to occupy a two-person cabin, and pay a surcharge (because published prices are typically based on double occupancy).

Although a ship cabin offers similar amenities to a hotel room, the size of the cabins tends to be smaller than a typical hotel room. There's also a difference between inside cabins, cabins with windows (ocean view), and cabins with a balcony. An inside cabin has no windows and is typically the smallest and least-expensive option. A mid-priced option is a cabin with a non-opening window that offers a view of the sea. Cabins with a balcony or a suite tend to cost more.

Based on your budget, how many people you're traveling with, and your personal preferences, choose a cabin type that will be comfortable and meet your wants and needs. After you choose a specific ship, research the cabin types and their locations within the ship.

Some passengers choose to book a cruise on a lower-cost, less-luxurious cruise line, but they reserve a higher-end cabin rather than paying the same money on a more expensive cruise line and having a smaller, inside cabin.

Doing Research

Because every cruise ship offers a different experience for passengers at a different price point, you need to do research before booking to ensure you'll have the most memorable, comfortable, and exciting cruise possible. When you've narrowed down your cruise line, ship, and itinerary and have visited the cruise line's website to get as much information as possible, turn to some of the online services that publish passenger ratings and reviews to read about the experiences of past passengers.

You'll find the largest collection of passenger ratings and reviews at the CruiseCritic.com or TripAdvisor.com websites or mobile apps.

Use CruiseCritic.com

To help you choose the best cruise options at the most affordable rates, consider visiting CruiseCritic.com to do your research, which includes free articles about cruising and thousands of ratings and reviews. You'll also discover tools for finding and booking money-saving deals on upcoming cruises and shore excursions.

1. From your computer, launch your favorite web browser, and type **www.cruisecritic.com** in the address field.

2. If you already know what cruise line, cruise ship, and itinerary you want, click the Reviews option to read reviews.

3. Select the All Cruise Reviews option from the Reviews pull-down menu. (Not shown.)

4. To find reviews based on cruise line, select the desired cruise line from the Search by Cruise Line pull-down menu, and then click the Search button.

5. To find reviews based on a ship's name, select the desired ship from the Search by Ship pull-down menu, and then click the Search button.

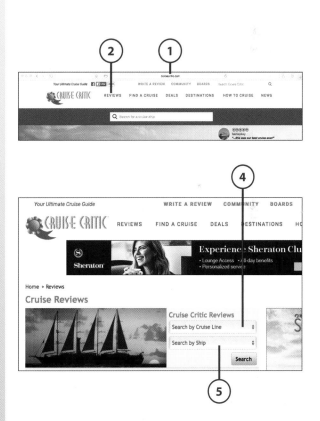

(6) You see a review for the selected cruise line or ship. Click one of the tabs to read about that specific aspect of a cruise ship.

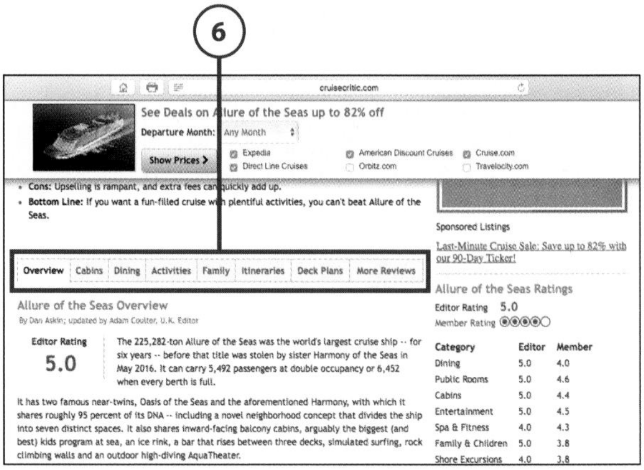

(7) Price upcoming cruises by selecting the desired departure month and year. Add a checkmark to the Expedia.com, Direct Line Cruises, American Discount Cruises, Orbitz.com, Cruise.com, and/or Travelocity.com options to quickly compare prices for a specific ship and sailing offered by each of these services. Click Show Prices.

(8) To read reviews by past cruisers (fellow travelers), first click on the Reviews option that's displayed along the top of the screen. Next, click one of the options under the Cruise Reviews heading (shown here), and choose one of the options from that pull-down menu. For example, click the Search By Ship pull-down menu, select the name of a specific cruise ship, such as Allure of the Seas, and then click the Search button. Average ratings for that ship, along with individual detailed reviews from past passengers, are displayed.

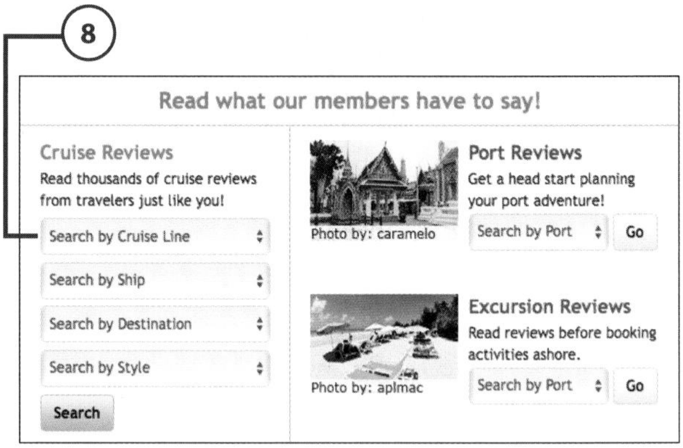

9 You see a collection of reviews written by past travelers.

10 Click the Find a Cruise button to use the tools offered by the Cruise Critic website.

11 Click one menu option at a time and make a selection from that menu to narrow your cruise options.

12 Click the Find a Cruise button to view a detailed listing of potential cruises that match your search criteria.

13 When you come across a listing for a sailing that's appealing, click the Show Prices option to quickly and simultaneously search multiple online travel websites to compare pricing for that cruise.

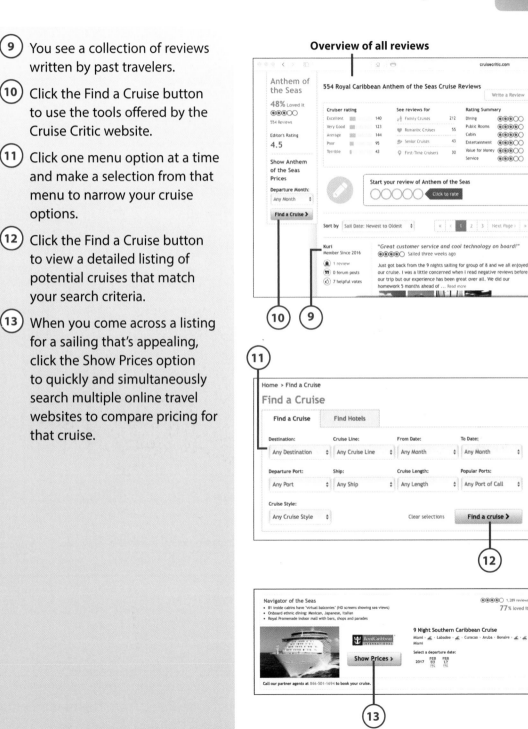

Overview of all reviews

(14) The pricing matrix displays prices based on specific cabin types, such as Inside, Oceanview, Balcony, or Suite.

(15) When applicable, use the Filter Results options to fine-tune your search results even further.

(16) Click a travel service tab to look up available rates using that service.

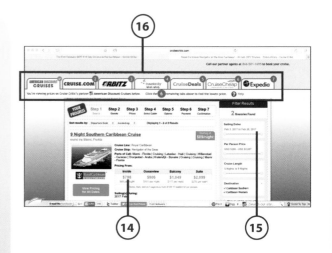

CruiseCritic.com Offers Many Tools and Resources

Other useful tools from CruiseCritic.com help you find last-minute cruise deals (click the Deals option) or learn about destinations and ports of call (click the Destinations option).

If you're new to cruising, be sure to read the articles in the How to Cruise area of the site. After you've experienced a cruise, feel free to click the Write a Review option and share your own opinions, travel tips, and experiences with the other CruiseCritic.com users.

Shopping for a Cruise

With many travel services, such as AAA Travel (www.aaa.com/travel), AARP Travel Center (travel.aarp.org), Expedia.com, or Travelocity.com, you can quickly search for a cruise and compare prices across multiple cruise lines. From the main menu of whichever service or app you use, click or tap the Cruises option to shop for a cruise online and find a discounted price.

In addition to shopping for a cruise using one of the online travel services that allow you to compare rates across multiple cruise lines, you can visit a specific cruise line's website to book a cruise with that cruise line. Working directly with a cruise line is more streamlined, especially if you're a repeat cruiser with that cruise line and have already set up a free account on that cruise line's website.

Use Travelocity.com

This example uses Travelocity.com on the computer, but most other travel services and their apps will work in a similar way.

1. From your computer, launch your favorite web browser and type **www.travelocity.com** in the address field.

2. Click Cruises from the service's main menu.

3. Click the Select Destination field, and choose where you'd like to cruise to. Keep in mind that many cruises offer several ports of call in one or more countries or regions.

4. Click Select Date and use the pull-down menu to choose the month and year you'd like to depart.

5. Click Search.

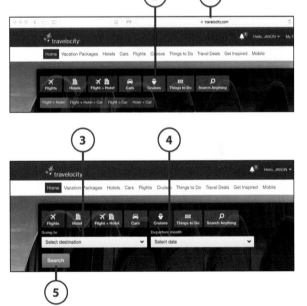

(6) You see a list of potential cruises. Each listing offers a brief synopsis of the cruise, including the cruise line, ship name, cruise duration, departing city, the sailing's itinerary, destination city (if applicable), total price for the cruise, and daily rate for the cruise. The rating from Travelocity's customers is also displayed.

(7) Click What's Included? to learn more about the specific offer.

(8) Click Show Dates to select a specific sailing (departure date), and then skip to step 10. Alternatively, move on to step 9 to narrow your results.

(9) Click on any of the options on the left side of the browser window to further refine the results. The listing of options will update based on your changes. Click the Show Dates button pointed out in step 8 when you find a cruise that matches your criteria.

(10) Scroll through the options on the Availability screen. When you find a sailing (departure date) you like, click Select for that listing.

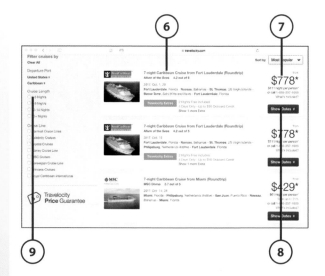

Basic Details

Each sailing listing includes starting rates for an Inside, Oceanview, Balcony, or Suite cabin.

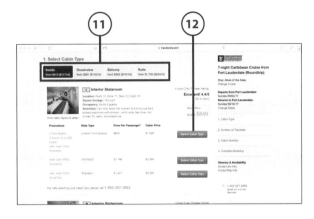

(11) Select the tab for the cabin type you want to see details about amenities, available promotions, rate type, and average rating.

(12) Click the Select Cabin Type button for the option you want.

(13) Use the pull-down menus to select the number of adults and children who will be sharing the cabin. Click Continue to see a list of available cabins.

(14) Review the details for the available cabins, including the deck number. Scroll down to use the deck layout map to help you determine the location on the ship where each available cabin is located (not shown). Click the Select button that corresponds to the cabin you desire.

(15) Complete the booking by providing details about each traveler, including their name, address, email address, phone number, citizenship, date of birth, and gender. (Not shown.)

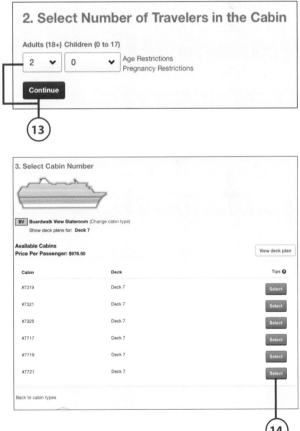

16 Scroll down to provide your payment details and billing address.

Payment Options and Cancellations

Based on how far in advance you're booking the cruise, you might have the option to pay a down payment immediately and then pay off the balance prior to the cruise. Alternatively, you can pay the total balance due upon booking your reservation.

Changes and cancellations are typically not possible after you've booked your cruise.

17 Click the Complete Booking button to finalize your reservation. You will receive a confirmation email shortly. (Not shown.)

Getting Answers

As you're working through the booking process, if you have any questions, call the phone number displayed on the screen or call the cruise line directly.

Make sure you understand whether round-trip airfare and ground transportation to and from the ship are included. If airfare is not included, you'll need to book your flights separately, which typically adds several hundred dollars to the per-passenger price of the cruise.

16

Payment Options
✔ We use secure transmission ✔ We protect your personal information

Choose a payment option

⦿ Pay in full today: $2,203.32

○ Make a deposit today: **$500.00**
Final payment due Jun 4, 2017 $1,703.32
Your credit card will be charged the deposit amount

VISA

Cardholder name *

Debit/Credit card number *

Expiration date *
Month ⌄ Year ⌄

Security code * ❓

Country *
United States ⌄

Billing address 1 *

Use RoyalCaribbean.com

Regardless of which specific cruise line's website you visit, the process for finding and booking a cruise is pretty much the same. For demonstration purposes, this example shows how to find and book a cruise using Royal Caribbean's website.

① From your computer, launch your favorite web browser and type **www.royalcaribbean.com** in the address field.

② Click the Discover Cruising or The Experience menu options to read information, view photos, and watch promotional videos from Royal Caribbean.

③ If you're a returning Royal Caribbean customer and have previously set up a free account on the website (or you're a member of the Crown & Anchor Society loyalty program), click the Log-In option and enter your account information when prompted.

④ If you already know where you want to go, when you want to leave, or where you want to leave from, use the pull-down menus under Find a Cruise. Click Search and skip to step 6.

(5) For help deciding where you want to go or which ship you want to cruise on, click the Plan a Cruise menu option and then select an option.

Looking for a Quick Trip?

Use the Quick Cruises option if you're searching for a weekend-long or short-duration cruise.

(6) You see a selection of available cruise options that are based on your search criteria. Each listing describes the cruise length, itinerary, ship, and starting price. Use the filter tools on the left side of the browser window to further narrow your search results.

(7) When you discover a listing for a cruise you're interested in, click the Learn More button to read more about that cruise option and what's offered. To book a reservation for the listed cruise, click the listing's Book Now button.

(8) Use the left and right arrows to scroll between available sailing dates.

(9) When you find a sailing date that suits your schedule, scroll down and click the Select & Continue button for the cabin type you want. Keep in mind that prices displayed are per-person, based on double occupancy per cabin. Prices do not include taxes, fees, or port expenses.

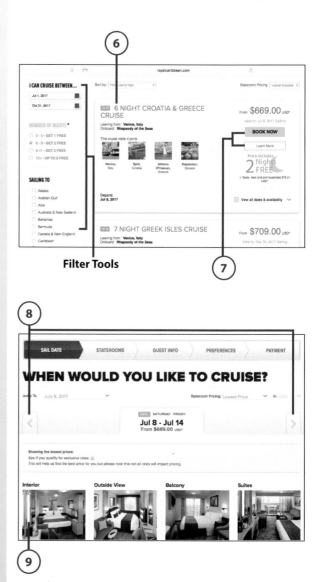

Get Help Making Decisions

Visit CruiseCritic.com or TripAdvisor.com to read personal reviews on cruise line, ship, itinerary, cabin type, cabin location, or dining preferences. Travel guide publishers, such as Fodor's and Frommer's (and their respective websites), also offer articles, reviews, and information that can help you make more educated decisions when choosing a cruise.

(10) Fine-tune the options related to your cabin selection, and then click Update.

Do You Qualify for an Additional Discount?

While using the Royal Caribbean website to seek out and book a cruise, after you've selected your cruise sailing date, cabin, and other details, you see an option labeled See If You Qualify for Exclusive Rates. Click this link to determine what additional discounts you're entitled to. For example, discounts are offered to passengers over the age of 55; members of the military, police, and fire fighters; and members of Royal Caribbean's Crown & Anchor loyalty program.

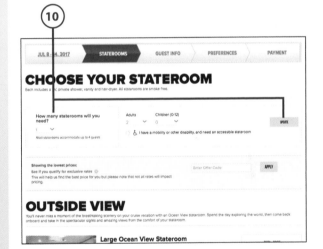

11 You see the details about the cruise you've selected. One at a time, provide the requested information about each traveler, starting with the primary guest. After entering details about the primary guest, click the Next Guest button to continue. After entering details about all guests, click the Continue button.

12 Choose your main dining preference and determine whether you want to prepay onboard gratuities. Scroll down the screen and indicate whether you want to purchase vacation protection. Click Continue.

Cruise details

>>>Go Further
VACATION PROTECTION

You can always purchase third-party travel insurance from a company like Travel Guard or Travelex. Whether you purchase trip protection from the cruise line or from a third party, having some type of insurance is highly recommended for a cruise. If there's a chance you'll need to cancel a cruise at the last minute—due to a personal situation or medical issue, for example—be sure to acquire travel insurance that includes a Cancel for Any Reason option.

For more information about travel insurance, see Chapter 12, "Finding and Purchasing Travel Insurance." Plan on spending about five percent of your total trip cost on travel insurance.

It's Not All Good

Understand the Cancellation Policy

Be sure to read the Cancellation Policy information displayed near the bottom of the screen before you finalize and pay for your reservation. Regardless of which cruise line you book with, understand that there is a financial penalty for canceling a reservation after it has been made.

If you have any questions, call the cruise line directly *before* finalizing your reservation. Royal Caribbean's toll-free reservation number is (866) 562-7625.

13 Enter your payment details and billing address. Choose an optional payment plan, if desired and applicable. Scroll down and click the Submit Payment button to finalize your reservation.

14 You'll receive confirmation for your reservation within minutes. (Not shown.)

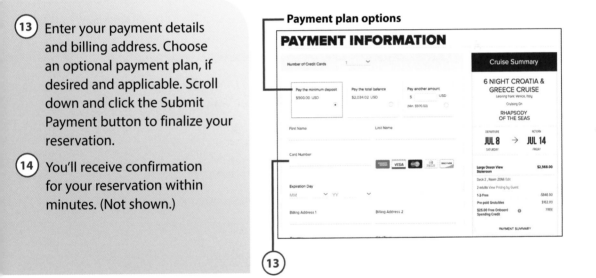

Mobile Apps That Enhance Your Cruise Experience

Mobile apps do more than help you find cruise opportunities and learn about what's offered aboard specific ships. You can also use them when you're actually aboard a ship and experiencing a cruise (or exploring a port of call). This section describes some of the apps that are most beneficial.

You can find all of these apps in the app store for your device.

The Ship Mate Mobile App

Ship Mate is a free app that's useful once you've booked a cruise. Before you leave, this app can help you acquaint yourself with your ship by providing deck plans, photos, your itinerary, and reviews and travel tips from past passengers. You also can learn about independently offered shore excursions and maintain an interactive packing list.

Apps for Shore Excursions

When it comes to finding and booking tours, activities, and shore excursions at each port of call, it's best to book them in advance. Still, in most cases, when you arrive at a port of call, there are opportunities to hire a tour guide or schedule an activity right on the spot.

If you like to make plans in advance, the cruise lines offer a selection of shore excursions from tour operators they have partnerships with. In addition, you'll find many independent tour operators and activities that you can pre-book with (often at discount), using one of these services:

- Cruising Excursions (www.cruisingexcursions.com)
- Shore Excursions Group (www.shoreexcursionsgroup.com)
- Shore Trips (www.shoretrips.com)
- ShoreExcursioneer (www.shoreexcursioneer.com)
- Viator (www.viator.com or its mobile app)

The Viator mobile app allows you to find and book independently operated tours, activities, and shore excursions.

Using one of these services, simply enter where you'll be visiting and the date of your visit, and you'll be provided with a list of available tours, activities, and excursions that you can reserve in advance (or in some cases, the day of your visit).

It's Not All Good

Not All Shore Excursions Are Suitable For Everyone

When reading descriptions for shore excursions, pay careful attention to the amount of walking or strenuous activity that's required. Also, read the section of the description that explains what you should bring with you.

For most tours, activities, and shore excursions in warm climates, wearing comfortable shoes, a hat, sunglasses, and sun block are all absolute musts. You'll also want to bring along bottled water to stay hydrated, as well as a snack.

If you have any physical limitations, such as trouble walking or climbing stairs, check with the ship's shore excursions desk or the tour operator before making your reservation.

Before booking any shore excursion, read the reviews and ratings from past travelers and make sure the schedule fits nicely with the scheduled time you'll be visiting that port. If the scheduled all-aboard time at a port is 5:00 p.m., for example, make sure the activity or tour you sign up is supposed to get you back to the ship by 4:00 p.m. at the latest so that you have a buffer for unexpected delays.

It's Not All Good

Proceed with Caution

Booking a shore excursion, tour, or activity independently often costs less than booking through the cruise line. However, if your tour or activity gets delayed and you miss the all-aboard time for your ship, your ship will depart without you. When you book a shore excursion through your cruise line, you're guaranteed that if you experience a delay, the ship will wait for you.

Apps for Cruise Lines

Many cruise lines have created their own proprietary mobile apps for use with the ship's onboard (Wi-Fi) Internet during your cruise. The functionality offered by these apps varies, but most apps let you do these things:

- Make dining reservations at premium restaurants aboard the ship
- Make show or entertainment reservations, when applicable
- View each day's schedule and plan your daily activities
- Send and receive text messages between passengers
- View interactive deck maps
- Learn about upcoming ports of call and book shore excursions

Depending on the cruise line, and when available, you can use these cruise line-specific mobile apps for free or a fee, even if you don't purchase a Wi-Fi Internet plan during the cruise.

Preinstall Desired Apps

Due to the slower Internet speeds offered aboard most ships, it's better to find, download, and install mobile apps you plan to use before departing on your cruise. To find the official app for your cruise line, visit the app store for your mobile device, and enter the name of your cruise line in the Search field.

Royal Caribbean's mobile app is called Royal iQ. The official Carnival Cruise Line mobile app is called Carnival Hub, and the Disney Cruise Line app is called Disney Cruise Line Navigator.

Many other mobile apps will come in handy when visiting various ports of call. To learn more about these optional apps, be sure to read Chapter 10, "Mobile Apps to Use at Your Destination."

>>>Go Further

TAKE ADVANTAGE OF THE MOBILE PASSPORT CONTROL APP

As you disembark from the ship for the final time at the end of your cruise, you are required to go through Customs (just like at an airport when you arrive back in the United States from abroad). Traditionally, this process requires filling out forms and waiting for up to an hour (or more) in line to be seen by and present your passport to a U.S. Customs officer.

As of early 2017, U.S. Customs and Border Protection offers a mobile app called Mobile Passport Control (MPC) that's useful to passengers traveling with a U.S. or Canadian passport. This optional app automates the Passport Control process, allowing passengers to complete the necessary forms on their mobile devices. Passengers then use a special kiosk to electronically submit their forms before seeing a customs officer.

If you create a profile in the app and fill out the digital forms in advance, using this mobile app shortens the time required to pass through U.S. Customs when returning from a cruise.

The mobile app was initially launched for use at Port Everglades (in Florida) and will eventually be available for use at all cruise ship terminals in the United States. For more information about Mobile Passport Control, visit www.cbp.gov/travel/us-citizens/mobile-passport-control.

Booking vacations at all-inclusive resorts or finding affordable travel packages is easy when you use an online travel service, such as AARP Travel.

In this chapter, you'll discover benefits of experiencing an all-inclusive vacation, as well as why it often makes sense to seek out package deals for travel to save additional money. You'll learn

→ How and where to learn about all-inclusive vacations
→ What perks and drawbacks exist with all-inclusive vacations
→ How to save money when booking vacation packages or a travel bundle

Finding All-Inclusive Vacations and Vacation Package Deals

An *all-inclusive vacation*, *vacation package*, or *travel bundle* can save you money and be simpler to plan and book. You can often find these using online travel services, such as AAA Travel (www.aaa.com/travel), AARP Travel (travel.aarp.org), Expedia.com, Kayak.com, Orbitz.com, Priceline.com, and Travelocity.com.

Read the Reviews

Just as you can read reviews of hotels on a service like TripAdvisor (www.tripadvisor.com), you can also find reviews of all-inclusive resorts. Use these reviews to help you find the best option based on your wants, needs, and budget.

As the name suggests, an *all-inclusive vacation* typically allows you to pay one price that includes multiple components of a trip, such as your flights, hotel or resort accommodations, meals, drinks, and/or some activities. This type of vacation package makes it easier to anticipate overall trip costs, plus eliminate much of the planning that goes into creating the perfect trip.

Meanwhile, an *all-inclusive resort* is a full-service resort that offers accommodations, activities, and meals, all on property, so there's seldom a need to leave the property during your stay. In some cases, flights to and from the resort, as well as ground transportation between the airport and resort, are included in the all-inclusive price.

Specialized online services can help you find, learn about, and book all-inclusive vacation packages. However, this type of vacation typically doesn't offer a lot of customizability. Instead, you can create your own *travel bundle* by booking flights, accommodations, rental car, and activities at the same time, using the same online travel service. This allows you to choose each component of your trip separately. The more components of your trip that you book simultaneously, the bigger discount the online travel service will provide, above and beyond being able to take advantage of the lowest prices possible for each component of your trip.

A *vacation package* is a collection of travel components (such as flights, accommodations, ground transportation, activities, tours, and meals) that an online travel service or individual travel provider (such as an airline or resort) puts together at a deeply discounted price. Because the travel package has been pre-created, there's typically less flexibility, but compared to booking each aspect of a trip separately, the savings are often significant.

Many online services, including AARP Travel, Hotwire, Orbitz, and Travelocity, continuously offer a selection of travel packages for destinations throughout the world. You'll also find these packages promoted through online services and mobile apps operated by Groupon and Travelzoo.

Understanding the Drawbacks of All-Inclusive Vacations and Travel Packages

The biggest problem travelers run in to when booking an "all-inclusive" vacation package is how a specific resort operator defines the term. In reality, an all-inclusive vacation doesn't actually include everything, so you should expect to incur additional charges.

Before booking an all-inclusive vacation, you should read all the fine print and determine exactly what is and is not included with the all-inclusive vacation you plan to book. The following are examples of what might *not* be included in the price of an all-inclusive vacation:

- **Activities that require specialized equipment:** The special equipment for any water-based activities—such as a boat rental, jet ski rental, parasailing, snorkeling or scuba gear, or fishing gear—typically costs extra, even if these activities are offered on the resort's property.

- **Dining at premium restaurants:** Some resorts have a dining room that serves three meals per day that are included in the all-inclusive price. However, this might be buffet-style dining or more casual dining with a limited menu offered for each meal. For an additional fixed rate per person, per meal (ranging between $10 and $50), it's possible to dine at one of the resort's premium restaurants that offers a more extensive or specialized menu, full table service, better quality food, and a more elegant environment.

- **Ground transportation between the airport and resort:** Although the resort typically provides car or shuttle bus transportation between the airport and resort, you need to make arrangements in advance and often pay a per-person charge for this service.

- **Off-property activities and tours:** Anything you have to leave the resort to do costs extra, including organized tours that can be booked through the resort.

- **Premium alcohol and specialty drinks:** Some all-inclusive resorts promote unlimited alcoholic beverages, as well as coffee, tea, and soda, but this typically does *not* include top-shelf alcohol, specialty drinks, bottled water, or canned soda (as opposed to complimentary fountain soda that's served by the glass).

- **Private instruction:** Although you might be able to play tennis or golf, snorkel, scuba dive, or participate in other sports for free as part of an all-inclusive vacation package (especially if you bring your own equipment), private or group instruction from a tennis pro, golf pro, or dive pro costs extra.

- **Spa and salon services:** Any spa or salon services, including massages, haircuts, manicures, and/or pedicures cost extra.

- **Tips and gratuities:** Some all-inclusive resorts include all tips and gratuities for the housekeeping, dining, concierge, front desk, and bell desk staff, but others don't. Over the course of a 7- to 14-day vacation, these tips can add up.

- **Wi-Fi Internet access:** Wi-Fi Internet service is typically available throughout an all-inclusive resort, but an hourly or daily fee for accessing it may apply.

It's Not All Good

Once You're There, It Costs to Leave

Because most all-inclusive resorts are typically located on large plots of land away from towns, tourist attractions, and other popular off-property activities, if you do opt to leave the resort property, you'll probably have to pay for taxi or other transportation (each way) and the cost of tours or other activities.

Pay Attention to Guestroom Details and Amenities

Every all-inclusive hotel/resort typically offers a selection of guestroom types or configurations, and each includes a different selection of amenities. As a whole, a resort will have a star-based rating, which has a direct effect on the cleanliness, size, configuration, comfort, and overall quality of the guestrooms and their amenities. What you should expect from a three-star hotel/resort will be inferior to what a four- or five-star hotel/resort offers. In general, the higher the rating, the more you'll pay.

Finding and Booking All-Inclusive Vacations

A few of the popular online travel services, including Expedia.com (www.expedia.com/All-Inclusive-Vacations), allow you to shop for and compare prices and offerings related to all-inclusive vacation packages and all-inclusive resorts located throughout the world. Using any of these services, you can typically choose whether to include round-trip flights as part of the package.

All-inclusive resorts tend to be popular throughout the Caribbean (including Jamaica, Barbados, Aruba, St. Maarten, St. Croix, and the Bahamas), Mexico (including Cancun and Playa del Carmen), the Dominican Republic, Costa Rica, and Panama, although you can also find all-inclusive resorts in other popular travel destinations, including within the United States (in Florida, for example).

Location Doesn't Really Matter

Most all-inclusive resorts are designed for guests to spend their entire vacation on property because they'll be sleeping, dining, participating in activities, and experiencing daily entertainment there. Thus, the location of the all-inclusive resort is less important than the service, cleanliness, amenities, level of luxury, and selection of activities that are offered.

Yet another option when shopping for this type of vacation deal is to visit, one at a time, the websites operated by all-inclusive resort operators to discover what's being offered. Some of the popular all-inclusive resort operators include

- Beaches (www.beaches.com)
- Club Med (www.clubmed.com)
- Divi Resorts (www.diviresorts.com)
- Palace Resorts (www.palaceresorts.com)
- RIU Resorts (www.riu.com/en/posts/videos-youtube/all-inclusive-hotels-resorts.jsp)
- Sandals (www.sandals.com)
- Superclubs (http://superclubs.com)

Searching for All-Inclusive Resorts

To find individual all-inclusive resorts operated in a specific country, type **all-inclusive resort, [*insert location*]** in the Search field of any search engine (such as Google or Yahoo!). Click any of the search results to learn about a specific all-inclusive vacation option.

There are also many online travel services that focus exclusively on all-inclusive resorts and vacation packages, including the following:

- All-Inclusive Outlet (www.allinclusiveoutlet.com)
- All-Inclusive Vacations (www.all-inclusive.com)
- All-InclusiveResort.com (http://all-inclusiveresort.com)
- AllInclusiveResorts.com (www.allinclusiveresorts.com)
- Resorts and Lodges (www.resortsandlodges.com/resort-type/all-inclusive)

Another option is to check with vacation home rental services, such as HomeAway or VRBO, to determine whether either of these services has listings for all-inclusive resorts in the region where you'll be traveling.

Use Expedia to Book an All-Inclusive Vacation

Expedia is one of the popular online travel services that allow you to find, learn about, and book all-inclusive vacations or all-inclusive resorts. Regardless of the service you use, the steps are pretty similar to what's given here. However, with the websites operated by a specific all-inclusive vacation resort, the process of making a reservation is somewhat streamlined because you won't be able to compare travel offers among resorts operated by different companies.

1. From your computer, launch your favorite web browser and type **www.expedia.com/All-Inclusive-Vacations** in the address field.

2. From under the All-Inclusive Vacations & Resorts heading, scroll through the listings of all-inclusive resorts and all-inclusive vacation packages currently being offered by Expedia.com. Continue to the next step to customize your all-inclusive vacation package. Alternatively, click the Mexico & Central America or Caribbean tab to narrow the listing by region, and then skip to step 13.

3. Choose either Hotel Only or Flight + Hotel.

4. Enter your home city or the closest major airport.

5. Enter the date when you'd like to depart.

6. Enter your desired destination. You see a list of countries and regions where all-inclusive resorts and vacations are offered. Click your choice. Alternatively, enter one of these places manually into the Going To field.

7. Enter a returning date.

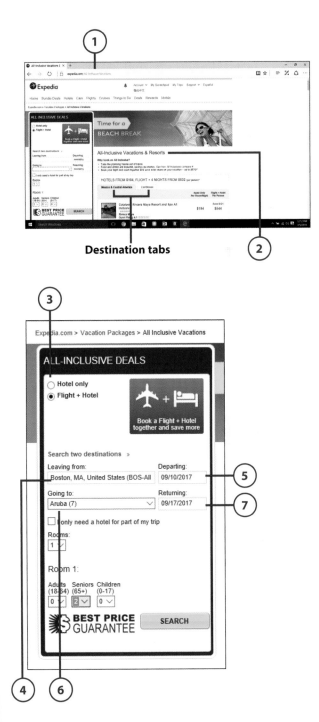

Destination tabs

(8) Use the pull-down menu to select how many rooms you require.

(9) Enter how many adults, seniors, and/or children will be staying in each room.

(10) Click the Search button to view a list of available all-inclusive resort and all-inclusive vacation options that meet your criteria.

(11) Scroll through the list to find an offer that looks interesting, click on the listing for more information, and then skip to step 13. Alternatively, further narrow your search options by continuing to step 12.

(12) Use the Filter Results tools to narrow your search. For example, you can choose all-inclusive resorts with a specific rating or that offer specific amenities and accessibility options.

Compare Prices with Other Services

In the right margin of the Expedia.com web browser window are buttons that let you compare rates with other travel services using the same criteria you're using on Expedia.com. Click any of the buttons for other services, such as Hotwire.com or Travelocity.com. Choose the service(s) you want to do a price comparison with, and then click on the Search Now button.

Perform a price comparison using other travel services

13 From the listing of all-inclusive resorts or all-inclusive vacations that meet your criteria, click a listing to view more details about the offer.

14 You can view photos of the resort, details about the resort's average rating from Expedia, and quickly access reviews of the resort from TripAdvisor.

15 Scroll down on the screen to select a specific offer within the selected resort. From here, you can choose the room type and style you want (which may affect the price). Click the Select button associated with a room type to select it, or scroll down to read more about the resort and view a full list of amenities and activities offered.

Look for Extra Costs

When viewing a listing on Expedia.com for an all-inclusive resort, scroll toward the bottom of the description to view a comprehensive listing of the services, amenities, activities, and dining options that are offered. As you review this listing, pay careful attention to what's included and what costs extra at each particular resort. Also, be sure to review what's described below the Fees and Optional Extras heading to learn more about what will definitely cost additional money.

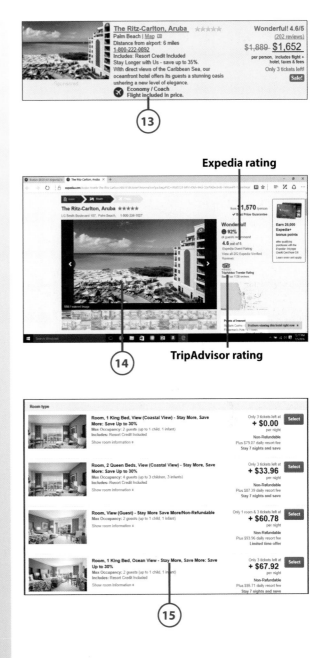

Expedia rating

TripAdvisor rating

(16) Select your flight options. Notice that some flight options cost less and some cost more than the rate that's already been quoted. Unless otherwise noted, all flights are for Economy class seats.

(17) Use the Filter Results tools displayed in the left margin of the browser window to narrow down your flight options. (Not shown.)

(18) Click the Select button associated with the flight you like. In some cases, you might depart and return on different airlines to secure the lowest rates possible.

(19) Review your flight details, as well as the details you've selected related to the all-inclusive resort. Pay attention to rates listed, as well as cancellation or change fee policies that are described. (Not shown.)

(20) Scroll down to review options you can pre-book related to your trip, including a rental car, optional shuttle transportation between the airport and resort, and/or offers for independent activities and tours in the area. All of these options require an additional per-person fee. Click the Add to Trip button for any options you want to include.

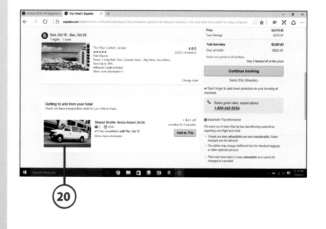

Review the Details

Before you proceed with step 21, if you have any questions, call the toll-free number that's displayed on the screen. Many reservations cannot be changed and are nonrefundable, so you must be certain you have all the details before you book the vacation.

21

23

(21) Click the Continue Booking button to make and pay for your reservation.

(22) Enter the traveler information for each person you'll be traveling with, and then click the Continue Booking button. (Not shown.)

(23) Decide whether you want to include travel protection (for an extra fee), and then enter your payment information.

(24) Carefully review all of the trip information. Click the Complete Booking button to finalize the reservation. (Not shown.)

(25) You will receive a confirmation email in a few minutes that outlines all the details and costs associated with your trip and that provides separate confirmation numbers for your flights, resort reservation, and any other optional services or activities you booked. (Not shown.)

It's Not All Good

Changes or Cancellations Might Not Be Possible

Based on the policies of the airline, resort, and other travel providers you selected, after you click the Complete Booking button you might not be able to change or cancel your reservations. If changes or cancellations are allowed, additional fees will be imposed. In some cases, Expedia.com offers free cancellations within 24 hours of booking an all-inclusive resort vacation. Look for this information below the Review and Book Your Trip heading, which you see just before clicking the Complete Booking button.

If you need to cancel or change the reservation *and* you have purchased Trip Protection insurance (either from Expedia.com or a third party, such as Travel Guard or Travelex), you will have additional options and changes may still be possible.

For more information about travel insurance, see Chapter 12, "Finding and Purchasing Travel Insurance."

Finding and Booking Vacation Packages

Most of the popular travel services offer vacation package options that include a variety of trip components gathered together and offered at a discounted price. Some of these vacation packages include round-trip flights, whereas others include a meal plan, ground transportation, and/or activities and tours. When visiting any travel website, click the Packages (or equivalent) option on the home page.

Individual hotel/resort operators or chains, airlines, some credit card issuers, and independent services—such as AAA Travel, AARP Travel, Groupon, and Living Social—offer vacation packages. Travelzoo also seeks out the best deals for vacation packages and publishes its findings via its website and mobile app.

Vacation Packages Might Not Be All-Inclusive

There is a difference between an "all-inclusive vacation" and a "vacation package," so make sure you understand what you're booking. A vacation package includes a group of trip-related components that are bundled together and offered at a special price. Additional fees will apply if you add components to the trip. Vacation packages typically do not include a meal plan, for example.

One Advantage to Vacation Packages

Compared to booking your flights, accommodations, and rental car separately, a travel package bundles everything together and saves you time in researching travel opportunities. You often save money compared to booking the individual components of your trip separately.

When comparing various travel packages, make sure you pay attention to what's actually being offered in terms of individual travel components (flights, accommodations, and so on). For example, one travel package that costs significantly more than another may be offering Business class or First class flights and/or four-star accommodations while another package includes Economy class flights with three-star accommodations.

Vacation Packages Through Airlines

Almost all major airlines have a special vacations department that specializes in creating and offering discounted vacation package deals and travel bundles with their promotional partners. One perk of booking a vacation package through an airline is that you earn bonus frequent flier miles, especially if you use the airline's credit card to pay for the trip.

The easiest ways to find these deals is to visit the website for your favorite airline and select the Vacations (or equivalent) option in the main menu.

Some of the popular airlines that offer vacation packages include the following:

- American Airlines Vacations (www.aavacations.com)
- Delta Vacations (www.deltavacations.com)
- JetBlue Getaways (www.jetblue.com/vacations/deals)
- Southwest Vacations (www.southwestvacations.com)
- United Vacations (http://vacations.united.com)

Find a Vacation Package Using Kayak

This example shows you how easy it is to find, learn about, and book a vacation package using Kayak. Using another service, the information you need to provide and the steps to follow are similar, although the package offerings and prices may vary dramatically.

What Is Kayak?

Kayak is an online service that lets you search across many other online travel services to find the best deals. When you select an offer, you're transferred to the specific online service that's promoting that vacation package.

1. Using your computer, launch your favorite web browser and type **www.kayak.com** in the address field.

2. Click Packages.

3. Enter your home city or airport.

4. Click the Enter Destination field to see a list of popular destinations where vacation packages are currently available. Click one of these options or manually type your desired destination.

5. Click on the Depart Date and Return Date fields, one at a time, and choose your desired departure and return dates.

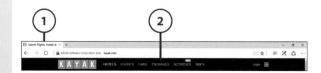

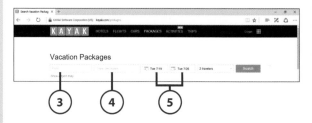

6 Select how many people you'll be traveling with.

7 Click Search.

8 You see a list of available travel packages that meet your criteria.

9 Search for offerings from other services—such as Apple Vacations, BookIt, CheapCaribbean, Delta Vacations, and Travelocity—by adding a check mark to the check box that's associated with each service listed below the Compare Sites vs. Kayak heading. When applicable, a separate web browser window opens to show search results from each service you select.

10 Narrow your options using the Search Result Filter tools. The results list is automatically updated when you change the criteria.

11 Click the Select button associated with a listing that looks appealing. Notice that each listing briefly describes whether Flight + Hotel is included in the displayed price.

12 Kayak redirects your web browser to the online service that's offering the listed vacation package. You then follow the booking procedures for that service. (Not shown.)

Pay Attention to Change and Cancellation Policies

The change and cancellation policies, as well as the booking procedures, for each service will vary, so read all of the information that's displayed carefully before confirming and paying for a vacation package. Pay close attention to the ratings and reviews that are listed with each offer, but determine the source of the ratings and reviews that are displayed, so you know how much credibility they have.

As always, before finalizing your reservation, compare rates from three or four different sources, including other travel services and/or the website for the vacation package provider.

Creating Your Own Travel Bundles

All the popular travel services enable you to manually create your own travel bundles by booking flights, accommodations, rental car, and/or activities/tours from the same service at the same time. Regardless of which service you opt to use, click the Bundle Deals or Flight+Hotel main menu option that's listed. Alternatively, you might be given the choice from the service's main menu to highlight which trip components you're looking for, and you might be able to add a check mark to all that apply (such as flights, hotel, rental car, activities, tours, and so on).

Remember, the more trip components you book simultaneously with the same service, the bigger the discounts you'll receive. Creating your own travel bundle often gives you more flexibility and options than booking a pre-created travel package.

Use AARP Travel

This example explains how to create and book a travel bundle using AARP Travel, although the process is similar regardless of which online travel service you use (providing that service offers this option).

(1) Using your computer, open your favorite web browser and type **travel.aarp.org** in the address field. (Notice that the domain extension is .org, not .com.)

(2) Click either the Book Travel Online or Contact a Travel Agent areas.

(3) If you're booking online, click each trip component you're interested in booking. Your options include Flight, Hotel, Car, Cruise, and Activities.

(4) Based on the trip components you selected, additional fields are displayed to collect the necessary information, such as where you're leaving from, where you want to travel to, your desired departure date/time, your desired return date/time, and, if applicable, the number of rooms you'll need. (Not shown.)

(5) Enter how many adults, seniors, and kids you'll be traveling with.

(6) Click Search.

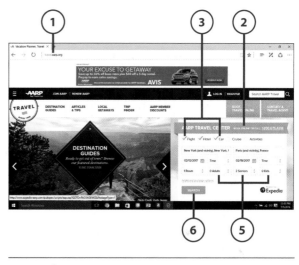

Special Discounts

At AARP Travel, all the content, including destination guides and travel tips, is available to anyone, but the special AARP discounts are available only to AARP members.

What's Included in the Price?

If you requested flights as part of your bundle, the prices are for Economy class airfares. Also, taxes and fees are already included in the displayed price, although additional fees may be added later (such as a daily hotel resort fee).

(7) You see a list of personalized travel bundles.

(8) Narrow down your search results by using the Filter Results options.

(9) Click a listing to view more detailed information and potentially make a reservation.

(10) If accommodations are part of your travel bundle, you'll be asked to select a specific guestroom configuration or room type, which could impact the cost of the trip. Click the Select button associated with the option you want.

Flight Options

In some cases, different airlines might be suggested for each segment of your flight to save you money.

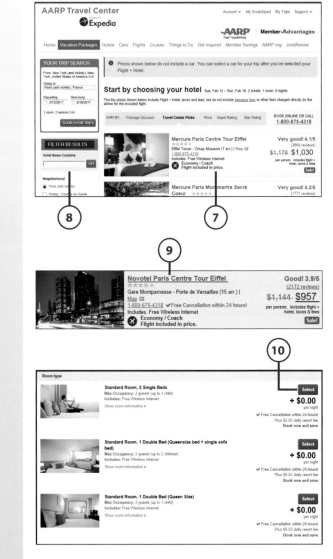

11 If flights are a part of your travel bundle, search through the flight options and select departing and return flights, keeping in mind that some flight options will impact the travel bundle price. Click the Select button to choose each flight option. Additional Filter Results tools are available to help you narrow down your flight options.

12 If a rental car is part of your travel bundle request, select a car type. Click the car offer that you want to add to your travel bundle.

Separate Flights	Show Roundtrip Flights				
SORT BY:	Departure Time	Arrival Time	Stops	Duration	Price

Our Best Pick: ✔ Cheap Flight

JFK 9:10PM → CDG 12:20PM +1 day	1 stop	9h 10m	Economy / Coach	✔ Free Cancellation within 24 hours! + $0 per person SELECT
Flight arrives Feb 13. 2017; package includes 6 hotel nights instead of 7.				
EWR 5:40PM → CDG 9:40AM +1 day	1 stop	10h 0m	Economy / Coach	✔ Free Cancellation within 24 hours! + $0 per person SELECT
Flight arrives Feb 13. 2017; package includes 6 hotel nights instead of 7.				
JFK 5:30PM → CDG 9:40AM +1 day	1 stop	10h 10m	Economy / Coach	✔ Free Cancellation within 24 hours! + $0 per person SELECT
Flight arrives Feb 13. 2017; package includes 6 hotel nights instead of 7.				
EWR 5:40PM → CDG 12:20PM +1 day	1 stop	12h 40m	Economy / Coach	✔ Free Cancellation within 24 hours! + $0 per person SELECT
Flight arrives Feb 13. 2017; package includes 6 hotel nights instead of 7.				

	Exclusive! AVIS In Terminal	enterprise In Terminal	Hertz In Terminal	SIXT In Terminal
Mini	$553 + $206 $347 Savings Manual	$677 + $170 $507 Savings Manual	$564 + $236 $328 Savings Manual	No Results
Economy	$560 + $227 $333 Savings Manual	$852 + $179 $673 Savings Manual	$572 + $248 $324 Savings Manual	$609 + $261 $348 Savings Manual
Economy Special	$561 + $237 $324 Savings Manual	$885 + $199 $686 Savings Manual	No Results	No Results
Compact	$578 + $255 $323 Savings Manual	$727 + $209 $518 Savings Manual	$592 + $271 $321 Savings Manual	$630 + $286 $344 Savings Manual
		$978		$658

(13) Review each component of your trip and, if necessary, make any additional selections that are required. At the bottom of the screen, be sure to click the Review Full Rules and Restrictions option to read details about each component of the trip, keeping in mind that some or all of the components might not be refundable or changeable.

(14) You see the total price for your travel bundle.

(15) Click the Continue Booking This Package option or Accept This New Price and Continue Booking option (whichever is applicable).

(16) Indicate whether you want to add trip protection for each component of the trip. You can add this option through AARP Travel Center (Expedia.com), or later buy travel insurance for the entire trip separately from a company like Travel Guard or Travelex. (Not shown.)

(17) Click Continue Booking This Package. (Not shown.)

(18) If you haven't already done so, sign in to your AARP Travel Center powered by Expedia account, or create a free account by clicking the appropriate option.

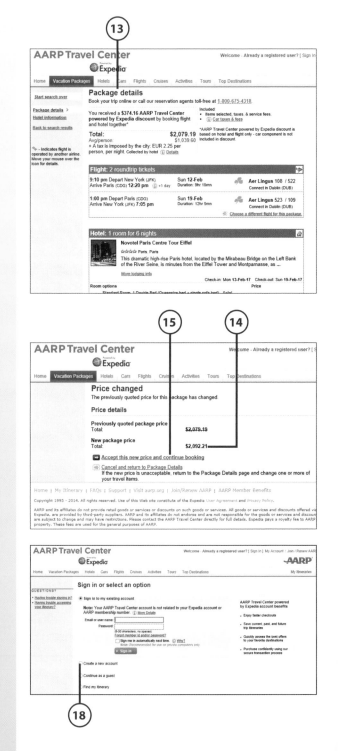

Check Out As a Guest

It's also possible to complete your booking as a guest of AARP Travel, although you'll ultimately need to provide the same information to finalize your booking as you would to create an account. When you create a new account, all of your personal information will be remembered so you won't have to reenter it when you use the site in the future.

(19) Follow the on-screen prompts to enter details about the individual travelers and your payment information. What information is requested varies based on which trip components are part of your travel bundle. Be sure to include your AARP membership number when it's requested, to receive the maximum discounts you're entitled to.

Getting Help Before You Confirm

Before confirming the reservation(s), be sure to call the toll-free number that's displayed on the screen if you have any questions.

(20) After you finalize the reservation, you receive a confirmation email. (Not shown.)

(19)

Trip Preferences

| Total: | $2,079.19 | Included: |
| Avg/person: | $1,039.60 | • This total includes selected items, taxes, and service fees. Unless specified otherwise, rates are quoted in USD. Car taxes and fees included. |

+ A tax is imposed by the city: EUR 2.25 per person, per night. Collected by hotel ⓘ Details

1 Who will be traveling on this trip?

✈🏨🚗 **Vacation package:** New York to Paris — Total travelers: 2

Flight information: New York (JFK) to Paris (CDG)

Make sure the name matches the name on your passport and driver's license. Flight requires a name of an adult or a senior to be the main contact.

You must fill in the boxes marked *

Senior (age 65+ over)*
Select from the list ∨ or Add a new traveler — Flight Contact

Senior (age 65+ over)*
Select from the list ∨ or Add a new traveler

We will forward your preferences and requests to the airline, but we cannot guarantee that they will be honored. Free and special meals are not available on many flights. Please confirm your requests directly with the airline before departure.

Hotel: Novotel Paris Centre Tour Eiffel, Paris

To book the reservation, the hotel requires the name of an adult for each room.

You must fill in the boxes marked *

Room contact (adult)*
Select from the list ∨ or Add a new traveler — Guests: 2 adults

Traveler information for — ✎ Edit Traveler Information

Phone numbers:
Country: — Area: — Phone#:

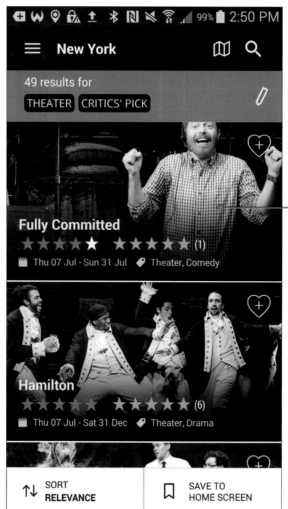

There are plenty of mobile apps, like interactive travel guides, that can help make your trip more organized and less stressful.

This chapter introduces you to a handful of smartphone and tablet apps that you can take advantage of when you reach your travel destination. You'll learn about apps that can be used to

→ Manage airline, lodging, and rental car reservations

→ Find restaurants and make dining reservations

→ Schedule food delivery to your lodging from local restaurants

→ Quickly find attractions, stores, businesses, and services you need, when you need them, wherever you happen to be

→ Handle a wide range of other tasks, including navigation, language translation, and currency conversion

Mobile Apps to Use at Your Destination

Chances are, you already know how helpful and versatile your smartphone or tablet can be in your everyday life. Well, that same device can become an indispensable tool during your travels.

Whether you use an Apple iPhone or iPad or have an Android-based smartphone or tablet, this chapter introduces you to ways of using your mobile device during your travels. You'll learn about a handful of specific apps that are worth installing on your mobile device for use during trips, and you'll also become acquainted with app categories you might find useful.

Internet Connectivity Is Useful When Traveling Abroad

To get the most use from your mobile device when traveling abroad, consider investing in a way to connect to a cellular data network, as opposed to having to remain within the range of Wi-Fi hotspots to maintain Internet connectivity.

Chapter 14, "Connecting Your Computer, Smartphone, or Tablet While Traveling," explains several options for establishing Internet connectivity from your mobile device when you're away from home.

Where You'll Find These Apps

When you see a specific app mentioned that you want to download and install on your smartphone or tablet, launch the app store app for the device you're using, and enter the exact title of the app in the Search field. When you locate the app in the search results, select it, and either download it for free if it's a free app or purchase it. All iPhone and iPad apps can be acquired from the App Store, which is accessible using the app store app that comes preinstalled on your mobile device. If you're an Android mobile device user, acquire apps from the Google Play Store, via the Play Store mobile app.

On the iPhone/iPad, tap the App Store icon to access the App Store.

On an Android device, tap the Play Store icon to access the Google Play App Store.

When a type of app is suggested, such as a currency converter or language translator, rather than a specific app, you can just enter a description of the app (such as **currency converter**) in the app store's Search field to view listings for multiple apps that offer similar functionality. Review the ratings and the features of each to determine which app is best for you.

Internet Access Required

Unless otherwise noted, all the apps you'll read about in this chapter require your mobile device to have Internet access via a cellular data connection or Wi-Fi. To get the most out of navigation apps that use your smartphone or tablet's GPS, a cellular data connection (3G/4G/LTE) is required. This allows the mobile device to remain connected to the Internet while you're moving around on foot or in a vehicle.

However, if you'll be relatively stationary when using an app (for example, if you're aboard an aircraft or in a hotel or airport), connecting to the Internet via a Wi-Fi hotspot works for any app as long as you remain within the signal radius of that hotspot.

Apps to Help You Get Where You're Going

During any trip, two categories of apps will be useful: apps to help you get to your destination and apps that can be used to help you enjoy your destination. Both often save time or money in the process.

Airline, Hotel, and Rental Car Company Apps

Even if you've booked all of your trip-related reservations using an online service or its mobile app, you can and should also take advantage of the various mobile apps offered by the specific airline, hotel, and/or rental car company you'll be using, to take advantage of additional functionality. Virtually all the major airlines have their own proprietary apps that can be used to help you find, book, prepare for, check in, and then enjoy a flight. The same is true for all the major hotel chains and rental car companies.

For example, from an airline-specific app, such as the one for American Airlines or JetBlue, it's possible to manage each of your flights using the tools available by tapping My Trips. It's also possible to book a new flight directly from your mobile device, check in to an existing flight, manage your frequent flier account, or check the status of any flight.

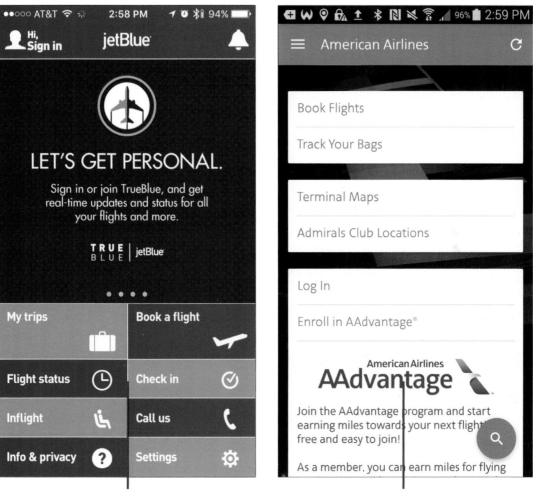

The JetBlue app's main menu on an iPhone

The main menu of the American Airlines app on an Android smartphone

While you're aboard the aircraft, use the airline's app to do things such as see a listing of available in-flight TV and audio programming, plus select what drinks and snacks you'd like to request. Also check for an option that lists functions you can use while aboard an aircraft (even if you don't pay the fee for in-flight Wi-Fi Internet access). (On the JetBlue app this option is called Inflight.)

Using the SPG: Starwood Hotels & Resorts mobile app, it's possible to find and book a Starwood hotel reservation from anywhere in the world. Some of the popular hotel chains associated with Starwood Hotels & Resorts include aLoft, Four Points, Le Meridian, Sheraton, St. Regis, and W Hotels.

As you're making a reservation using this app, be sure to tap the Rate Preference option and select the discount(s) you're eligible for, such as Senior & AARP (shown here).

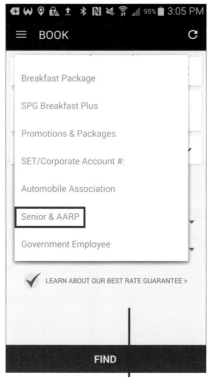

SPG: Starwood Hotels & Resorts Mobile App

Once you set up a free account and have a hotel reservation booked, you can manage all aspects of that reservation (and your loyalty program membership) from your smartphone or tablet, including remotely checking in to a hotel, and then using your smartwatch (that's linked with your smartphone) as your room key.

With mobile apps offered by rental car companies, you can find rental car availability anywhere that company operates, select a vehicle type, and book a reservation. If you already have a reservation that was not booked using the mobile app, launch the app and tap the My Rentals (or equivalent) menu option (shown here on the Enterprise Rent a Car mobile app running on an Android smartphone). When prompted, enter your reservation confirmation number to retrieve and display your reservation details.

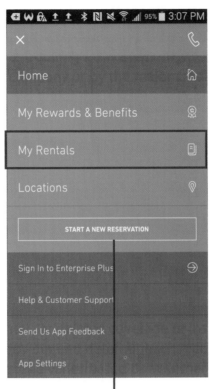

Enterprise Rent A Car Mobile App

After the app loads your reservation information, you can update or change the reservation as needed, plus manage your loyalty program account.

Keep in mind that, regardless of which airline, hotel, or rental car app you're using, you are able to manage itineraries and reservations for multiple trips you have booked with that travel provider. For example, if you have three round-trip flights booked with American Airlines, each reservation has its own confirmation number (also referred to as a "record locator"). Once you sign in to your account for the American Airlines' website or mobile app, using the app's Find Trip feature, one at a time, to retrieve and store each separate itinerary within the app as a separate trip by entering your first name, last name, and record locator for each trip. It's then possible to manage all of your upcoming travel that involves that travel provider.

Manage Your Flight Information

The following steps explain how to manage a flight you've already booked with Southwest Airlines from your mobile device. The process is similar on any smartphone or tablet, regardless of which airline's mobile app you use.

Confirmation Number

(1) If you booked your travel using an online service (such as AARP Travel Center, Expedia.com, Hotwire.com, Travelocity.com, or the Southwest.com website), and then want to view and manage your flight information using that airline's mobile app, first make your reservation and acquire your flight-related confirmation number from the confirmation email you receive from the airline or online travel service, as shown in the figure.

(2) Launch the airline's mobile app, and sign in to the app or tap the Continue as Guest button. You see the app's main menu.

(3) Tap Manage Travel (or an equivalent option).

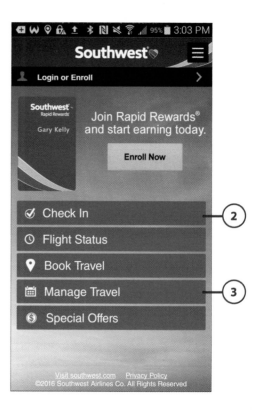

4 Enter your flight confirmation number, first name, and last name. Tap the Retrieve Reservation button to continue.

5 Once your reservation information is retrieved via the Internet, the mobile app displays all information relevant to your current or upcoming flights related to that trip. You then have the ability to check in for flights, create an electronic boarding pass, check a flight's status, change your seat assignment, prepay for checked luggage, or change the flight, for example. Using some airline apps, you can also upgrade from Economy class (when available) for an additional fee. (Not shown.)

Navigation Apps

Built in to your iPhone or iPad is the Maps app that comes preinstalled on the mobile device. If you're using an Android smartphone or tablet, the Google Maps mobile app comes preinstalled.

As discussed in Chapter 6, "Finding Ground Transportation," either of these apps, or another navigation app that you download and install from the app store, can be used with the GPS and Internet capabilities of your mobile device to help you navigate almost any city or region of the world while you're driving, walking, or, in some cases, taking public transportation.

In addition to helping you find your way around during a trip, these apps can help you find, learn about, and obtain directions to popular tourist attractions, points of interest, restaurants, hotels, or other services you may need (such as a bank/ATM machine, pharmacy, or local hospital).

Use the Maps App to Find a Restaurant

Use the following steps to use your iPhone or iPad to find a nearby restaurant that serves the type of food you're in the mood for, learn about that restaurant, read reviews about it, access its menu, and sometimes even book a reservation.

Use the Latest Version of the Maps App

The steps shown here are for an iPhone/iPad with the iOS 9.3.2 version iOS. With iOS 10.1 (released in late 2016), additional features have been added to the Maps app, so some screens look slightly different.

1. Make sure your mobile device has Internet access.

2. Tap the icon to launch the Maps app.

3. Tap the Location icon to allow your smartphone or tablet to pinpoint your exact location.

Quickly Find Information About Other Businesses and Services

You can find more than restaurants with the navigation apps. You can just as easily type the specific name of a local business, point of interest, tourist attraction, or type of service, such as an ATM, gas station, or pharmacy.

4 Enter the type of food you're in the mood for. For this example, I used **Steak Restaurant, Boston, MA**. If you're already in Boston, you can simply type **Steak Restaurant** to find nearby steak restaurants.

5 Tap Search.

6 Displayed on the map are virtual red pushpins, each of which indicates a steak restaurant.

7 On the lower half of the screen are individual listings for restaurants that meet your search criteria. Each listing includes the restaurant name, the type of restaurant it is, the average cost per person for a meal (using between one and four dollar signs), the town/city where the restaurant is located, its average rating, and a related thumbnail photo. Tap a pushpin or one of the listings to view more information about that establishment. Note that if you perform a search based on your current location (as opposed to a general search), the distance from your current location is displayed instead of the town/city when viewing a search result.

8 You see detailed information about the restaurant. Tap Directions to obtain driving or walking, turn-by-turn directions from your current location to the restaurant. Tap the phone number or phone icon to call the restaurant. Tap the website address to visit the restaurant's webpage.

Customer Ratings

The star-based rating displayed at the very top of the information screen is the establishment's average rating on Yelp!. The number that's displayed in parentheses next to the average star-based rating is the total number of reviews the average rating is based upon.

9 Swipe through the information screen to view the restaurant's hours of operation, more information about that establishment, and photos taken by past guests of that restaurant.

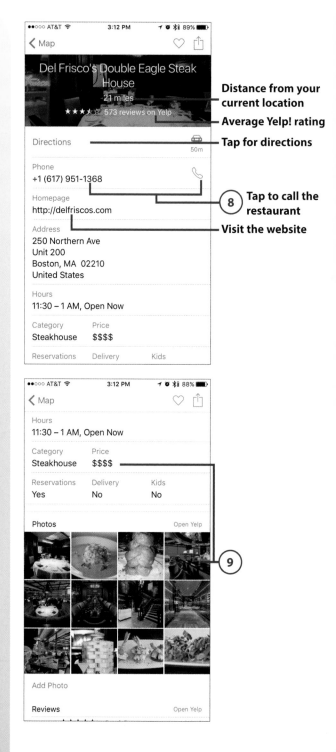

Distance from your current location

Average Yelp! rating

Tap for directions

Tap to call the restaurant

Visit the website

10 Read detailed reviews from past customers and view customer ratings.

Reviews   Open Yelp

★★★★★ by **Derek B.**   6/6/16
Went here for a birthday dinner and let me tell you, the Bone-In Prime Strip is to die for. Awesome selection of cuts, seafood and sides (o...

★★★★☆ by **Robert H.**   5/29/16
Wow. Atmosphere is definitely excellent with an exceptional job by waitstaff. It has been over six months since I went and I can still vividly remem...

★★★★★ by **Scott R.**   5/28/16
Top notch steak. Everything was perfect, and we had a group of 14 people. One of the finest steaks I have had.

Check In   Write a Review

More Info on **yelp**

>>>Go Further
THE MAPS APP WORKS WITH OTHER POPULAR APPS

To get the most out of the Maps app when it comes to looking up and learning about restaurants, points of interest, tourist attractions, businesses, and services, also download and install the free Yelp! and Open Table apps. Tapping certain fields in the information screen of the Maps app launches the Yelp! app to display additional information, such as the restaurant's menu and more detailed reviews.

Thanks to integration with the OpenTable app, if you want to book a reservation for the restaurant you've found using the Maps app and it's a participating restaurant, tap the Reservations option to launch the Open Table app. You're then able to enter how many people you'll be dining with, as well as the date and time of the reservation you'd like to make. Within seconds, you'll receive an on-screen confirmation for your reservation without having to call the restaurant.

Read more about the Yelp! and OpenTable apps later in this chapter.

Use the Google Maps App to Find a Restaurant

(1) Make sure your mobile device has Internet access.

(2) Tap the icon to launch the Google Maps app.

(3) Tap the Location icon to pinpoint your current location.

(4) Tap the Directions banner along the bottom of the screen for detailed directions between two locations you select. (The default is to begin a trip from your current location, but you can modify this field.)

(5) Tap a tab for Explore Food & Drinks In This Area to find dining establishments located near you.

6 Alternatively, in the Search field, enter the type of food you're in the mood for. For this example, I typed **Seafood Restaurant, London**. If you're already in London, you can simply enter **Seafood Restaurant** to find nearby restaurants that specialize in seafood. Tap the Search key on the keyboard (not shown).

7 Food icons are displayed on the map to indicate restaurants that meet your search criteria.

8 On the lower half of the screen are individual listings for the restaurants. Each listing includes the restaurant name, the type of restaurant it is, the average cost (using between one and four dollar signs), the town/city where the restaurant is located, its average rating, its hours of operation, and a related thumbnail photo. Tap an icon or one of the listings to view more information about that establishment.

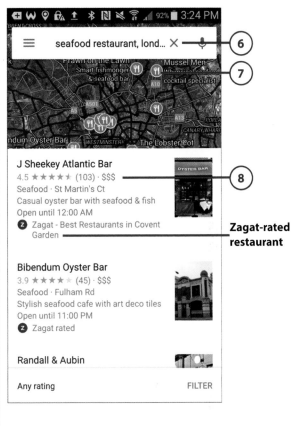

Zagat-rated restaurant

Zagat-Rated Restaurants

If the restaurant has been reviewed by Zagat, you see a Z icon in the listing.

(9) You see the detailed restaurant listing. Tap the Call button to initiate a call to that restaurant. Tap the Website icon to view the restaurant's website. Tap the restaurant's address to get detailed driving or walking directions to it from your current location.

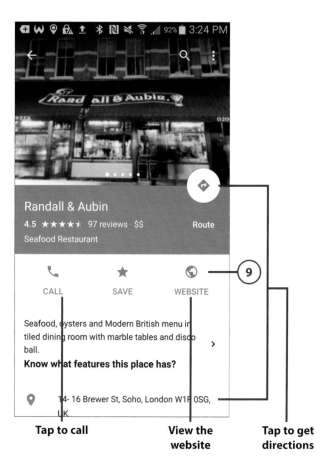

Tap to call

View the website

Tap to get directions

(**10**) Swipe through the information screen to view a chart that depicts the restaurant's busiest times, see photos of the restaurant (taken by past customers), view its ratings and reviews, and, if applicable, read its Zagat review.

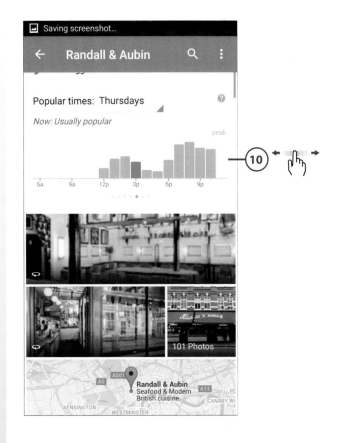

Google Maps Is Also Available for iOS Devices

From the App Store on your iPhone or iPad, you can download and install the free Google Maps app and then use this app rather than the Maps app that comes pre-installed on your smartphone or tablet. Both Google Maps and the iOS 10.1 edition of the Maps app enable you to take a virtual tour of a city or region and quickly see an animated view of an area, landmark, or popular tourist destination. This tool can help you decide what you want to visit and prepare for the terrain you'll encounter.

Finding Restaurants and Making Dining Reservations

The app store for your smartphone or tablet includes a selection apps that will help you find, learn about, and potentially book a reservation for a restaurant almost anywhere in the world. The following are some dining apps worth installing onto your mobile device:

- **Foursquare:** This free social media and interactive travel guide app allows people from all over the world to review and share their experiences at restaurants. From the app, you can access more than 60 million reviews of places to eat, drink, shop, or visit, plus keep track of places you've been or want to go.

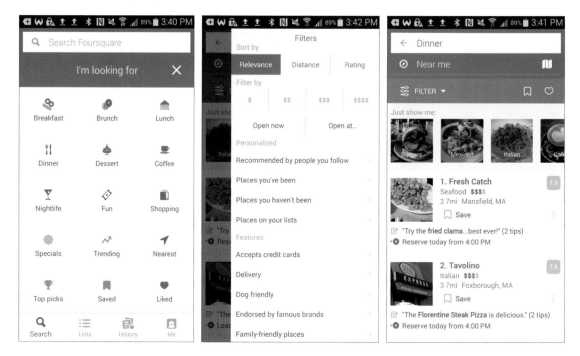

- **Groupon:** When used with the GPS capabilities of your mobile device, this app allows you to find discount coupons and offers from restaurants, bars, and businesses offered in specific cities throughout the world.

Living Social

The Living Social app is another app for finding discounts from businesses, services, and restaurants near wherever you happen to be. (Not all cities are supported by the Living Social app.)

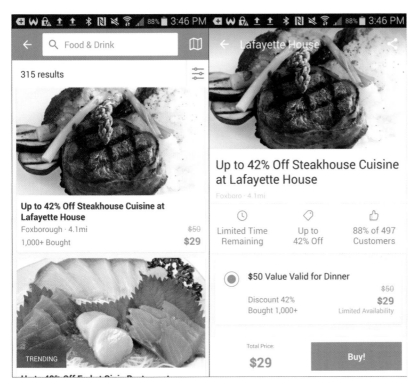

- **OpenTable:** This app helps you find and learn about nearby restaurants and then make a reservation directly from your Internet-connected smartphone or tablet. It works in many cities around the world, including almost all major metropolitan areas within the United States.

- **Trip Advisor:** This app includes reviews of dining establishments throughout the world. You can use the search tools built in to the app to find the types of restaurant you'll enjoy when visiting almost any city in the world. Trip Advisor also offers reviews of hotels, tourist attractions, activities, and tours, for example.

OpenTable

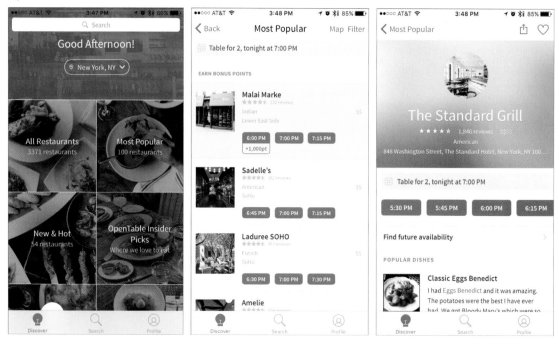

Trip Advisor

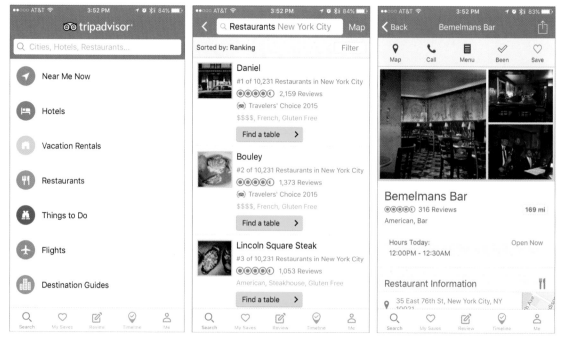

- **Yelp!:** From this app, you can gain access to more than 100 million reviews of restaurants, hotels, tourist attractions, tours, and travel-related services located around the world. Yelp! allows you to pinpoint your current location and then use adjustable filters to find nearby restaurants based on food type, price, or average rating. It's then possible to read detailed reviews from past customers and preview menus. You can also obtain directions to the restaurant from your current location.

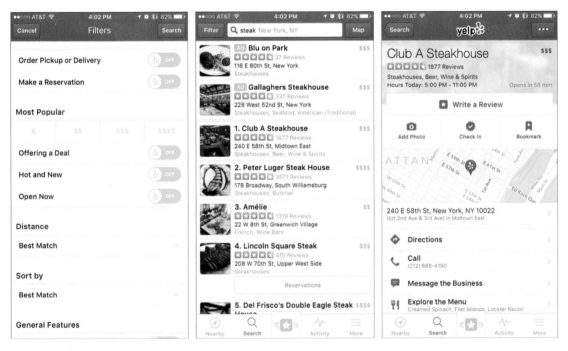

- **Zagat:** This app gives you easy access to thousands of reviews for popular dining establishments in major cities around the world from one of the most respected sources for professional written restaurant reviews. You can easily find nearby restaurants using a variety of search tools (based on cuisine type, rating, cost, features, or location), and then learn all about the dining experience that's offered by reading detailed but concise reviews and viewing the restaurant's menu. This app integrates with the OpenTable app, so you can then make dining reservations directly from your mobile device.

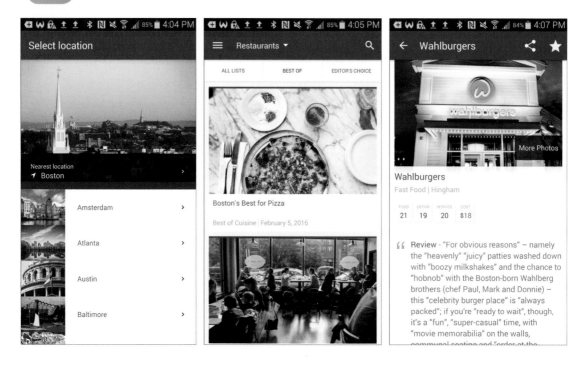

- **Zomato** (formally Urban Spoon): With information available about more than 1 million restaurants around the world, this app determines your location and then makes recommendations based on the type of food you're looking for. Using filters, narrow your search results using specific criteria, such as price, average rating, popularity, cuisine type, or location. After you choose a dining option, the app provides directions to help you get there from your current location. (See the next page.)

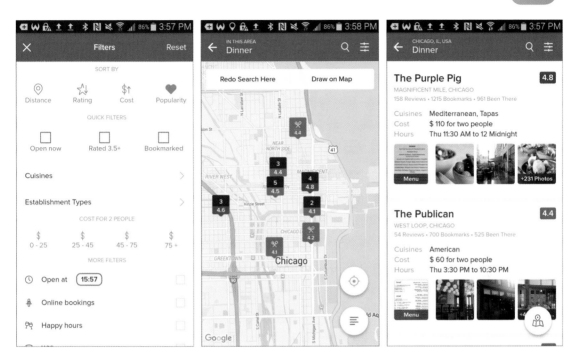

Use the Yelp! App

Yelp! offers a comprehensive and ever-expanding database that contains more than 100 million reviews of restaurants, businesses, services, tourist attractions, and tours offered throughout the world. The Yelp! mobile app puts this vast amount of information at your fingertips, allowing you to quickly find and learn about whatever it is you're looking for.

(1) Download and install the optional Yelp! mobile app onto your smartphone or tablet. (Not shown.)

(2) Tap the icon to launch the Yelp! app. (Not shown.)

3 From the main menu, tap the Restaurants option to see a listing of nearby restaurants (based on your current location).

4 Alternatively, in the Search field, enter the type of restaurant you're looking for, followed by a comma, and then continue by typing the city, state, and/ or country. Alternatively, type the name of a restaurant. For this example, I used **Seafood restaurant, Boston, MA**. Tap the Search key on the keyboard (not shown).

5 You see a list of restaurants that meet your initial search criteria. Each listing displays the name of the dining establishment, its address, its average rating, average price (using between one and four dollar signs), and the type of food that's offered.

6 Tap a listing for a restaurant you want to learn more about.

7 Tap the Directions field to obtain detailed directions from your current location, or tap the Call option to initiate a call to the restaurant.

8 Tap on the More Info option to see more details about the restaurant.

9 You see additional information about the restaurant. Swipe through this screen to read more about the restaurant.

10 Swipe up to see the Review Highlights section, which provides a quick overview of the dining experience you can expect. These are reviews written and posted by past customers. Swipe up again to read more detailed reviews.

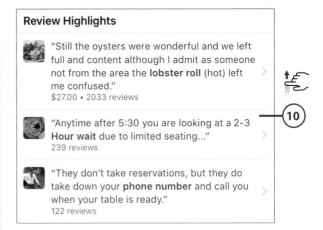

Use the OpenTable App

The OpenTable app works very much like Apple Maps, Google Maps, Yelp!, or Zomato (formally Urban Spoon) to help you find and learn about restaurants, but this app offers one additional feature—the ability to instantly make a confirmed reservation at more than 32,000 participating restaurants around the world. OpenTable can be installed onto any smartphone or tablet and requires an Internet connection to work.

Set Up a Free Account

By setting up a free account in the OpenTable app, your smartphone or tablet can remember your personal preferences and information, plus keep track of where you've dined in the past.

1 Download and install the free OpenTable app onto your mobile device.

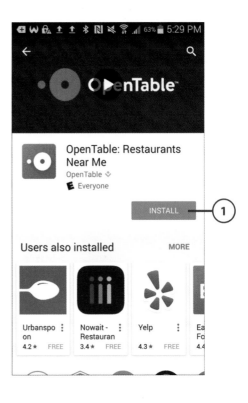

2 Tap the icon to launch the app. (Not shown.)

3 The app uses the GPS capabilities built in to your smartphone or tablet to pinpoint your current location. If necessary, update this location by tapping the Location icon.

4 Customize how you want restaurant listings sorted and displayed by tapping the Customize icon (Android only). On the iPhone/iPad, enter what you're looking for in the Search field, or swipe up and tap one or more of the menu buttons, such as Dinner Tonight, Near Me Now, Italian, Seafood, Mexican, Romantic, Outdoor Seating, or Good for Groups, to fine-tune your search.

5 Adjust the Sort By options (choose between Best, Distance, Name, or Rating) or Distance, plus narrow down average price listings (choose All, or between two and four dollar signs), select a Cuisine type, and/or seek out restaurants offering a special offer through the app. Make your customizations by tapping the appropriate options, and then tap Done.

6 Tap the Search icon.

(7) Enter a specific type of cuisine or the name of a restaurant in the All Restaurants field.

(8) In the Current Location tab, leave the default if you're already in the region where you're looking for a restaurant. Alternatively, tap this field and enter the city, state, and country where you want to search.

(9) Tap the Reservation details field and select the total number of people dining (between 1 and 20), the desired day (choose Today, Tomorrow, or the desired date), and the desired reservation time. Tap Done (not shown).

(10) Tap Search to locate restaurants that meet your search criteria and that have a reservation available on the date and time you selected.

(11) Swipe through the restaurant list to see information about restaurants that match your criteria. Tap a restaurant listing to view more details about that restaurant. Alternatively, if you desire, tap the Map icon located near the top-right corner of the screen to view a map with pushpins that represent restaurants that meet your search criteria.

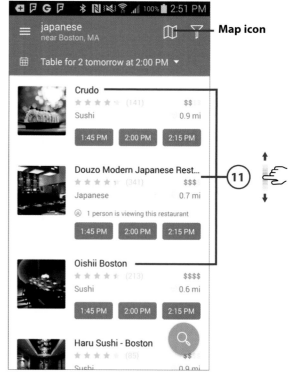

Map icon

12 Tap the left arrow icon in the top-left corner of the screen to return to the restaurant listing, or tap on a virtual pushpin to view that restaurant listing.

Make a Reservation

If you don't need further details before making your decision, tap a time button to make a reservation at a restaurant.

13 The restaurant information screen offers detailed information about the dining establishment. You can learn about its hours of operation, payment options, available parking, and dress code. Tap a time button to make a reservation if you have not already done so, or if the time you previously selected is not available.

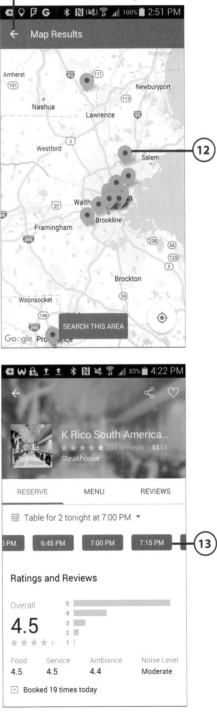

Return to restaurant listing

(14) Select the number of people the reservation is for, the day of the request reservation, and the time you want to dine. Tap Done.

(15) Upon requesting a reservation, if you have already signed in to the OpenTable app using your account details, a reservation will be made and confirmed within seconds. If you have not already signed in to the app, you'll be prompted to do so, or you'll be asked to enter your first name, last name, email, and smartphone phone number. You can also fill in the Special Request field. For example, you can request a table near a window or ask for a high-chair or booster seat. Tap Reserve to make and confirm your reservation.

(16) As the reservation time approaches, use the OpenTable app to obtain driving or walking directions (via the Google Maps app on an Android device) from your current location to the restaurant.

(17) When you arrive at the restaurant, tell the host you have a confirmed reservation made using the OpenTable app. (Not shown.)

Pay Using the OpenTable App and Android Pay

If you have an Android Pay account set up on your smartphone, at participating restaurants you can pay for your restaurant bill directly from the OpenTable mobile app.

Using Food Delivery Apps

Even if you're staying at a hotel and can order room service, you might want to order food from someplace else. Now you can order from a nearby restaurant (even if that restaurant does not typically offer delivery) using a mobile app.

With the app, you view the full menus of participating restaurants, place your order, pay for your order using a credit or debit card you link with the app, and then have your order delivered. You can even add a tip for the delivery person when paying via the app.

What's great about these food delivery apps is that they work with many restaurants throughout supported cities. There's rarely an added delivery surcharge, although some restaurants have minimum order requirements. Your food is usually delivered within 30 to 60 minutes.

A handful of apps offer this functionality, and each app works with a different selection of participating restaurants. Two of the most popular apps that offer food delivery from the broadest range of restaurants in cities around the world are GrubHub and Yelp 24 Eats (which is separate from the Yelp! app described earlier.)

Find a Food Delivery App

If the GrubHub or Yelp 24 Eats app does not support the city you're visiting, access the App Store (iOS) or Google Play Store (Android), and type **Food Delivery, [Insert City, Country]**. Read each listed app's description, and download an appropriate app.

Locating Attractions, Stores, Businesses, or Services

In addition to the Maps or Google Maps apps that allow you to enter whatever type of business, service, local attraction, or point of interest you're looking for into the Search field, you can find other apps that also allow you to quickly find what you're looking for nearby, wherever you happen to be in the world.

For example, the free AroundMe app (shown here on an Android smartphone) pinpoints your location and then offers an easily accessible menu that allows you to quickly find what you're looking for, whether it's a bank/ATM, bar, coffee shop, gas station, movie theater, pharmacy, public parking lot, hospital, or hotel. The app also offers interactive local guides for popular cities around the world. Once you find a listing for what you're looking for, the app helps you get there and provides detailed information about what you selected.

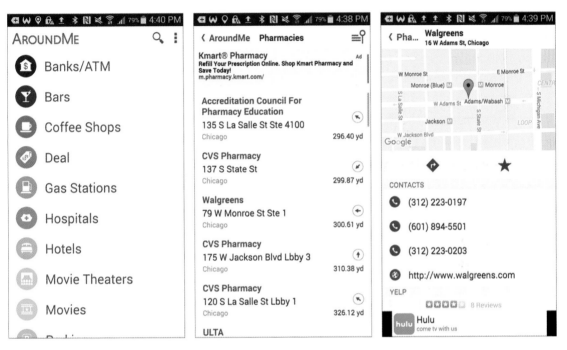

Other apps similar to the AroundMe app are the Around-You, Find Around Me, Find Near Me, Nearby, NearMe Places, and Places Around Me apps. All offer similar functionality when it comes to finding points of interest, businesses, restaurants, and services that are located around your current position, or the location you specify. All these apps require Internet connectivity and your mobile device's built-in GPS capabilities (Location Services).

More Ways to Use Your Mobile Device While Traveling

If you spend a little time browsing the App Store (iOS) or Google Play App Store (Android), you can easily find apps that add functionality to your smartphone or tablet that is particularly useful during a trip. The following list describes a few types of apps that are worth installing on your mobile device. To find a selection of apps that fall into each category, type the category name—such as **currency converter** or **language translator**—in the Search field.

- **Currency converters:** In a foreign country that uses a different currency, having a currency converter on hand that knows the current exchange rate will make it easier to quickly determine how much you're paying in dollars. Most of these apps allow you to quickly select two currencies. When you type in an amount of money in one currency, the app converts it into the other currency within seconds. Apps like Currency Today, GlobeConvert, My Currency Converter, and XE Currency are all free and make currency conversions easy.

The GlobeConvert currency converter app running on an iPhone

Siri and Google Voice Search Handle Currency Conversion

Instead of using a currency converter app, press and hold down the Home button of your iPhone or iPad to activate Siri (iOS) or activate Google Voice Search (Android) by tapping the microphone icon in the Google Search field of your Home screen. When prompted to speak, say something like, "Convert 25 Euros into U.S. Dollars." Internet connectivity is required.

- **Interactive travel guides:** Whether you want to learn all about a city you're visiting or determine the top tourist attractions and historic landmarks to visit, there are numerous interactive travel guide apps available for virtually every city in the world. To find them, access the app store for your mobile device and type **travel guide, [*insert city, state, country*]**. Each interactive, city-specific travel guide app offers a different selection of features and functions to help you explore that location.

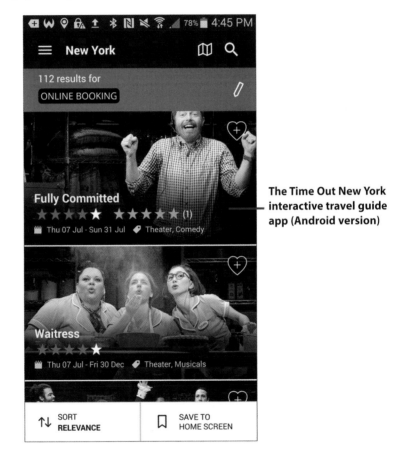

The Time Out New York interactive travel guide app (Android version)

- **Language translators:** When visiting a foreign country where you're not fluent in the local language, consider installing a language translator app. In some cases, when you speak into the app, it translates what you say into the foreign language you select, or you can manually type a word or phrase so the app can translate it. These apps typically require Internet access. To find the app that offers the language translation functionality you want or need, type **language translator** into the Search field of your app store.

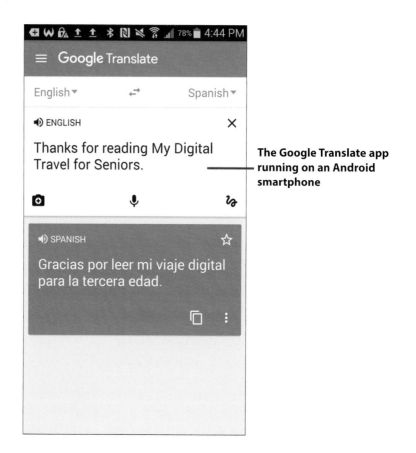

The Google Translate app running on an Android smartphone

- **Shopping apps:** If you enjoy shopping at retail stores, countless optional apps can help you find the location of stores that sell what you're looking for, plus help you find the lowest price possible on those items. If you're in a store and want to find a lower price on a specific item, price comparison apps allow you to type the name of the item (or scan its barcode using the camera built in to your smartphone), and then find nearby stores that sell the item for less. You can either go to that store or ask the store you're in to match their competitor's price for the item(s) you want to buy.

Price Comparison Mobile Apps

Apps like Amazon, Magic Scanner, NowDiscount, Price.com, Price Check, Price Scanner, Quick Scan, RedLaser, and ShopSavvy allow you to compare prices for products while you're in a store. There are also apps, such as RetailMeNot, that pinpoint your location as you're out and about, and then notify you when you are in close proximity to a retail store that has some type of coupon or special offer going on.

Apps That Save You Money

If you belong to an organization that gives you discounts at stores, restaurants, tourist attractions, and other types of businesses, you can use that organization's mobile app to determine what discounts are available near your current location. If you're a AAA member, the AAA Mobile app also helps you discover a wide range of discounts you're entitled to. As an AARP member who enjoys traveling, be sure to install the AARP Member Advantages and AARP NOW apps on your smartphone or tablet.

Find Discounts with Your Computer

Chapter 11, "Online Travel Discounts by Association," covers how to find discounts using your desktop or laptop computer.

Use the AAA Mobile App to Save Money

For members of AAA, one of the tools offered by the AAA Mobile app is the ability to find and view nearby businesses and services that offer discounts to AAA members. To use this app (shown here on an iPhone) to save money, follow these steps:

1. Download and install the AAA Mobile app onto your smartphone or tablet. (Not shown.)

2. Tap the icon to launch the AAA Mobile app. (Not shown.)

First Time Only

The first time you use the app, you must enter your ZIP code, agree to the service terms, and sign in to your account. On subsequent uses of the app, you won't need to do this.

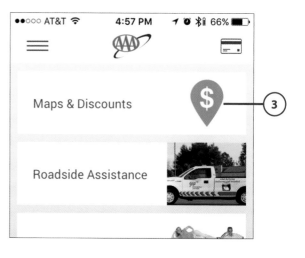

(3) From the app's main menu, tap the Maps & Discounts option.

(4) The displayed map includes a bunch of red dots, each of which represents a local business (based on your current location) that offers some type of discount to AAA members. To view a list of these businesses and their offers, tap the List option.

See the businesses as a list

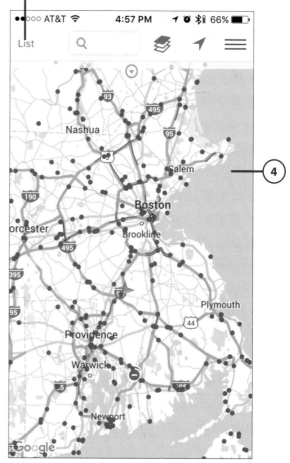

5) Swipe through the list to review the businesses. Businesses are categorized—Lodging and Dining are examples—to help you discover specific types of offers. Tap a listing to view details about that business or service.

AAA Travel Guides Also Available

When using the AAA Mobile app, you can download a travel guide for the place you're visiting by tapping the Menu icon in the top-right corner of the screen and then tapping the AAA Travel Guides option (Android). From the menus, select the guide you want. You'll discover guides for cities throughout the United States, separate guides for national parks, and guides for destinations in Canada, the Caribbean, and Mexico.

Access free travel guides on an iPhone by tapping the Menu icon (in the top-left corner of the screen), selecting the Maps & Directions menu option, and then tapping the Guides option (displayed at the bottom center of the screen). From the AAA Travel Guides menu, select which travel guide you want to view.

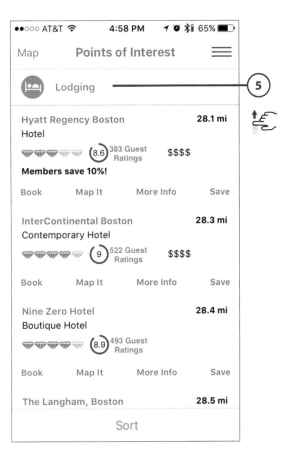

6 You see the AAA Diamond Rating (if applicable) along with details about the discount the business/service/attraction/ restaurant offers to AAA members, when applicable.

7 Tap Directions to obtain detailed directions to that business, or tap Save to save the information to quickly access it later.

Use the AARP Member Advantages App to Save Money

To use the AARP Member Advantages app on your smartphone (the iPhone version is shown here) or tablet, follow these steps:

1 Download and install the AARP Member Advantages mobile app onto your smartphone or tablet from your app store. (Not shown.)

2 Tap the icon to launch the AARP Member Advantages app. (Not shown.)

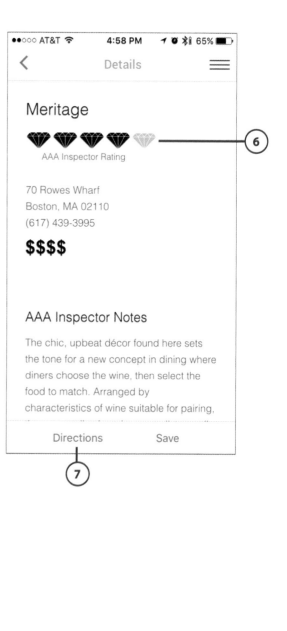

(**3**) On the Select Location screen, enter the city and/or ZIP code where you are (or will be visiting), or tap on the Use Your Current Location option.

(**4**) The first time you use the app, adjust options displayed on the Settings menu to determine what type of money-saving deals you're interested in and give the app permission to generate notifications when it finds applicable offers.

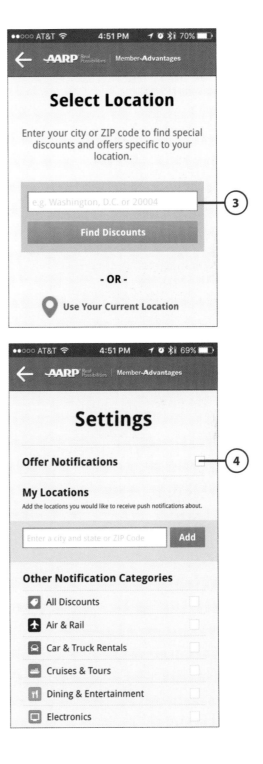

(5) Unless you've customized the app's settings, you will see a general listing of all local businesses, restaurants, services, and attractions that offer an AARP discount to customers displayed on the Discounts Home screen.

(6) Narrow down this list by tapping the Categories option and then tapping a subcategory, such as Air & Rail, Dining & Entertainment, Health & Wellness, or Shopping. The default selection is All Discounts. Tap Apply Filter after you've made your selection.

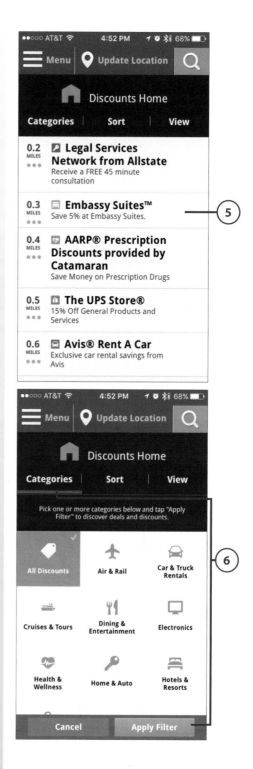

7. Tap Sort to narrow down the listing by nearby offers, online-only offers, or limited time offers.

8. Tap View to select the format used to display the offers.

9. Tap any listing to view that offer.

10. You see details about location(s) where the offer is valid, as well as applicable terms and conditions. Use the buttons at the bottom of the screen to call the business, obtain more details, get directions, or display a digital version of your AARP membership card (needed to receive the special deals).

Enter Your AARP Membership Number Once

The first time you use the AARP Member Advantages mobile app, tap the Menu icon and select the My AARP Card option. When prompted, enter the email address and password you used to set up your online AARP account, and then tap the Log In button. The app automatically loads your membership number and creates a digital version of your membership card that you can access and display anytime from within the app.

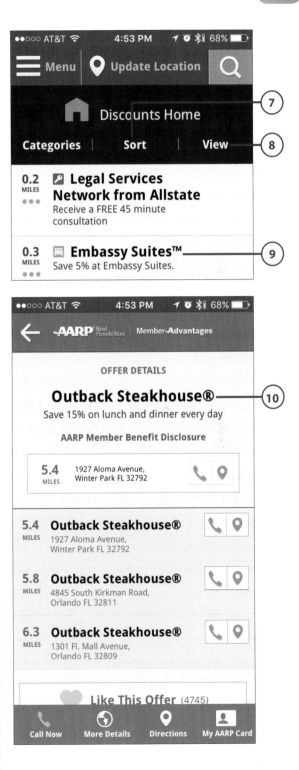

Many Other Types of Apps Are Available

When you visit the App Store for your iPhone/iPad or the Google Play App Store for your Android mobile device, you'll find many other types of apps in the Travel category that you might find useful. For example, there are apps that can help you track the status of flights (Flight Aware, Flight Track 5, and GateGuru), help you find the cheapest flights (eSoon Travel, Hopper, Jetradar, Skiplagged, SkyGuru, Skyscanner), as well as apps that can help you find the closest (and least expensive) gas stations (Fuelzee, GasBuddy, or GasGuru).

Many national parks, popular tourist attractions, and museums, for example, also have their own proprietary mobile apps that can help you get the most out of your visit. In the Search field of the App Store (iPhone/iPad) or the Google Play App Store (Android), type the name of the tourist attraction, landmark, or museum you plan to visit to find applicable apps.

If you're planning a visit to a national park, for example, some of the apps you might find useful include National Parks by National Geographic, Passport to Your National Parks, Pocket Ranger National Park Passport, or REI—National Parks Guide and Maps.

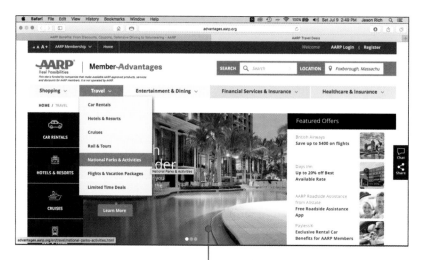

Use your device to save money with your membership in groups like AAA, AARP, the military/government, and USAA, and with a service like Groupon or Living Social.

In this chapter, you'll discover how to use your Internet-connected device to take advantage of travel-related discounts you're entitled to as a member of groups like AARP, AAA, the military/government, and USAA, plus learn how to use Groupon, Living Social, and similar services. Topics covered include how to

→ Find and take advantage of discounts on travel-related expenses offered by AARP

→ Find and take advantage of discounts offered to AAA members using your computer

→ Discover travel-related discounts using other services, like Groupon and Living Social, from your computer

Online Travel Discounts By Association

Other chapters have explained how to use AARP Travel website to shop for and book flights, accommodations, rental cars, cruises, vacation packages, and vacation bundles and how the AARP Member Advantages and AARP Now mobile apps can help you find discounts while you're out and about or traveling. Beyond what the AARP Travel Center (which is powered by Expedia.com) offers, AARP's Travel Benefits web page (www.aarp.org/benefits-discounts/travel-benefits) and AARP's Member Benefits webpage (www.aarp.org/benefits-discounts) offer additional ways to find and take advantage of available discounts.

Ways to Access the AARP Travel Benefits Website

In addition to using your favorite web browser on your computer to explore the AARP Travel Benefits or AARP Member Benefits web pages, you can use the web browser built in to your smartphone or tablet to access this information. You can also find these benefits through the AARP Now mobile app.

This chapter also explains how to use your Internet-connected computer to access other websites operated by AAA, AARP, American Express, Groupon, Living Social, and other credit card issuers to find and take advantage of discounts as you're planning your trip's itinerary and deciding what activities you'll experience, what tours you'll take, and where you want to enjoy your meals.

The Benefits of Membership

To take advantage of discounts offered through AAA, AARP, and USAA, it's necessary to first become a member of these organizations, all of which offer perks, benefits, and discounts that go well beyond what you'll use when traveling. To learn more about AARP membership, visit www.aarp.org and click the Join option. To learn more about AAA membership, visit www.aaa.com/membership, and click the Join option.

Available to veterans, active military personnel, and their families, USAA (www.usaa.com/inet/pages/travel_main) offers a selection of money-saving opportunities in a wide range of product and service categories, including travel.

AARP Travel-Related Resources Beyond AARP Travel

Beyond the discounts you receive when making your vacation arrangements through the AARP Travel Center, you're entitled to many other discounts and perks, some of which can be useful when preparing for a trip or while you're actually traveling. From your computer, launch your favorite web browser and type **www.aarp.org/benefits-discounts/services_discounts_list** in the address

field. You go to AARP's Travel Benefits web page, where you'll discover discounts offered by specific airlines, hotels, rental car companies, cruise lines, rail lines, and travel agencies that you can take advantage of by working directly with those travel providers rather than going through the AARP Travel Center.

Travel Benefits

CAR RENTALS	CRUISES	FLIGHTS & VACATION PACKAGES	RAIL & TOURS
AARP® Travel Center powered by Expedia®	AARP® Travel Center powered by Expedia®	AARP® Travel Center powered by Expedia®	AARP® Travel Center powered by Expedia®
Avis Rent A Car	Collette Cruises	British Airways	Collette Explorations
Budget Rent A Car	Grand European Travel	Collette	Grand Canyon Railway
Budget Truck Rental	Windstar Cruises	Collette Explorations	Grand European Travel
Payless Car Rental		Grand European Travel	Vacations By Rail
Zipcar		Liberty Travel	
		MedjetAssist	

Scroll down this page to find the Everyday Discounts heading where you'll discover restaurant chains, entertainment options, and various services that you could benefit from while vacationing. For example, if you're planning a road trip, signing up for AARP Roadside Assistance could be useful. If you have the need for a car repair or tire replacement, presenting your AARP membership card at participating tire centers or auto repair centers entitles you to a discount.

Everyday Discounts

APPAREL, AUTO & HOME	APPAREL, AUTO & HOME CONT.	DINING & ENTERTAINMENT	DINING & ENTERTAINMENT CONT.
AARP Auto Buying Program	Monro Muffler	Bonefish Grill	McCormick & Schmick's
AARP® Roadside Assistance from Allstate	Mr. Tire	Bubba Gump Shrimp Co.	Outback Steakhouse
	RepairPal	Burger King	Rainforest Cafe
AARP® Roadside Assistance from Allstate premier plans	Tanger Outlets	Carrabba's Italian Grill	Regal Cinemas
AutoTire Car Care Center	The Tire Choice & Total Car Care	Chart House	Saltgrass Steak House
Everyday Savings Center powered by NextJump	The UPS Store®	Cirque du Soleil	sweetFrog Premium Frozen Yogurt
HomeServe	Tread Quarters Discount Tire & Auto Service Centers	Claim Jumper Restaurant & Saloon	The Oceanaire Seafood Room
Ken Towery's Tire & Auto Care		Denny's	TeeOff.com
		Dunkin' Donuts	Ticketmaster®
		Landry's, Inc., Restaurants	

Here are some other examples of discounts that are available through AARP Travel Benefits:

- If you enjoy shopping at outlet stores, present your AARP membership card at the Shopper Services or Management Office of any Tanger Outlet location to receive a coupon book worth $1,000 in savings.

- Present your AARP membership card at any UPS Store to save money when shipping packages to your destination or home (or anywhere else).

- Many people enjoy relaxing with a good book while on vacation or during travel time. If you want to catch up on your reading, Amazon.com offers discounts to AARP members on Kindle eBook readers and eBooks, as well as audiobooks from Audible.com. And members can often get special discounts on AARP books, including *My Digital Photography for Seniors* and *My Digital Entertainment for Seniors*, at AARP.org/Bookstore.

- Many of America's national parks also offer a wide range of discounts to AARP members. This includes accommodations located near national parks and admission and program fees offered within the parks. To learn more, visit http://advantages.aarp.org/en/travel/national-parks-activities.html.

Get Recommendations from AARP and Expedia

With Expedia.com, AARP Travel offers an interactive Fun Things to Do tool that you can access using your computer and any web browser. Here's how to use it:

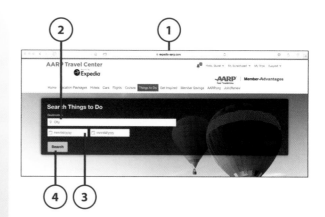

1. Type **www.expedia-aarp.com/Activities** in the address field of your web browser.

2. Enter your destination city in the Destination field.

3. Select when you'll be visiting.

4. Click Search.

5 Use the filter tool to narrow your search results. A list of potential activities, shows, events, and tours that are available during your travel dates is displayed. Click any listing to see more information or to pre-book tickets/reservations.

6 The description page for an activity includes details about it, such as when and where it's available, and information about the discount you'll receive by booking your tickets or reservations online from this website. To make a reservation and pay for it using a credit or debit card, click the Book button.

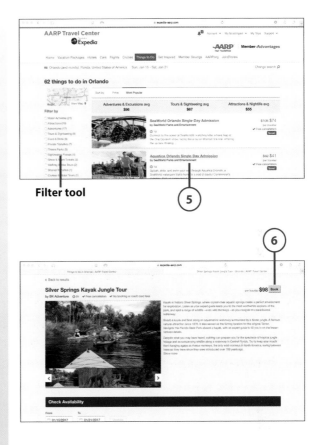

Filter tool

Don't Forget Your Card

Be sure to have your AARP membership card with you, and download the free AARP Now app to receive perks and discounts you're entitled to.

Finding Discounts Offered to AAA Members

If you're a AAA member, from www.aaa.com you can easily find, learn about, and, in some cases, book reservations and get tickets for activities and tours that offer discounts to AAA members. You'll also discover what restaurants, stores, businesses, and activities offer discounts when you present your membership card. You can also use the AAA Mobile app (covered in Chapter 10, "Mobile Apps to Use at Your Destination") to find discounts.

Use the AAA Website to Find Discounts

Depending on your home state, the appearance of the local AAA website will differ from what's shown here (for New England). However, the following steps give you an overview of how to find local discounts you're entitled to. To use the AAA website to discover member discounts that will be useful when planning a trip or actually traveling, follow these steps:

(1) Type **www.aaa.com** in the address field of your web browser.

(2) Click the Discounts main menu option.

(3) Two separate categories are displayed—Where to Save and Ways to Save. Each offers a submenu that allows you to find money-saving offers.

(4) For example, as you're planning what you want to do during an upcoming trip, from the Where to Save menu, click the Entertainment & Attractions menu option. Or, from the Ways to Save menu, select the Movie & Theme Park Tickets, Travel Discounts, or Concert Tickets option.

(5) You see a list of nearby options (based on your current location) that offer discounts to AAA members.

(6) Click the Advanced option to change locations.

(7) Select Entertainment & Attractions from the Category pull-down menu.

(8) Enter where you'll be visiting.

(9) Select a distance option to narrow the search to what's offered within a specific radius of the city and state you selected.

(10) Click Search to view updated listings.

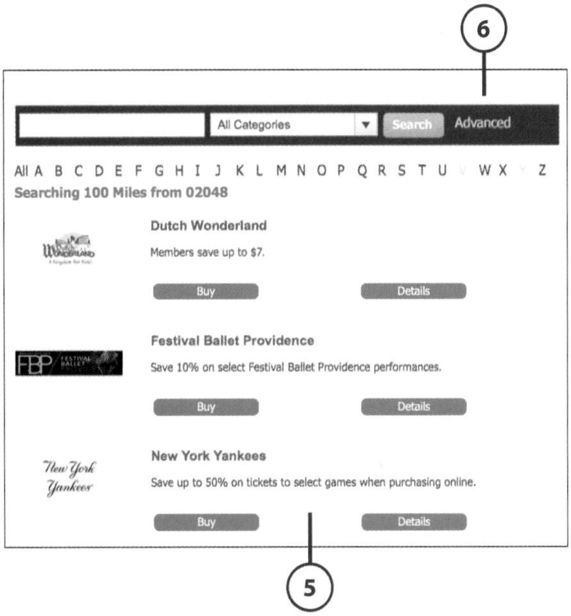

| | All Categories ▼ | Search | Advanced |

All A B C D E F G H I J K L M N O P Q R S T U V W X Y Z
Searching 100 Miles from 02048

Dutch Wonderland
Members save up to $7.

Buy   Details

Festival Ballet Providence
Save 10% on select Festival Ballet Providence performances.

Buy   Details

New York Yankees
New York Yankees
Save up to 50% on tickets to select games when purchasing online.

Buy   Details

Advanced Search   x
Keyword:

Category:
Entertainment and Attractions   ▼

City/State:
Mansfield,MA

Distance:
Any Distance   ▼

Search

11 Click on the Details button for any listing to view more information about a specific offer and find out how to take advantage of it.

12 From any of the offer description screens, it's possible to purchase the tickets or make your reservations, plus take advantage of the AAA discount that's offered. Follow the on-screen prompts to do this.

Discovering City-Specific Discounts

Groupon and Living Social are independent online services that work with local merchants, restaurants, services, attractions, and travel providers around the world to offer special discounts. A membership is not required to use Groupon or Living Social, but you do need to set up a free account while using the website or mobile app.

Every week, Groupon and Living Social offer a different selection of discounted offers. When you find an offer that's appealing, you purchase a coupon that allows you to take advantage of that offer. For example, a restaurant in New York City might offer a coupon that you buy from Groupon or Living Social for $25.00. You redeem the coupon at that restaurant for $50.00 worth of food and drinks. You've just saved 50 percent on your meal.

Groupon or Living Social work with an ever-changing selection of local businesses, restaurants, and services in many cities. So if the city you're traveling to is supported by Groupon or Living Social, it's possible to quickly find and prepurchase special deals from restaurants, spas, salons, dry cleaners, activities, or tourist attractions, for example, which you can take advantage of when you reach your travel destination.

It's Not All Good

Groupon and Living Social Offers Have Their Restrictions

Before purchasing any offer from Groupon or Living Social, carefully read the fine print associated with that offer. Every offer has an expiration date, and some have blackout dates. Make sure you'll be able to redeem the coupon you purchase during the dates you want or need to. Also, determine whether an advanced reservation is required, and make sure you'll be able to book a reservation during the dates you'll be visiting the area.

For example, if you purchase an offer for a discounted one-hour massage at a spa located in the city where you'll be vacationing, contact the spa to make sure it'll be open and has appointments available during your travel dates. The coupons you purchase from Groupon or Living Social are typically not refundable or exchangeable.

Use Groupon and Living Social to Find Discounts

Groupon and Living Social work very much the same way. You can browse through the offers using your computer's web browser or download and install the Groupon and Living Social mobile app on your mobile device. This example shows how to purchase a coupon on Groupon.

Access Living Social's Website

To access Living Social's website and browse what's offered, visit www.livingsocial.com.

① From your computer, launch your favorite web browser and type **www.groupon.com** in the address field.

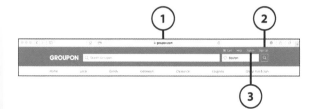

② The first time you use the service, click Sign Up to set up a free account. This will involve entering your full name and email address, and creating a password or using your Facebook or Google account.

③ If you already have an account, click Sign In, and then enter your email address and password.

Facebook and Google

If you created your account using your Facebook or Google account, click the Login with Facebook or Login with Google button.

④ You see a comprehensive listing of available offers based on your current location.

⑤ Select a different location, such as where you'll be traveling to, by clicking the Location field and entering your travel destination. The listing of available offers will be updated to reflect the newly selected location.

6 Scroll down to browse through the listings, or click a category along the left margin of the browser window to narrow down your search. For example, if you're looking for a discounted massage offer, click the Beauty & Spas category. To find a local dry cleaner, click the Local Services option or Local tab (depending on the mobile device you're using).

7 Click any listing to view the details of the offer and learn more information about the company, service, or travel provider that's offering the deal.

8 Read through the offer's description, including the fine print. If you want to purchase that offer, click Buy! and follow the on-screen prompts.

9 The coupon or certificate you purchased that's related to the offer will be accessible via the Groupon website or Groupon mobile app. However, in most instances, you can also print the certificate, and then present it when and where you want to redeem it. (Not shown.)

>>>Go Further
THE GOODS AND TRAVEL CATEGORIES

The preceding example showed you how to purchase a coupon through the Local category. The Goods option shows you deals for items you can purchase. These are offers that you can redeem at specific retail stores through websites.

The Getaways option includes deeply discounted deals from hotels, resorts, and travel providers offering travel packages. Click on one of the submenu options to narrow your search based on the geographic region where you want to go, such as USA & Canada; Mexico, the Caribbean & Latin America; or Europe, Asia, Africa & Oceania.

Be sure to read all the fine print before clicking the Book button to purchase an offer. Pay careful attention to restrictions that are listed, as well as the information found under the Policies & Fees heading, which outline additional charges you might incur.

Scroll down on a travel offer's information screen to read detailed TripAdvisor reviews of the hotel, resort, or travel package you're considering.

In some cases, you'll be able to make your travel reservation directly from the Groupon website. In other cases, you receive your Groupon coupon for that offer and then you need to contact the travel provider directly to redeem the coupon and make your reservation.

The Goods category   **The Getaways category**

Getting Perks from Your Credit Card

As an American Express (AmEx) cardholder, you're automatically entitled to free travel-related services offered by American Express, plus you qualify for discounts when booking travel, purchasing travel and rental car insurance, and, if you're traveling abroad, exchanging foreign currency. Depending on which American Express card you possess, you may earn frequent flier miles on your favorite airline anytime you make purchases and/or receive other travel-related perks while on your trips.

Also Search for Lower Rates Elsewhere

Think of American Express Travel as another online travel service, like Expedia, Orbitz, or Priceline. American Express Travel offers exclusive discounts and perks to American Express cardholders; however, they might not always be the lowest prices available, so it's important to shop around.

Like the other online travel services and websites, American Express Travel displays fares or rates for a variety of its partners. These deals will vary, and they might not always be better than what the other online travel services offer. Always check with two or three other services to see if they offer more competitive rates or fares, just as you would when using any other online travel service or website. You must shop around to get the best travel deals.

The following websites help you discover and use the various travel-related services and discounts that American Express has to offer:

- **AmEx Card Options (www.AmericanExpress.com):** Discover the different types of AmEx cards you can apply for, what travel-related perks each offers, and then apply for a card online. If you don't already have an AmEx card, apply for a new AmEx card at least several weeks before a planned trip if you want to take advantage of travel-related benefits and perks while on that trip.

- **Travel Discounts for AmEx Cardholders (https://travel.americanexpress. com/travel-offers):** American Express manages its own online travel agency (American Express Travel) that provides discounts on flights, accommodations, rental cars, cruises, vacation packages, and vacation bundles to cardholders. Use this website to find and book your travel, plus take advantage of often exclusive travel discounts that are offered.

- **Foreign Currency Service (www.americanexpress.com/us/content/ astrology/index.html):** Before leaving for a foreign country, you can order local currency for that country, have it delivered to your home or office, and take advantage of low currency exchange rates offered to AmEx cardholders.

American Express Travelers Checks

Instead of carrying large amounts of cash while traveling, you have the option to acquire American Express Traveler's Cheques from: www.americanexpress.com/travelerscheques. These travelers cheques can typically be used throughout the world as cash, they never expire, and they can often be replaced if they're lost or stolen. You do not need to be an AmEx cardholder to purchase and use American Express Traveler's Cheques. Another option is to use your AmEx card in foreign counties to obtain cash (in the local currency) from ATM machines, without paying high currency conversion fees.

- **American Express Global Assist (www.americanexpress.com/globalassist):** Receive free telephone assistance if you run into trouble while traveling. American Express Global Assist can help if you lose your passport or wallet, help you recover lost luggage from an airline, or assist in coordinating emergency medical services you require while traveling abroad, for example.

- **Travel Insurance (www.americanexpress.com/travelinsurance):** Through a partnership with Travelex, you can acquire travel insurance prior to an upcoming trip and receive special coverage offered only to AmEx card holders.

- **AmEx Rental Car Insurance (www.americanexpress.com/carrental):** Acquire rental car insurance for a flat fee per rental as opposed to a daily fee. Learn more from the "Understand Your Rental Car Insurance Options" section of Chapter 6, "Finding Ground Transportation."

>>>Go Further
OTHER CREDIT CARD ISSUERS OFFER TRAVEL PERKS AND DISCOUNTS

Many credit card issuers, including MasterCard, Visa, and Discover, also offer a variety of discounts and perks to travelers. This applies only to credit cards, however, not to prepaid credit cards or debit cards that have the MasterCard or Visa logo.

Keep in mind that each individual credit card comes with its own selection of perks and discounts, and only some credit cards, including those issued through an airline, cater specifically to travelers. If you're a frequent traveler, seek out a credit card that lets you earn frequent flier miles with one or more airlines for every dollar you spend and that offers perks, such as no foreign transaction fees and low currency conversion rates. Some credit cards also let you check your first piece of luggage for free or obtain preboarding privileges on a specific airline.

Visit these sites to learn more about the travel-related perks offered to cardholders:

- www.mastercard.us/en-us/consumers/features-benefits/card-benefits.html
- www.cardratings.com/bestcards/travel-rewards-cards.php
- www.creditcards.com
- https://usa.visa.com/support/consumer/card-benefits.html
- www.discover.com/credit-cards/member-benefits

Find Travel-Related Discounts Offered By AmEx

To find travel discounts and book travel through American Express Travel (using your computer), follow these steps:

(**1**) Launch your favorite web browser and type **www.americanexpress.com** in the address field.

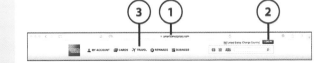

(**2**) Log in to the website using your American Express website account information. If you don't yet have an online account, but you do have an American Express card, click the Create New Online Account option and then follow the on-screen prompts.

(**3**) Click Travel.

4 Click Book a Trip under the Personal Travel heading.

5 Click the tab for Flights, Hotels, Flight+Hotel, Cars, or Cruises, based on the type of travel you want to book. (This example uses the Flights option.)

6 Fill in the fields with the requested information.

7 Use the pull-down menu to select the number of travelers for whom you want to purchase airline tickets. Select the number of infants, children, youth, adults, and seniors separately, because you might qualify for different pricing for each type of passenger.

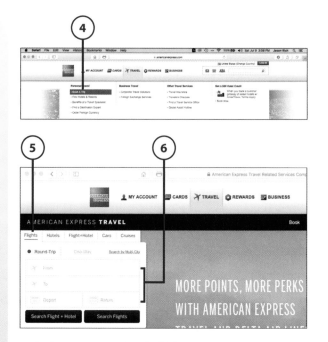

8 Use the pull-down menu to select between Economy, Premium Economy, Business class, or First class.

9 Click on the I Prefer Non-Stop Flights check box if you want to fly direct, which may limit your flight options or cost extra.

10 If you can be flexible with your travel dates, click the Show Me +/− 3 Days option to compare airfares based on alternative departure and return dates.

11 Click Search Flights to browse available flights that meet your search criteria.

12 Scroll through the displayed flight listings to compare airfares between airlines and flight options.

13 Use the filter tools displayed to fine-tune your search results for flights. Then, select specific flights you want by clicking the Select button that's associated with its listing.

14 Follow the onscreen prompts to provide traveler information, pay for the reservation, and complete the booking, just as you would with any other travel-related website. When you pay for travel using certain American Express cards, you earn extra frequent flier miles for each dollar you spend on flights, for example. (Not shown.)

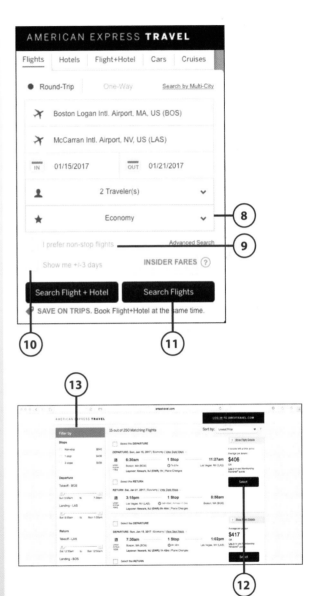

Purchasing travel insurance before any trip may be a good investment.

In this chapter, you'll learn about optional travel insurance and why it could be an important investment. Topics covered include

→ What travel insurance is, what's covered, and why it might be useful
→ How to shop for travel insurance online
→ How to initiate a claim online

Finding and Purchasing Travel Insurance

As you make travel arrangements and book travel and accommodations, the online travel service or airline website you use will typically offer you optional travel protection for an additional fee. Likewise, when you rent a car, you'll be offered optional vehicle protection or loss/damage waiver protection from the rental car company for an additional daily fee.

Because online travel services, airlines, and rental car companies are not insurance agents, what's being offered to you is typically "trip protection," "travel protection," or "vehicle protection" coverage rather than comprehensive "travel insurance." In many cases, the actual coverage you receive might be similar, although it might not be as comprehensive as travel insurance.

Trip protection for a flight, for example, typically covers issues that occur that are somehow related only to the flight and little else. So, before purchasing any trip protection coverage, read the fine print carefully to determine what's covered and how much coverage is offered.

For more comprehensive coverage, make all your travel arrangements and then purchase travel insurance from an independent insurance company that specializes in travel insurance, such as Allianz, Travel Guard (AIG), or Travelex. Each offers a variety of coverage plans that includes much more comprehensive coverage related to all aspects of your trip. You can find details about these three companies later in this chapter in the "Shopping for Travel Insurance" section.

Purchase Optional Travel Insurance Before You Depart

If you're interested in acquiring optional travel insurance, you must purchase it before you depart for your trip.

In general, the one-time cost for travel insurance is approximately 10 to 20 percent of the overall trip cost. The cost depends on where you live, your age, where you're traveling to, the overall cost of your trip, the level of coverage (or maximum benefit payouts) you select, and the additional coverage options you choose.

The price of the policy is also affected by whether you include a Cancel for Any Reason option to the plan. That option costs more, but it offers a lot more flexibility and coverage if you need to cancel your trip for a reason that's covered by the policy.

When You Travel, Things Can Go Wrong, So Be Prepared!

No matter how much time and effort you invest to make sure every aspect of an upcoming trip is planned perfectly, sometimes things go wrong. When something unexpected happens just prior to a trip or during your travels, the negative financial implications can be significant. Travel insurance might help you avoid incurring hundreds or often thousands of dollars in extra costs to rectify the problem, obtain medical help that's needed, and return home safely.

Travel Insurance Coverage

The following are some of the things that can go wrong just prior to or during a trip:

- Your credit cards, driver's license, or passport are lost or stolen.

- A cancelled or significantly delayed flight dramatically disrupts your trip and prevents you from making a connecting flight or from boarding a cruise ship before its departure.

- Severe weather (such as a hurricane) forces you to unexpectedly change or cancel your travel plans or end your trip prematurely.

- A travel provider you paid goes bankrupt.

- You arrive at your destination but your luggage is delayed or lost by the airline.

- Your hotel room gets robbed, or you get mugged during a trip and some of your personal property gets stolen.

- You have a personal injury, accident, or emergency medical issue before the trip. (In this case, your medical expenses would not be covered but you would be able to recover the cost of your trip, even if it was otherwise nonrefundable or non-changeable.)

- On your trip, you're involved in an accident that requires emergency medical treatment, hospitalization, and/or evacuation.

- Your prescription medication gets lost, and you need an emergency refill while traveling abroad.

- During a cruise, you get off the ship at a port of call, something happens to cause a delay on land, and you miss the ship's departure.

- You have prepaid for a trip and have nonrefundable reservations, but you need to cancel the trip prior to departure for personal or medical reasons.

The insurance plan you select determines what situations related to a trip are covered. As with any type of insurance, the hope is that you purchase it but never need to file a claim and actually take advantage of it. However, if something does go wrong before or during a trip, especially if you're traveling abroad, travel insurance is a relatively small investment that you'll be very happy you made.

When you acquire optional travel insurance from a company like Allianz, Travel Guard, or Travelex, depending on the plan you choose, most or all aspects of your trip are covered.

Keep in mind that some travel insurance policies include a "cancel for any reason," provision, which often costs a bit extra. If this is the case, you can cancel the trip prior to your departure and recover a significant portion of the money you spent on nonrefundable and non-changeable airline, hotel, rental car, resort, or cruise reservations, for example. Be sure to read the fine print before purchasing travel insurance to understand exactly what's covered under the "cancel for any reason" provision.

It's Not All Good

Regular Insurance Doesn't Always Cover You When Traveling

Even if you have comprehensive health insurance that covers health issues and emergency medical situations when you're at home, you might have little or no coverage when you travel, especially if you travel abroad. Be aware that Medicare and Medicaid will not cover you outside the United States. Thus, it's important to understand what insurance coverage you already have and what supplemental insurance you need to have adequate protection when you travel.

Likewise, if you opt to rent a car and rely on your own auto, homeowner's, and health insurance policies to provide the coverage you need for yourself, your belongings, your passengers, the rental vehicle, and any other people involved in an accident, you may discover you have some coverage, but it's limited.

By determining what coverage you have, you can easily acquire additional insurance prior to a trip to fully protect yourself.

Because travel insurance is a one-time purchase that covers your trip, there's also no worry that your annual premium will go up if you need to file a claim with the travel insurance company.

Most comprehensive travel insurance you acquire from a company like Allianz, Travel Guard, or Travelex offer some or all of the coverage you need in one policy, for a flat fee, that includes protection for the duration of your trip. After you acquire travel insurance, the coverage remains active from the time you purchase it until you return home (based on the dates you provide when acquiring the policy). If after acquiring a policy you change your departure or return date, it's essential that you contact the company you purchased the travel insurance from and amend the policy to maintain full coverage for the duration of your entire trip.

Comprehensive Travel Insurance

Comprehensive travel insurance offers a wide range of coverage. Be sure to visit the website of the travel insurance company you work with to determine the level of coverage offered and to acquire definitive and detailed explanations for each type of coverage. The descriptions offered here are for general reference purposes only.

Also, some activities might not be covered by your comprehensive insurance plan. If your vacation involves certain dangerous activities—such as skiing, skydiving, scuba diving, hot air ballooning, piloting an aircraft, or driving a race car—you might need additional insurance to have coverage if something goes wrong while you're engaged in that activity.

When choosing a travel insurance policy, look for the following types of coverage and choose the ones that are important to you:

- **Accidental Death and Dismemberment:** This aspect of the insurance includes a predetermined amount of coverage if the insured person is injured or killed during the trip as a result of an accident. (Certain types of accidents resulting from the participation of dangerous activities, such as skydiving, are not covered unless additional coverage is added to the policy.)

- **Baggage Delay:** This covers your checked luggage if it's delayed by your airline for more than a predetermined number of hours.

- **Cancel for Any Reason:** This option allows you to decide that you simply don't want to go on the trip after it's been booked and paid for.

- **Cancel for Work Reason:** This option allows you to cancel the trip, if the reason relates to a work-related issue that's covered by the policy.

- **Car Rental Collision Coverage:** This is equivalent to the Loss/Damage Waiver Protection offered by rental car companies. It covers the rental vehicle if it's stolen or damaged.

- **Emergency Evacuation:** This covers the costs of being evacuated and transported to a hospital for emergency medical treatment.

- **Emergency Travel Assistance:** This is an added benefit offered by travel insurance providers that allows you to call a special phone number anytime during your trip if you require help.

- **Lost, Stolen, or Damaged Baggage and Travel Documents:** This covers your luggage, personal belongings, and travel documents (up to a certain value specified by the policy) if they are lost, stolen, or damaged during your trip. This is in addition to any coverage offered automatically by an airline.

- **Medical Expenses:** This covers any medical attention you require during your trip.

Existing Medical Condition?

If you have an existing medical condition, special requirements apply if you want to obtain maximum insurance coverage and benefits during your trip. The Allianz website offers an informative article about what you need to know when acquiring travel insurance. You can find the article at www.allianztravelinsurance.com/travel/medical/existing-medical-conditions-coverage.htm.

- **Missed Connection:** This covers the additional expenses or financial loses as a result of missing a connecting flight, train, or ship that results in a disruption of your trip.

- **Trip Cancellation:** This means if the trip gets cancelled for a covered reason that's outside your control, you can recover your financial losses.

- **Trip Delay:** This covers the additional expenses or financial losses as a result of a trip that's delayed due to a covered reason.

- **Trip Interruption:** This covers you if something happens that causes your trip to end early.

Always Pay Attention to the Level of Coverage Offered

Every travel insurance policy offers different coverage levels or maximum benefit amounts for each specific type of coverage. Based on your needs, make sure the policy you purchase offers ample coverage. Emergency medical attention involving emergency evacuation and/or hospitalization, for example, can easily wind up costing tens of thousands of dollars or more.

Shopping for Travel Insurance

The easiest way to shop for and purchase optional travel insurance prior to a trip is to call a travel insurance provider, or visit a company's website to get details about coverage and purchase a policy for yourself and your family members.

Table 12.1 provides contact information for Allianz, Travel Guard, and Travelex, three popular and highly reputable travel insurance providers.

Emergency Calls from Abroad

When you make an emergency assistance call to one of these insurance companies from outside the United States, make a collect call to the number listed in the right column of Table 12.1.

Table 12.1   Travel Insurance Company Contact Information

Travel Insurance Company	Toll-Free Information Number	Website	Emergency Assistance Phone Numbers
Allianz	1-866-884-3556	www.allianztravelinsurance.com	1-800-654-1908 1-804-281-5700 (from outside the U.S.)
Travel Guard	1-800-826-4919	www.travelguard.com	1-800-826-1300 (U.S.) 1-715-345-0505 (from outside the U.S.)
Travelex	1-800-228-9792	www.travelexinsurance.com	1-855-892-6495 1-603-328-1373 (from outside the U.S.)

As you shop for travel insurance among various providers, you'll see varying levels of protection and coverage, as well as varying prices. Make sure you're acquiring the most comprehensive coverage, with the maximum level of benefits you might need, at the best value.

Allianz Mobile App

If you purchase Allianz Travel Insurance, you can manage the policy, access the TravelSmart Hotline, and have useful information at your fingertips by downloading and installing the free TravelSmart Mobile App for iOS and Android smartphones and tablets.

Purchase Travel Insurance Online

For demonstration purposes, this section explains how to shop for travel insurance from Travel Guard (AIG) by visiting this company's website. If you choose a different insurance provider, the requested information will be similar, but the plans that are offered, their respective prices, and the level of benefits offered will vary. The entire process for finding and purchasing optional travel insurance should take less than 10 to 15 minutes.

① Make all of your travel reservations as you normally would, and calculate your total trip cost by adding up the cost of airfare, accommodations, rental car, cruise, and/or vacation package. Include everything trip-related that you've paid for thus far or will pay for before you depart. (Not shown.)

2 From your computer, use your favorite web browser and type **www.travelguard.com** in the address field.

3 Click the Get a Quote tab.

4 Select where you live from the State of Residency drop-down menu.

5 Select your destination country.

6 Fill in the fields displayed below the Trip Details heading.

7 Enter the trip cost and birth date for each traveler for whom you're purchasing the same travel insurance policy.

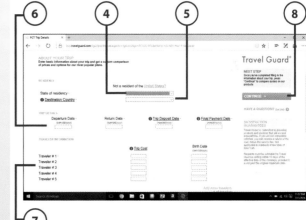

A Policy for Each Traveler

Each person you're traveling with requires his or her own policy, but it's easy to purchase the same policy for multiple people at the same time online.

8 Click Continue.

9 Review the plan options and the circumstances that each covers.

10 Click the Customize button associated with the plan you want to acquire.

(11) Click the check box for each option that you want to add to the policy. In some cases, additional information will be required from you once you select an option.

(12) Click the Re-Calculate Quote button to see the updated price of the plan.

Full Description of Coverage

To see a detailed description of coverage for the plan you've selected, click the Please Read Description of Coverage Here link.

(13) Click Continue.

(14) Provide the information requested for each traveler. Notice that their birth dates and trip costs (that you entered earlier) are also displayed. Make sure this information is correct. Scroll down.

(15) Use the pull-down menus to select answers to all questions that apply to your trip. If a question doesn't apply, from the pull-down menu, select the None option.

(16) Click the Add Beneficiary button to enter the full name of the beneficiary you want to designate for the life insurance aspect of the policy.

(17) Click Continue.

Click to see a full description of the selected coverage

18 Select how you'd like to receive your insurance documents. The By Email option is the most convenient.

19 Enter your payment information.

20 (Optional) Click the Description of Coverage, Terms and Conditions, Privacy Notice, Alerts, Strike List, and Fraud Notice options to review additional information about the plan before purchasing it.

21 Click the check box to acknowledge that you have read and agree to the terms and conditions of the policy.

22 If you have any questions about the insurance plan or what it covers, click the Have a Question? button.

23 Click Complete Purchase to finalize your purchase. In a few minutes, you will receive a confirmation email that includes your policy number and related information. Keep this email safe in your inbox until after you return from your trip, in case you need to reference it.

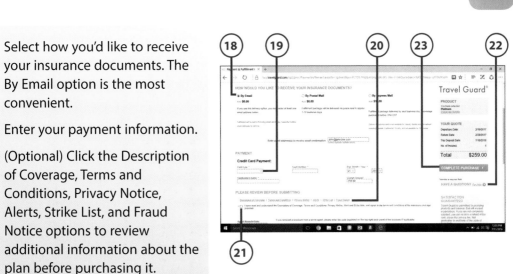

Print Out Your Insurance Documents

Be sure to print the insurance documents that are provided. Included with this paperwork will be an insurance card that lists your name, insurance policy number, and phone numbers to call in case of an emergency. Keep this paperwork with all your other important travel documents. Put the card in your wallet for easy access during your travels. You might also want to keep a copy with your loved ones at home, email a copy to yourself, and store it in the cloud for safekeeping.

Filing a Claim Online

In the best-case scenario, you'll purchase travel insurance, nothing will go wrong, and you will never need to file a claim with the insurance company. But if something does go awry, call the emergency assistance phone number for the insurance company immediately—or as soon as you are safely able to. You will be asked to provide your policy number, name, and other related information. Follow the instructions given to you during the call.

To file a claim, follow the directions given to you when you call the emergency assistance phone number, or return to the insurance company's website and follow the directions provided here:

- **Travel Guard (AIG):** Visit www.travelguard.com, click the Customer Service main menu option and then the Claims option. Click Create an Account. Follow the on-screen prompts to continue. Be sure to watch the instructional video, "How to File a Claim," and click the Required Documentation option to determine what paperwork you need to provide.

Click Claims to file a claim with Travel Guard insurance.

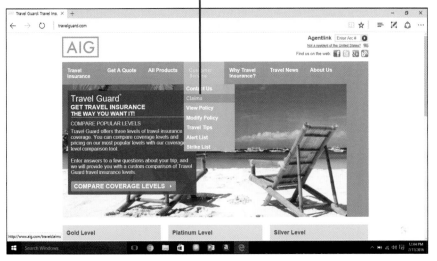

- **Allianz:** Visit www.allianztravelinsurance.com and click the File a Claim option. Follow the on-screen prompts to continue.

Click here to file a claim with Allianz.

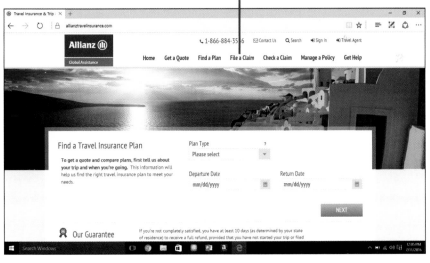

- **Travelex:** Visit www.travelexinsurance.com, click the Plan Holders main menu option, and choose the File a Claim option. Follow the on-screen prompts to continue.

The File a Claim option is on the Plan Holders tab.

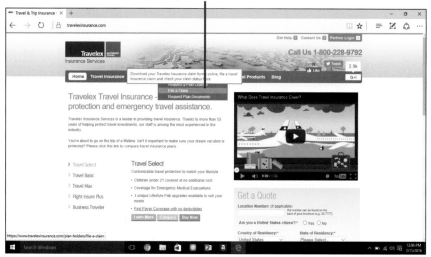

Based on the type of claim you are filing, you will be required to provide completed forms provided by the insurance company, as well as related documentation (medical bills, letters from medical professionals, police reports, and so on) and receipts for expenses incurred. Failure to provide everything that's requested will result in delays in the processing of your claim—or the inability to process your claim altogether.

Once all of the correct paperwork has been submitted with your claim, based on the insurance company, allow 7 to 30 days for the claim to be reviewed. You can check the status of the claim any time by visiting the company's website or by calling its customer service phone number.

Keep Detailed Records

If you need to file a claim with your travel insurance provider, be sure to keep detailed notes of all related information, including a timeline, what actions were taken, who you spoke with (doctors, police officers, witnesses, and so on), and what expenses you incurred. Also, be sure to obtain a copy of any printed police, hospital, or accident reports that were created. The more information you gather in advance, the easier it will be to reconstruct the events when filing a claim. Also keep a record of communications you have with the insurance company—whom you spoke with, when, and what their representatives said.

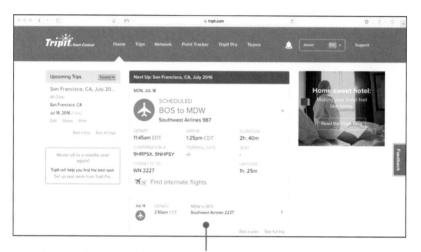

Use an online service like TripIt.com (or the TripIt mobile app) to manage all aspects of your travel itinerary.

This chapter introduces you to websites and mobile apps that you can use to manage all aspects of your travel itinerary. You'll learn about

→ Online services and mobile apps used to create, manage, and share your travel itinerary

→ Tools for solo travelers who want to meet other solo travelers

Services for Managing Travel Itineraries

Anytime you book a flight, accommodations, or rental car using an online travel service or a specific website or mobile app from an airline, hotel, or rental car company, it's possible to manage those aspects of your travel itinerary through the website or mobile app where you made the booking. In addition, online services and mobile apps, such as Travefy and TripIt.com, let you manage all aspects of a trip itinerary from a single website or mobile app. With these services, you can easily share an entire itinerary (or portions of it) with specific other people. Services like Travefy and TripIt.com also allow you to store and manage multiple itineraries at the same time.

>>>*Go Further*

DON'T OVERSCHEDULE YOUR TRIPS

Many people discover that their fondest and most exciting travel experiences are the ones that weren't planned but that just happened, so be sure to leave time in your schedule for spontaneity.

Instead of planning how you'll spend every minute of every day, consider planning your time in morning, afternoon, and evening chunks. This gives you time to fit in unplanned activities that you discover during your travels, or spend more time engaged in activities you're thoroughly enjoying.

Also, when you're planning multiple activities in a single day, allow ample time to travel between those activities. Ultimately, if you overplan your time so that you can see and do everything possible, but you encounter an unexpected delay, you'll find yourself stressed out and rushing to get back on schedule. This takes away from the overall travel experience.

Mobile Apps for Managing Your Travel Itineraries

In the app store for your device, you can find a handful of smartphone and tablet mobile apps to manage your travel itineraries and share details about your travel-related plans with other people.

The sharing functionality offered by these mobile apps comes in handy when you're having someone pick you up at the airport, when you're traveling with a group of people, or when those staying at home want to know where you are.

These same mobile apps allow you to easily track aspects of your trips; receive automatic alerts of flight delays or cancellations, airplane gate changes, or weather problems that could impact your travel; or generate alarms to remind you of check-in times at airlines, hotels, rental car companies, tours, or activities.

The following sections cover five mobile apps that I like to use for itinerary management. To find others, visit the app store for your device. In the Search field, type **travel itinerary** or **travel planner**.

Drift

When it comes to planning how you'll spend your time during a trip, the free Drift app for the iPhone/iPad offers a simple tool that helps you create a plan and navigate between activities. The app keeps track of where you're going and where you've been. It's a scheduling, research, and navigation tool that can help you make the most of your time during any trip.

When you first launch the app, select a destination. Then, use the Search tool to look up points of interests, attractions, businesses, or restaurants that you want to visit. The app uses the Internet to look up details about each activity you discover and displays pertinent information on the screen. Then, for each item, tap the Add to Schedule button to include it in your itinerary for the date you select.

Find things to do, and then add those activities to your itinerary.

Excursion

With Excursion, you can select a destination and then use built-in tools to help you discover what there is to see and do in that area. Using search filters, you can quickly browse through categories—such as Attractions, Nightlife, or Food & Drink—find what you want to experience, and then place these items into your virtual itinerary, which you manage in the app on your smartphone or tablet.

The Excursion app also has a social component for travelers to write reviews, travel tips, and itineraries that are shared with the online community. Thanks to the Share tools, it's easy to create your travel itinerary and then email it to specific people, or post your plans on social media sites, like Facebook.

After you've selected how you want to spend your time, the Excursion app displays the locations of your destinations on detailed maps (which can be viewed offline) to help you navigate.

After installing the Excursion app, create a free account (or log in to the service via the app using your Facebook account details). Next, tap the Make A New Plan or List. When prompted, enter your destination (city, state, country), and then tap the Attractions, Activities, Food & Drink, Coffee, Nightlife, Shopping, Sleep, or Transport buttons to start researching how you can spend your time. Once an itinerary is created, you're able to give it a custom name.

Each time you tap a listing, you see detailed information about it. Tap the Add to Plan button for any listing to include it on your itinerary. After you've added multiple activities to your itinerary, it's easy to move them around and more precisely plan out your time. Use the Plan Route feature, which can help you figure out the most efficient routes to take between activities.

As of summer 2016, Excursion was available exclusively for iOS mobile devices, although an Android version was in development.

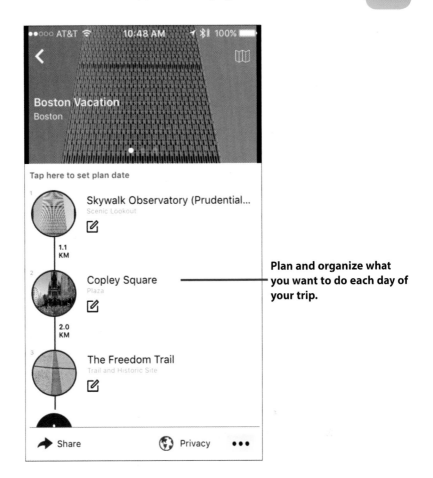

Plan and organize what you want to do each day of your trip.

FlightTrack 5

FlightTrack 5, available for iOS and Android, is a full-featured tool for managing all flight-related information pertaining to one or more separate itineraries. The app also helps users handle tasks like tracking flights, and viewing alerts when an upcoming flight is delayed, cancelled, or has a gate change.

Using the Share tools, it's easy to share flight details with others, which is useful if someone is picking you up at the airport, for example.

Sygic Travel: Trip Planner

Available for Android devices, this free personal trip planner app allows you to choose a destination for your trip, discover places to visit (such as tourist attractions and landmarks), and plan each day of your itinerary. While you're traveling, you can use it to help you navigate from place to place. This app works with Fodor's travel guides for a handful of major cities around the world, plus it gathers information from the Internet.

Sygic lets you download your itinerary, maps, and related information, and store it on the smartphone or tablet, so it's readily available for offline viewing if you're traveling abroad and don't have Internet access. It's also possible to print your itineraries and create PDF files from them so you can view them on other devices.

Also built in to the app is the ability to obtain current weather forecasts for where you'll be visiting, time and distance calculators to help you plan your travel time between activities more efficiently, and templates that make it easier to create your itineraries.

To get started using the app, you must set up a free account.

Trip Boss Travel Manager

In addition to helping users plan and organize their daily itinerary prior to and during a trip, this $9.99 app, for iOS devices, offers an integrated expense tracker component, so it's easy to keep track of spending and manage a trip budget.

Using the navigation tools built in to the app, you can determine the most efficient way to plan your activities based on their locations. Then you can make your way between locations using interactive maps.

The app includes a tool for splitting restaurant bills and calculating tips, a travel time calculator, and a currency converter.

Maintain a Digital Travel Diary

The app developer that created Trip Boss Travel Manager offers a separate app called Journal: Trip Boss Travel Manager, which is an itinerary-planning tool with an integrated digital diary. It allows users to chronicle their travel adventures. You can also find many other digital diary apps in both the App Store (iOS) or Google Play Store (Android) so you can create journal entries that combine text, digital photos, and audio or video clips to chronicle your travel adventures.

Read Chapter 15, "Chronicle and Share Your Experiences," to learn about the Moleskine Voyage travel journal, which nicely integrates a traditional paper-based journal with the digital world.

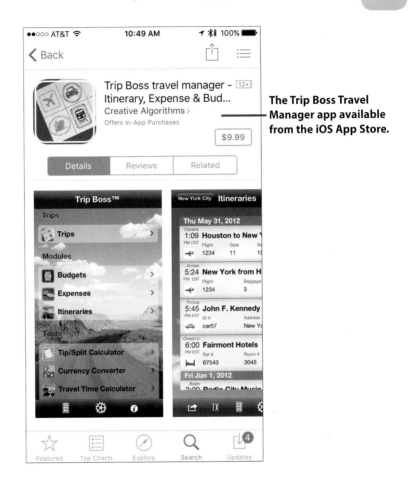

The Trip Boss Travel Manager app available from the iOS App Store.

TripCase

This iPhone/iPad and Android mobile app (which offers smartwatch integration) allows you to store all your flight, accommodation, rental car, activity, tour, and other travel confirmations and details in one place. Then during your trip, the app will alert you of upcoming check ins and provide real-time flight information.

After you arrive at your destination, the TripCase app can help you discover what's available near you, call an Uber car, and share your itinerary details with other people.

After you set up a free TripCase app using your existing email address, anytime you receive a confirmation email from an airline, hotel, rental car company, or any other travel provider, simply forward it trips@tripcase.com. It will recognize your email address and automatically import the confirmation details into the app, so manual entry of travel details is seldom required.

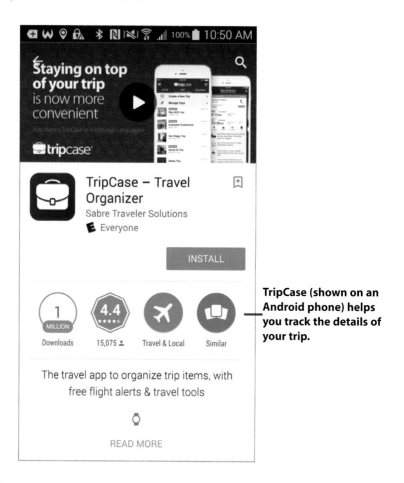

TripCase (shown on an Android phone) helps you track the details of your trip.

>>>Go Further

CREATE A NICELY FORMATTED TRAVEL ITINERARY USING MICROSOFT WORD

If you're coordinating a trip for a group, such as your extended family or a handful of friends, one easy way to manually create a well-organized, shareable itinerary is to create it in Microsoft Word using a free travel itinerary template.

From the SampleWords.com website (www.samplewords.com/travel-itinerary-template) download the travel template. Open the template in Word and fill it in with all your travel information. What you wind up with is an easy-to-read, and nicely formatted document that you can print or share electronically with others.

Travel Itinerary Management Options for Your Computer

The following is a selection of travel itinerary managers that are available for your computer or a mobile device with Internet access. To access any of them, instead of using an app, you'll use your computer or mobile device's web browser to visit the service's website.

Travefy

You can create and organize your itinerary using the free online Travefy service (www.travefy.com). After you've created an itinerary, you can sync and view it with a mobile device via the free Travefy Personal Itinerary Viewer app.

Travefy is designed for group travel planning. After you create an itinerary, you can invite the people you'll be traveling with to contribute to and view it. Trafey online offers a chat feature, so the people you'll be traveling with can participate in text conversations as the itinerary is being created.

To begin using this service, visit the Travefy website and set up a free account. Then, follow the directions offered in the next section to create an itinerary for an upcoming trip.

Click the Discover icon, select your destination city, and then click the Hotels, Activities, Food & Drink, or Vacation Rentals to discover what there is to see and do, as well as where you can stay. As you discover listings you want to incorporate into your itinerary, simply click the Add to Itinerary button.

Travefy integrates with services like TripAdvisor, so you can read reviews of activities, tours, attractions, and accommodations. It also integrates with Trivago.com, so it's possible to find and book accommodations, and often save money in the process. (Refer to Chapter 7, "Finding and Booking Accommodations," for more information about Trivago.com.)

Another way that Travefy is useful for planning group travel is the Collect & Pay for Expenses tool. This tool enables the primary trip planner to calculate how trip-related expenses should be divided among the travelers, and it then keeps track of who has paid what and when they paid.

Manage Your Travefy Account

After you create a free Travefy account from the website, click the Your Account option to personalize your account by adding your photo. To do this, click the Profile option on the Your Account menu. Click the Wallet option to link a credit or debit card to the account. When you have payment information linked to the account you can quickly book and pay for activities and/or accommodations while using the service's built-in research tools. Click on the Trips option to create, switch between, and manage multiple itineraries, or view past itineraries.

After you have created an itinerary using the Travefy website from your computer, install the Travefy mobile app and sign in to the app using your existing Travefy account information. Your itinerary will automatically sync with your smartphone or tablet, so you can view and access the information while on the go.

Manage and Share Travel Itineraries Using Travefy

To begin using the free Travefy.com service from your Windows PC or Mac computer (shown), follow these steps:

(1) Launch your favorite web browser, and type **www.travefy.com** in the address field.

(2) Click the Personal option near the top-right corner of the browser window, and then click the Start Planning button.

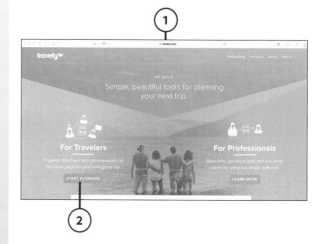

(3) If you do not already have an account, click Create a Free Travefy Account option and provide the requested information. You'll then be signed in to the service automatically.

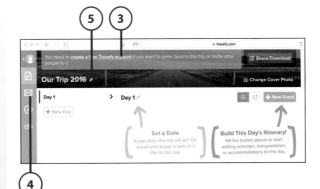

(4) Click the Invite Collaborators button to invite specific people you'll be traveling with to have access to the itinerary and chat room associated with it. Provide each invitee's email address, and he or she will receive an email invitation to become part of the online group.

(5) Click the pencil-shaped icon and create a custom name for the itinerary, such as Family Reunion Trip 2017. If you want, further customize the appearance of the itinerary by clicking the Change Cover Photo option, and select a digital photo that's stored on your computer that you want to display.

(6) Click the Day 1 heading and enter the specific date that represents the first day of your trip. Otherwise, the default is "Day 1."

(7) Click the +New Day button once for each extra day you want to add. These will be referred to as Day 2, Day 3, and so on. If you entered a start date for the trip in step 6, the additional days you add automatically display the appropriate dates.

(8) Select a day for which you want to plan an event and then click on the +New Event button.

(9) Select between the Activity, Lodging, Flight, Ground Transportation, or Cruise option to categorize the event.

(10) Enter the pertinent details for the event, starting with a title for the event.

Adding Formatting and Attachments

In the Notes section for each event, you can add bold text, bulleted lists, numbered lists, or website hyperlinks. It's also possible to add attachment files—such as photos, confirmation letters, or documents—to each event by clicking the Upload a File button.

(11) Click the Done Editing button to store the new event in your itinerary.

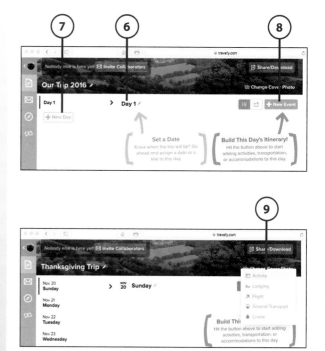

12 Once a listing is created and placed in a Day, you can drag it around to adjust the order of multiple events. Click the Rearrange option and then drag an event listing up or down (in a day's itinerary), or drag it into another day altogether.

13 Add as many separate New Events as you want in each day of the itinerary.

14 Chat via text messages with other people invited into your group.

15 Click the Discover button and type your destination city to find and research hotels, activities, restaurants, or vacation rentals.

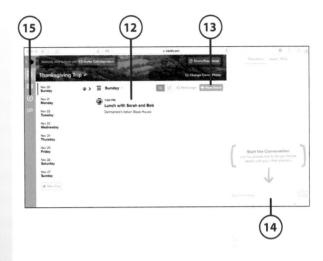

16 Click the Hotels, Activities, Food & Drink, or Vacation Rentals option to narrow the search results. Click any of the search results to view a detailed information screen about item.

17 In some cases, you'll be able to book your reservations right from the Travefy service and have that reservation added to your itinerary. Alternatively, click a listing, and then tap on the Add to Itinerary button to add it to your itinerary. (Not shown.)

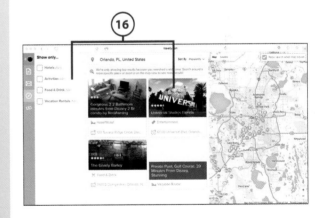

(18) Click the Share/Download to share your itinerary with your mobile device, your own computer(s), or with other people.

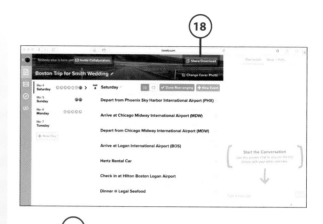

Working with Your Itinerary

Before and during actual trip, you can view, edit, print, and share your itinerary. After your trip, the itinerary is archived. Use the command icons displayed along the left margin of the screen when viewing the Trips menu.

(19) Click the Your Account option, and select the Trips option from the Your Account menu to access past itineraries.

(20) Launch the Travefy mobile app on your smartphone or tablet (shown here on the iPhone), sign in to your Travefy account, and be able to access, view, and share your itineraries while you're on the go.

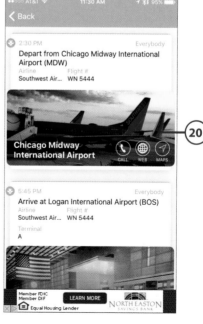

TripIt

TripIt is both an online service that can be accessed from any computer's web browser and a full-featured mobile app that works with the iPhone, iPad, and Android devices. TripIt.com offers a comprehensive tool for managing all aspects of a travel itinerary, including flights, accommodations, and rental cars.

Each time you compile an itinerary, the service organizes and displays everything by date and time, and syncs the information between your devices, as well as any calendar or scheduling software or mobile app you use.

After you set up a TripIt account, forward your confirmation emails from airlines, accommodations, and rental cars, for example, to plans@TripIt.com. TripIt recognizes your email address and imports the details into your travel itinerary. It's possible to simultaneously manage multiple itineraries at once and give a unique name to each.

Using the service's Share tools, you can share your entire itinerary (or parts of it) with specific people via text message or email, or publish aspects of your itinerary on social media services, like Facebook. TripIt.com also integrates nicely with other apps, like Flight Track 5, the Calendar app that comes preinstalled on all Macs and iOS mobile devices, and Outlook for Windows PCs, for example.

Manage flight (shown here), rental car, and accommodation details for one or more itineraries using TripIt.com.

TripIt.com's basic functionality is free, but if you want to take advantage of all of the travel-related tools the service and mobile app offer, you need to purchase a TripIt Pro account for $49.00 per year.

Among the additional tools offered to TripIt Pro users are the ability to get real-time flight alerts and notifications. In other words, you're automatically alerted of upcoming check-in times, and then the app tracks your flight information in real time, so you're alerted to delays, cancellations, and gate changes. You're also given the ability to find alternative flights (if your original flight gets cancelled), plus track frequent flyer and loyalty program points.

To begin using TripIt, set up a free account by visiting www.tripit.com from your computer's web browser. Or if you're using a smartphone or tablet, download and install the free TripIt mobile app and set up your account there.

Ways to Meet Fellow Solo Travelers

If you enjoy venturing out on your own and traveling solo but you enjoy meeting and interacting with other travelers, a handful of mobile apps can help with the initial introductions. Try one of these mobile apps:

- **BadooFly:** This app, when used with an Internet-connected mobile device, finds and displays details about the people around you who are also using the app. You're then able to see each person's profile and initiate a text-based chat from within the app. With more than 300 million registered users, if you're traveling in a popular city, you're apt to find others who are using the app and looking to interact with fellow travelers.

- **FlipTheTrip:** Use this iOS app to choose your destination and enter your trip dates, and then meet locals and fellow travelers by browsing through their profiles. You can then connect with those people through the app and perhaps set up an in-person meeting.

- **Ship Mate:** If you're traveling on a cruise ship, the Ship Mate app allows you to see profiles of other people on your ship who have checked in via the app for your sailing dates. With the app, you can communicate with those people via text messaging prior to and, if you have Wi-Fi, during a cruise. This same app also offers built-in tools for managing your cruise itinerary, booking independent shore excursions, and viewing deck maps of the various cruise ships.

- **SoloTraveller:** Like FlipTheTrip, SoloTraveller is an app-based social network that helps you find other people near you, view their profiles, and communicate with them via in-app text messaging. You can then opt to go sightseeing, take a tour, dine, or share ground transportation. The app takes advantage of your smartphone or tablet's GPS capabilities to determine your location and display detailed maps identifying the locations of other users.

- **Tripr:** By taking advantage of the GPS capabilities built in to your Internet-connected smartphone or tablet, this iOS app allows you to find and interact with people near you. Use this information to share travel tips, arrange meet ups, and explore together. Before leaving on your trip, manually enter your destination and travel dates to see profiles of other people who will be visiting that area when you are. You can then communicate via in-app text messaging.

It's Not All Good

Use Common Sense When Meeting Strangers

Using any of the apps designed to help you meet total strangers while you're traveling should go against everything you were taught as a child about speaking to strangers. If you opt to communicate, interact with, and potentially meet strangers during your travels, always use common sense. For example, meet strangers in a public place, and avoid sharing any personal or financial information with them.

While you may have good intentions, others may try to use the opportunity to target you for identify theft or other criminal activity, so always use caution.

>>>*Go Further*

USING FACEBOOK'S CHECK-IN FEATURE TO FIND PEOPLE NEARBY

Built in to the Facebook mobile app is a feature called Check-In. When you use it, details about your current location are shared in real-time with other Facebook users. Keep in mind that when you publish your current whereabouts online, people will know you're not home, or could potentially find you at your current location.

Depending on how you adjust the Facebook Privacy Settings (www.facebook.com/about/basics/what-others-see-about-you), it's possible to make your Check-In locations searchable by your existing Facebook friends. This allows people to know where you are, and then make contact with you to arrange a meet up, for example.

To see which of your Facebook friends are located nearby (based on their most recent Check-Ins), from the Facebook mobile app, tap the More menu option, and then tap the Nearby Friends option. Doing this displays a list of friends who have recently used the Check-In feature, so you can see their last Check-In location.

To find Nearby Places, sorted by category, such as Restaurants, Coffee Shops, Nightlife, Outdoors Attractions, Hotels, or Shopping, from the Facebook mobile app, tap the More menu icon, tap the Nearby Places option, and then select a category. Options close to your current location are displayed. Click any listing to view a detailed information screen, read reviews (if applicable), and find nearby events (if applicable).

When you're viewing an information screen related to a listing, tap the People tab to see a list of Facebook users (potentially strangers) who have recently checked in at that location.

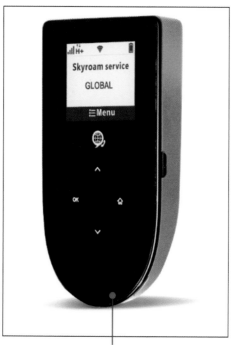

The Skyroam personal Wi-Fi hotspot

This chapter shows you the different ways you can stay connected to the Internet from your computer and mobile devices while you're traveling. You'll learn

→ How a cellular data (3G/4G/LTE) and a Wi-Fi Internet connection differ
→ When connecting to a Wi-Fi hotspot can be useful
→ How to take advantage of a personal Wi-Fi hotspot

Connecting Your Computer, Smartphone, or Tablet While Traveling

Now that you're becoming savvy about using your gadgets to plan and manage your travel, you're going to want to take advantage of travel tools and resources while you're away from home. Doing this requires Internet access.

Internet Access Is Typically Required

Many of the tools and resources you've learned about thus far in this book require Internet connectivity to be fully functional. This chapter covers some of the more cost-effective ways to obtain Internet access while traveling.

If you're staying in your home country, chances are the cellular plan for your smartphone allows you to connect to the Internet via your cellular service provider's cellular data network from just about anywhere. You also can make and receive calls or send and receive text messages from anywhere in the country. Of course, you can supplement this connectivity (and conserve your cellular data usage, often saving you money) by taking advantage of Wi-Fi hotspots in airports, hotels, restaurants/cafes, tourist attractions, libraries, and other public areas.

If you're using a computer or tablet that offers only Wi-Fi Internet connectivity, it's possible to connect to the Internet from any public Wi-Fi hotspot. You also can create your own hotspot almost anywhere in the world using your smartphone or a personal Wi-Fi hotspot device (which is covered later in this chapter).

Meanwhile, when it comes to making international calls from your smartphone, you also have a handful of options, some of which are free.

>>>Go Further
CONNECT YOUR COMPUTER TO THE INTERNET

To connect your computer to the Internet while you're traveling, you must find and use a Wi-Fi hotspot in a hotel, airport, café, or wherever you can find one.

You also have two other options. First, depending on your cellular service provider, you might be able to create a personal Wi-Fi hotspot using the cellular data connection from your smartphone. When you do this you can connect one or more Wi-Fi devices to the wireless personal network you create, but you will use up your monthly cellular data allocation a lot faster (and possibly incur international data roaming fees) when you do this.

Another option is to purchase a portable battery-powered personal Wi-Fi hotspot device. This device connects to a local cellular data network and establishes a password-protected wireless Wi-Fi hotspot that your computer and other Wi-Fi-compatible devices (such as your tablet or eBook reader) can connect to.

See the section called "Taking Advantage of a Personal Wi-Fi Hotspot," later in this chapter for more information about how to use either of these options.

If you'll be traveling abroad, you might need to purchase a power converter for your computer, so you'll be able to plug it into a local outlet to power the computer and recharge its batteries.

For Apple MacBook or MacBook Air users, the World Travel Adapter Kit is available from Apple Stores or Apple.com for $29.00 (www.apple.com/shop/product/MD837AM/A/apple-world-travel-adapter-kit).

For a Windows PC computer, international power adapters are available from office supply stores, computer stores, Brookstone (or Brookstone.com), or many shops in airports.

Cellular Data Versus Wi-Fi from Your Mobile Device

When you're in the coverage area of your cellular service provider, your cellular service plan for your smartphone includes talk, text, and cellular data service. The name of your provider is displayed at the top of your device's screen (shown in the figure on an iPhone that's connected to AT&T Wireless). Depending on your plan, you might have unlimited talk and texting, plus a monthly wireless data allocation of 1GB, 5GB, or 10GB.

Signal strength bars and cellular service

It's Not All Good

When in Rome, You Might Be Roaming

When using your smartphone in your home country, the name of your cellular service provider, along with signal strength bars, are displayed along the top of the screen when the device is turned on and connected to the cellular service.

If you're an AT&T Wireless subscriber, for example, but you go outside AT&T Wireless' coverage area in the United States, the name of another cellular service may be displayed at the top of your smartphone's screen. This means you are roaming (and pay extra for service).

If no cellular company's name appears near the top of the screen, and no signal strength bars are displayed, you're outside of any coverage area, and the phone's calling, texting, and cellular data Internet won't work until a connection to a cellular service provider is re-established.

Even if you're not within a cellular network's coverage area, however, you can still turn on your device's Wi-Fi feature, find a public Wi-Fi hotspot, and then connect to the Internet via a Wi-Fi connection. There is no charge to do this from your cellular service provider, unless the local Wi-Fi hotspot provider charges an access fee.

If the Wi-Fi hotspot charges an access fee, you'll either be prompted for a password (which you'll need to acquire from the hotspot operator) or you'll automatically be directed to a web page that instructs you to purchase online time by the minute, hour, or day. At this point, you can opt to pay the access fee or seek out a free hotspot elsewhere.

Whenever you go outside your cellular service provider's coverage area, your smartphone automatically roams, which costs extra. If you travel abroad, international roaming charges can apply. You could wind up spending between $.50 and $4.99 per minute to talk, between $.50 and $2.00 per text message, and up to $20.00 per megabyte (MB) for cellular data usage.

There are several ways to avoid these high international roaming charges:

- Contact your cellular service provider before you leave the country to sign up for a prepaid international roaming plan that offers discounted rates. The rates vary based on which countries you plan to visit. The following are the international roaming information websites for the major U.S.-based cellular service providers:

  - AT&T Wireless (www.att.com/shop/wireless/international.html)

  - Verizon Wireless (www.verizonwireless.com/landingpages/ international-travel)

  - Sprint PCS (http://shop.sprint.com/mysprint/services_solutions/ category.jsp?catId=service_international)

  - T-Mobile (www.t-mobile.com/optional-services/international.html)

Ways to Avoid International Roaming Charges

As you'll discover, as a traveler, you have a handful of options to help reduce or eliminate international roaming charges when you use your smartphone or tablet abroad. The following are some of the most popular options:

- **Purchase a SIM Chip Before You Leave**—Many online services sell prepaid SIM chips for smartphones or tablets that you can order before you leave home. In the international terminals of most U.S. airports are kiosks or electronics stores that also sell SIM chips for international use. To find companies that sell prepaid SIM chips, use your web browser to search for *prepaid SIM for Travel*. Simcorner.com, Telestial.com, Worldsim.com, and WorldTravelSim.com are websites that sell prepaid SIM chips. As you shop these sites, compare rates and make sure you acquire a SIM chip that's compatible with your mobile device.

- **Purchase a No-Contract, Pay As You Go SIM Chip When You Arrive**—When you get to the country you'll be visiting, you can purchase a no-contract, pay-as-you-go or pre-paid SIM chip for your unlocked smartphone, and pay local rates to use the phone for calls, texting, and cellular data Internet access. When you do this you're assigned a new local phone number to your smartphone, which you'll use until you replace your original SIM chip and return home.

- **Purchase a No-Contract, Pay-as-You Go Smartphone When You Arrive**—You can also purchase a prepaid cellular phone in the country you're visiting, and pay local rates to use it. Airport shops, local cell phone stores, consumer electronics stores, and, in some cases, local convenience stores will sell these low-cost smartphones that are ready to use.

- **Rely Only on Using Wi-Fi Hotspots**—Seek out and connect to free Wi-Fi hotspots where you travel. You can use your smartphone or tablet for text messaging and accessing the Internet, plus use a Voice-Over-IP (Internet-based) calling service to make and receive calls via the Internet. Skype (www.skype.com) or the Skype mobile app (or a service like it) allow you to do this easily. Facebook also allows you to communicate with other Facebook users, for free, via messaging, email, audio calling, or video calling. If you're an Apple user, you can use FaceTime to make and receive audio or video calls via the Internet, for free, from anywhere in the world.

To avoid unwanted international roaming charges when traveling overseas, place your phone into Airplane mode, and then turn on just the Wi-Fi feature. Or, if you want to be able to make and receive calls and text messages but not use cellular data to access the Internet, turn off the phone's Cellular Data Roaming option:

- On an iPhone, launch Settings, tap the Cellular option, tap Cellular Data Options, and then turn off the switch associated with Data Roaming.

- On an Android smartphone, launch Settings, tap the Data Usage option, tap the International Data Roaming option, and then make sure International Data and Enhanced 4G LTE Services are turned off. Do this by removing the check mark from the respective check box for each feature. This process might vary slightly based on the make and model of the Android device you're using.

International Roaming

By default, if you simply leave your home country and attempt to use your smartphone, chances are it will automatically connect to a local cellular service provider wherever you happen to be. You'll be able to make and receive calls and text messages, but you will pay high international roaming fees.

Depending on your cellular service provider, you might need to call your provider before you leave the country to ask to have the international roaming features turned on.

If you plan to use your smartphone overseas and rely on international roaming, be sure to prepurchase an international roaming plan for the duration of your trip by contacting your cellular service provider, or plan on using one of the other options described in this chapter.

Prepaid Sim Chips

Every smartphone—as well as tablets with cellular data connectivity—use a special SIM chip to access a cellular service provider. When you remove this SIM chip from your mobile device, and replace it with a SIM chip purchased in the country you're visiting, your mobile device is assigned a new phone number, and you pay local rates to make and receive calls, send and receive text messages, and access a local cellular data network.

How to Remove and Replace a SIM Chip

Based on the make and model of the mobile device you're using, locate the SIM card slot on your device. On an iPhone or iPad, for example, it's located on the side of the device. To open this slot, use a thin, unbent paperclip or the tool provided with your device. Insert the tool into the slot's hole and press gently. The card slot will open, and the SIM card tray will pop out, allowing you to insert a new SIM card or remove and replace the existing SIM card. Once the new SIM card is inserted into the tray, place it back into the card slot and press it in gently to lock it into place.

Make sure you acquire the correct size SIM card for your mobile device, and that you insert the card in the proper direction in the tray. Never force the card into the tray, or the tray into the card slot. Any cellular phone store can help you with this process.

You can purchase a prepaid SIM chip or a pay-as-you go SIM chip that will remain active for the length of your trip but that does not require a long-term contract or have automatically recurring monthly charges. How much you'll pay for this option depends on what the prepaid or pay-as-you-go plan includes in terms of talk minutes, text messages, and cellular data usage.

If you want to keep your existing smartphone as it is, you also have the option of purchasing a second smartphone locally in the country you're visiting, which comes with a pre-paid SIM chip already installed. This option will be a bit more expensive than simply acquiring a SIM chip for your existing (unlocked) smartphone or tablet. (Check with your cellular service provider to determine if you have an unlocked smartphone, or need to have it unlocked prior to your trip.)

Some Apple Mobile Devices Have a Universal Apple SIM Chip

Some Apple iPhones and iPads come with an Apple SIM chip preinstalled. When you leave your home network's coverage area, you're automatically given the option to purchase a pay-as-you-go or pre-paid cellular plan within the country you're visiting, without having to swap the SIM chip.

Wi-Fi Options for Making and Receiving Calls

As long as your smartphone or tablet has Wi-Fi Internet access, it's possible to use a service like Google Hangouts, Google Voice, MagicApp, Skype, Talk U, UppTalk, Voxofon, Viber, WePhone, or WeTalk or a service like FaceTime or Facebook to make and receive voice-over-IP (VoIP) audio or video calls, plus send and receive text messages, without using a cellular data connection. Many of these services are free, or charge just a few cents per minute of talk time when making or receiving international calls.

Wi-Fi Hotspots

All smartphones, tablets, and computers have the ability to connect to the Internet via a Wi-Fi connection. This is a wireless connection that allows the computer or device to connect to a signal generated by a wireless router that's connected to a modem, which then connects to the Internet in the location you're in.

A Wi-Fi hotspot has a signal radius of less than 100 feet, so if you move outside of the signal coverage area, your connection to the Internet will be lost. The good news is that when you travel, you'll discover Wi-Fi hotspots are pretty easy to find. When you use a Wi-Fi hotspot, it does not use up any of your cellular plan's cellular data allocation (if applicable), plus the Internet connection through a Wi-Fi hotspot is typically faster than using a 3G, 4G, or LTE cellular data connection.

Public Wi-Fi Hotspots

Public Wi-Fi hotspots can often be found in airports, hotel lobbies, fast food restaurants, coffee shops, Internet cafes, bookstores, libraries, and some tourist attractions. In many cases, access to a public Wi-Fi hotspot is free and does not require a special password.

Some hotels, restaurants, and local businesses, however, offer free access to their Wi-Fi hotspot only to customers. In this case, you have to have a special password and enter it when you attempt to connect to that hotspot.

Some places, such as hotels and Internet cafés, may charge a per-minute, per-hour, or daily fee to access their Wi-Fi hotspot. As you're choosing a hotel, consider whether it offers free in-room Wi-Fi to guests.

In-Flight Wi-Fi

More and more major airlines and trains provide Wi-Fi capabilities, which passengers can access from their computers, smartphones, or tablets free or for a fixed rate. This Internet connection is typically much slower than a regular Internet connection, and popular video streaming and calling services—such as Apple Music, FaceTime, Google Voice, Hulu, Netflix, Pandora, Skype, and Spotify—are typically blocked.

Plan on spending between $10.00 and $30.00 per flight (or per day) for in-flight Internet access, when it's available.

Access Aboard a Cruise Ship

Cruise ships all over the world now offer Internet access. Ships that use older wireless Internet services charge a hefty fee (up to $.75 per minute) for a very slow Wi-Fi Internet connection. But more and more ships are equipped with much faster speed Internet, allowing the cruise ships to offer unlimited Wi-Fi access per day, or for the duration of the cruise, for a fixed rate.

Plan on spending upwards of $30.00 per day for a daily cruise ship Internet plan. If you prepurchase an unlimited Wi-Fi plan for the length of your cruise, the rate often drops to around $10.00 to $15.00 per day, per device.

It's Not All Good

Beware of Cellular at Sea Charges

While at sea, your device may connect to the Cellular at Sea service that allows you to make and receive calls, send and receive text messages, and access a satellite-based cellular data network. Unless you've prepurchased a discounted plan from your home cellular service provider for Cellular at Sea, this service has higher rates than typical international roaming rates.

To avoid excessive Cellular at Sea charges, refrain from using your cellular capabilities for calls, texts, or Internet access while you're aboard a cruise ship, unless you're connecting only to the ship's Wi-Fi Internet via a paid Wi-Fi plan or have prepurchased a discounted Cellular at Sea plan. Make sure your smartphone or tablet is in Airplane mode and then turn on the Wi-Fi feature to connect to the ship's onboard Wi-Fi.

Taking Advantage of a Personal Wi-Fi Hotspot

A Wi-Fi hotspot can be created by a smartphone, tablet, or a standalone device that has 3G/4G/LTE cellular connectivity. These standalone devices that create a Wi-Fi hotspot using a cellular Internet connection are called personal

Wi-Fi hotspots, and they've become one of the most sought-after tools for international travelers. These devices are small and battery powered and offer quick, low-cost Internet access from hundreds of countries around the world.

If your cellular service provider allows you to transform your smartphone or tablet into a password-protected, personal Wi-Fi hotspot, that device will generate its own Wi-Fi hotspot signal that uses a cellular data connection for Internet access. Thus, if you have a cellular data usage allocation, when you connect other devices to your personal Wi-Fi hotspot, that cellular data allocation will get used faster. Keep in mind that if you're creating and using a personal Wi-Fi hotspot while traveling abroad, costly international cellular data roaming rates will apply.

Create a Personal Wi-Fi Hotspot Using Your iPhone or iPad

Use your iPhone or iPad (that's linked with a cellular service provider that allows it) to create and turn on a personal Wi-Fi hotspot.

 From your iPhone's Home screen, launch Settings.

② Tap the Personal Hotspot option from the main Settings menu.

3 Turn on the virtual switch associated with the Personal Hotspot option, and then set a Wi-Fi password, which you'll use to access this newly created hotspot from your other devices. (In some cases, a default password is created for you, but you can change it to something you're more apt to remember.)

4 When the Personal Hotspot feature is active, when you search for Wi-Fi networks in your immediate area from another device, such as your iPad, notebook computer, or an eBook reader, a password-protected hotspot that uses the name of your smartphone will be listed. Select it and enter the password you created. (Shown here, an iPad is connected to a personal Wi-Fi hotspot called Jason R. Rich's iPhone 6s ,which is being generated by a nearby iPhone.)

Tap here to set password.

Create a Personal Wi-Fi Hotspot Using Your Android Device

Use your Android smartphone or tablet (that's linked with a cellular service provider that allows it) to create and turn on a personal Wi-Fi hotspot.

(1) From the Home screen, launch
Settings. (Not shown.)

(2) Tap the Connections tab.

(3) Tap Tethering and Wi-Fi Hotspot.

(4) Tap Mobile Hotspot.

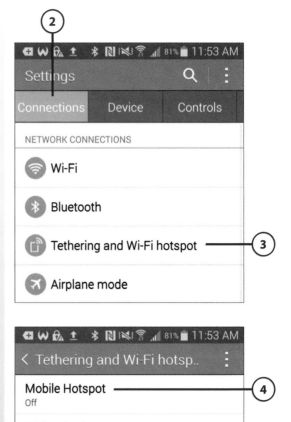

(5) Turn on the virtual switch associated with Mobile Hotspot. Assuming your mobile device has cellular Internet access and your cellular service provider allows it, a personal password-protected Wi-Fi hotspot will be created.

(6) From your other Wi-Fi devices, search for nearby Wi-Fi networks, and select the one associated with your Android device. When prompted, enter the password for the personal Wi-Fi hotspot that was created by your Android device, or that you were prompted to create when turning on this feature. When your other Wi-Fi devices are linked to the personal Wi-Fi hotspot, any access to the Internet will use some of your cellular data plan's usage allocation. (Not shown.)

Saving screenshot...

< Mobile Hotspot   OFF   — (5)

☐ Samsung GALAXY Note4 2603
Allow all devices to connect.

HELP

Use your device as a Mobile Hotspot to share Wi-Fi with up to 10 devices. Manage access to your Mobile Hotspot by creating a list of allowed devices. Remember to connect your device to a power outlet because Mobile Hotspot consumes more battery. Mobile Hotspot uses mobile data and can result in additional charges.

Purchase a Personal Wi-Fi Hotspot Device

Instead of using the cellular connection built into your smartphone or tablet to create a personal Wi-Fi hotspot, another option (which is often less costly, especially when traveling abroad) is to purchase a separate personal Wi-Fi hotspot device.

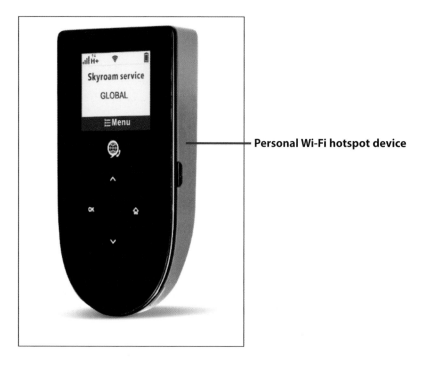

Personal Wi-Fi hotspot device

Personal Wi-Fi hotspot devices are battery-powered and about the size and weight of a pack of cigarettes. They have a SIM chip installed that allows them to connect to a local 3G/4G/LTE cellular data network wherever you are. After the cellular connection is established by the device, a password protected Wi-Fi signal is generated, and you can use it to connect your Wi-Fi devices to the Internet.

There are two types of personal Wi-Fi hotspot devices. One works in the United States, and you pay a flat monthly fee for a predetermined amount of wireless data usage (typically 5GB or 10GB per month).

A second option, which is ideal for travelers, is a personal Wi-Fi hotspot device that costs less than $150.00 from a company that has roaming deals established with cellular service providers around the world.

Skyroam Personal Wi-Fi Hotspot Alternatives

In addition to Skyroam, there are a handful of companies that sell personal Wi-Fi hotspot devices, as well as flat fee cellular data service that works around the world. For example, a company called GlocalMe (www.glocalme.com) sells a device that allows users to prepurchase flat-rate data packages that can be used in a one-year period.

Depending on which country its being used in, a 1GB data package (good for 365 days) costs between $10.00 and $30.00.

To find other options for personal Wi-Fi hotspot devices, using any web browser, type **personal Wi-Fi hotspot for travel**. Look for a device that offers 3G, 4G, and LTE service in as many countries as possible, for the lowest rate you can find. Keep in mind, some countries will only offer 3G or 4G connection speeds.

Once you own (or rent) the personal Wi-Fi hotspot device, you pay a flat fee for either a predetermined amount of online access (1GB, 5GB, or 10GB to be used within a 30-day or one-year period), or a flat fee per day for unlimited Internet access in any country that's supported.

The Skyroam personal Wi-Fi hotspot device (www.skyroam.com) costs $99.00. Day passes for Internet access that works in more than 120 countries around the world are priced as low as $8.00 per day (for unlimited access for up to five devices during each 24-hour period). These passes are available exclusively from the Skyroam website.

The benefit to using a personal Wi-Fi hotspot when traveling abroad is that you can carry the device with you, in a pocket, purse, backpack, or briefcase, and its signal radius goes where you go. Thus, you can still use the navigational (GPS) tools in your smartphone or tablet for real-time turn-by-turn directions, plus take advantage of Internet-based voice or video calling instead of paying international phone charges.

After you've acquired a Skyroam device, for example, and have set up an account (which takes about five minutes using any Internet web browser), you simply need to travel to a country where the device offers service, turn it on, and tap the Start button to being using one of your prepurchased day passes for a 24-hour period. When the 24-hour period expires, you can activate another day pass, as needed, with the touch of a button, and pay just $8.00 more (for the next 24 hours) to obtain unlimited Internet access wherever you happen to be.

Where to Purchase Personal Hotspots

Wi-Fi hotspot devices are also sold through Amazon.com. If you're an Amazon Prime subscriber, you can order one of these devices before your next trip, and receive free two-day shipping.

Glossary

AAA   American Automobile Association is a membership-based service that includes a wide range of services for travelers, including an online travel website that offers discounts on flights, hotels, rental cars, cruises, and vacation packages, as well as discounts on admission to museums and tourist attractions.

AARP Travel Center   This is an online travel service for AARP members that operates in partnership with Expedia.com. From here, you can find and book discounted flights, accommodations, rental cars, cruises, and vacation packages, plus use a handful of tools to research vacation opportunities and save money on other aspects of your travel.

Airbnb   Offered as a lower-cost alternative to traditional hotels and motels, Airbnb is a service that matches travelers with local hosts who charge a nightly fee for guests to stay in their home, condo, or apartment.

airline website   This is a website operated by a specific airline. You can use the website to research, book, and manage your flights. When you visit an airline-specific website, you can find and book flights only with that airline (or that airline's partners). When you use an online travel service, you can compare flight options and rates across many airlines simultaneously.

app store   An online store where you can find, acquire, and, when applicable, purchase apps. For iOS mobile devices, Apple operates the App Store. For Android mobile devices, Google operates the Google Play Store. If you're a Windows PC user, you can get software from the Windows Store, and Mac users can acquire software from the Mac App Store. An Internet connection is required.

Camera app   The app that's built in to every smartphone or tablet that enables users to take pictures using the mobile device's front- or rear-facing camera.

carry-on baggage   The luggage you carry onto an airplane; you store it in the overhead bin above your seat or under the seat in front of you. Every airline has size and weight limitations for carry-on luggage. Typically, in addition to one carry-on bag, a passenger can bring one personal item onto the aircraft, such as a purse, briefcase, messenger bag, laptop computer case, or backpack.

cellular Internet connection   All smartphones and some tablets use a cellular Internet connection, which is operated by cellular service providers. It enables mobile devices to access cell towers to access the Internet, make/receive calls, and send/receive text messages. 3G, 4G, and LTE refer to the speed of a cellular Internet connection.

checked baggage   Luggage that is checked with the airline and placed in the baggage compartment of an aircraft during a flight. On domestic flights, a checked bag can be up to 50 pounds, and it must meet specific size requirements or the airline charges additional fees. Most airlines now charge for all checked baggage.

confirmation number or booking number   When you make an online reservation for a flight, accommodations, rental car, or tour, you will receive a confirmation number or booking number that serves as proof that you paid for the reservation and that your payment has been accepted by the travel provider.

departure city   The city from which you're departing. When using an online travel service, instead of typing the name of a city or airport, you can typically type in an airport code. For example, SFO represents San Francisco International Airport and LGA represents LaGuardia International Airport (in New York).

destination city   The city to which you're traveling. When using an online travel service, instead of typing the name of a city or airport, you can typically type in an airport code. For example, BOS represents Boston and LAX represents Los Angeles International Airport.

hotel booking service   An online travel service that focuses exclusively on allowing users to find, compare, and book accommodations, often at a discount. Booking.com, GetARoom.com, and Hotels.com are popular examples of these services. Using one of these services, you can find available rooms and compare rates across many hotel and motel chains in the city to which you'll be traveling.

interactive travel guide   This can be a mobile app or website that offers interactive tools for helping travelers learn about and navigate their way around a popular tourist destination or city.

Internet-enabled   This refers to a computer, smartphone, or tablet that can connect to the Internet. A smartphone, for example, can use a Wi-Fi or cellular-based Internet connection.

mobile app   A standalone application that runs on a smartphone or tablet and that gives that mobile device additional features or functions.

mobile device   A smartphone (cellular phone) or tablet is considered a mobile device. These are battery-powered gadgets that, like a computer, have a microprocessor and internal storage, run an operating system, and run apps for added functionality. They also connect to the Internet via a Wi-Fi and/or cellular connection and have their own full-color (touchscreen) display.

online travel service   An online service that enables you to research travel destinations, compare rates for flights, accommodations, rental cars, cruises, travel packages, or travel bundles, and then book and pay for reservations (and often receive a discount). AAA Travel, AARP Travel Center, Expedia.com, Orbitz. com, Priceline.com, and Travelocity.com are examples of popular travel services.

personal Wi-Fi hotspot   Using a small, battery-powered device that connects to a local cellular data service wherever you happen to be, you're able to create a mobile Wi-Fi hotspot from which you can connect your computer(s) and mobile device(s) to the Internet.

Photos app   The app that comes preinstalled on smartphones and tablets that's used to view, organize, edit, enhance, print, and share digital images.

proprietary mobile app   A mobile app created by a specific company or service, such as an airline, hotel chain, rental car company, or cruise line.

rental car booking service   An online travel service that specializes in helping users find available rental cars and compare rates between multiple rental car companies. CarRentals.com, Rentalcars.com, and Silvercar.com enable visitors to find and rent a vehicle online.

shore excursion   An optional (paid) tour, activity, or adventure that cruise ship passengers experience on land when the ship stops at a port of call.

social media service   A service that enables people to communicate with each other and exchange information in a variety of ways. Social media can be used to share digital photos or to communicate with online friends via text messages, audio calls, or video calls, for example. Facebook is the world's most popular social media service, with more than 1 billion active users.

travel bundle   A travel package that saves you money because you book flights, accommodations, and/or a rental car at the same time and from the same online travel service or travel provider.

travel insurance   Insurance that covers a wide range of things that can go wrong before and during a trip. Travel insurance covers things like emergency medical expenses, financial loss due to lost or delayed baggage, or financial loss as a result of a missed, delayed, or cancelled flight. Especially when traveling abroad, having optional travel insurance is highly recommended.

travel itinerary   A detailed schedule of your travel plans, including details about flight, hotel, and rental car reservations, for example. Many people use a mobile app or online service to help them create and manage their travel itineraries.

travel or vacation package   Created by a travel provider, this is a discounted package that typically includes flights, accommodations, and other aspects of a trip (such as ground transportation, admission to attractions, and/or a meal plan).

Travelzoo.com   An online service that continuously searches the Internet for the very best travel and vacation package deals and then publishes its findings online and in its mobile app.

TripAdvisor.com   An online service with the world's largest collection of ratings and reviews for travel-related concerns, such as hotels, restaurants, tourist attractions, and tour operators. It's a free, powerful, and informative tool that aids in researching potential trips. It offers a public forum for travelers to share their advice, tips, ratings, and reviews, based on their firsthand travel experiences.

Uber   A lower-cost alternative to using a licensed taxi or limousine service, Uber is an app-based service that enables you to find a ride that's provided by a private individual using his or her personal vehicle.

vacation rental   An alternative to a hotel or motel where travelers rent an entire home, condo, or apartment when they travel.

web browser   The specialized software used to surf the Internet from a PC or Mac computer. Smartphones and tablets also have built-in web browsers.

Wi-Fi hotspot   A way to connect to the Internet using your computer or mobile device, from a hotel, airport, airplane, restaurant, cafe, tourist attraction, library, or any other business that offers a Wi-Fi hotspot. A Wi-Fi hotspot has a limited signal radius within which you must stay to maintain the Internet connection.

Index

A

REGISTER THIS PRODUCT
SAVE 35%*
ON YOUR NEXT PURCHASE!

☐ How to Register Your Product

- Go to quepublishing.com/register
- Sign in or create an account
- Enter the 10- or 13-digit ISBN that appears on the back cover of your book or on the copyright page of your eBook

🔓 Benefits of Registering

- Ability to download product updates
- Access to bonus chapters and workshop files
- A 35% coupon to be used on your next purchase – valid for 30 days
  To obtain your coupon, click on "Manage Codes" in the right column of your Account page
- Receive special offers on new editions and related Que products

Please note that the benefits for registering may vary by product. Benefits will be listed on your Account page under Registered Products.

We value and respect your privacy. Your email address will not be sold to any third party company.

* 35% discount code presented after product registration is valid on most print books, eBooks, and full-course videos sold on QuePublishing.com. Discount may not be combined with any other offer and is not redeemable for cash. Discount code expires after 30 days from the time of product registration. Offer subject to change.

quepublishing.com